MW00613632

Actual Malice

Actual Malice

CIVIL RIGHTS AND FREEDOM OF THE
PRESS IN *NEW YORK TIMES V. SULLIVAN*

Samantha Barbas

UNIVERSITY OF CALIFORNIA PRESS

University of California Press
Oakland, California

© 2023 by Samantha Barbas

Library of Congress Cataloging-in-Publication Data
Names: Barbas, Samantha, author.
Title: Actual malice : civil rights and freedom of the press in New York
    Times v. Sullivan / Samantha Barbas.
Identifiers: LCCN 2022015274 (print) | LCCN 2022015275 (ebook) |
    ISBN 9780520385825 (cloth) | ISBN 9780520385832 (epub)
Subjects: LCSH: Sullivan, L. B.—Trials, litigation, etc. | New York Times
    Company—Trials, litigation, etc. | Trials (Libel)—Alabama—
    Montgomery. | Civil rights—United States. | Freedom of the press—
    United States. | Libel and slander—United States.
Classification: LCC KF228.N4 B37 2023 (print) | LCC KF228.N4
    (ebook) | DDC 342.7308/53—dc23/eng/20220921
LC record available at https://lccn.loc.gov/2022015274
LC ebook record available at https://lccn.loc.gov/2022015275

Manufactured in the United States of America

32 31 30 29 28 27 26 25 24 23
10 9 8 7 6 5 4 3 2 1

Contents

Introduction

The fate of the *New York Times*, the nation's press, and the civil rights movement hung in the balance. In Montgomery, Alabama, in 1960, activists attempting to desegregate local lunch counters were persecuted by authorities and attacked by vigilantes. When a civil rights group called the Committee to Defend Martin Luther King and the Struggle for Freedom in the South placed an advertisement in the *New York Times*, exposing Alabama officials' role in this violence, the officials retaliated with libel suits against the *Times* and four ministers, leaders of Martin Luther King Jr.'s Southern Christian Leadership Conference (SCLC), who allegedly endorsed the ad. One of the libel suits was brought by L.B. Sullivan, public affairs commissioner, who oversaw the Montgomery police.

Segregationist officials had found a way to weaponize libel law against their critics. Libel law allows those who allege that their reputations have been injured by false and defamatory statements to bring claims for monetary damages. When Sullivan sued the *Times* and the ministers, the libel laws in most states were strict. The falsity of the defamatory statement was presumed, and the only defense was to prove the statement's truth "in all its particulars." First Amendment protections didn't apply to libel law at the time.[1]

1

L.B. Sullivan's claim would be considered spurious today. Sullivan alleged that his reputation was injured by accusations of police violence, although being known for committing brutality against civil rights protesters would have enhanced a police commissioner's reputation in Montgomery at the time. A few of the statements in the ad were incorrect, but the mistakes were so trivial that they didn't change the ad's overall meaning. Nevertheless, under Alabama's strict libel laws, an all-white jury awarded Sullivan $500,000, the largest libel verdict in the state's history to that time, and enormous by the standards of the day.

Sullivan's lawsuit was one of a string of libel lawsuits brought by Southern segregationist officials against Northern media outlets in a massive regional vendetta intended to intimidate them and to prevent them from reporting on the civil rights movement. The *New York Times*, the nation's newspaper of record, was despised in the South for its sympathetic coverage of the civil rights movement and its forthright support of integration. This segregationist "libel attack" on the press proved to be extraordinarily effective. Other Alabama officials sued the *Times* over the advertisement and the *Times*' civil rights reporting. By the end of 1961, the *Times* confronted over $6 million in potential libel judgments and the possibility of bankruptcy. The newspaper pulled its reporters out of Alabama to avoid further libel trouble. By 1964, CBS and the Associated Press, among other media companies, faced over $288 million in damages in libel cases brought by segregationist officials.[2]

The *Times* and the civil rights leaders appealed to the U.S. Supreme Court. In an opinion by Justice William Brennan, the Court shot down Sullivan's verdict, put state libel laws under First Amendment limitations, and freed the press to cover the civil rights movement. A unanimous Court declared that the right of citizens to criticize their leaders is the "central meaning" of the First Amendment, and that freedom of speech is foundational to a democratic society. There is a "national commitment" to "uninhibited, robust, and wide-open" debate on public issues, Brennan wrote, one that "may well include vehement, caustic, and sometimes unpleasantly sharp attacks on government and public officials."[3]

New York Times v. Sullivan is widely regarded to be one of the great opinions of constitutional law, "one of the most important free speech decisions of all time," and is one of the most-cited Supreme Court opinions.[4] *Sullivan* freed the press to report on the activities of public officials and to hold government accountable without fear of devastating libel suits. *Sullivan* has contributed greatly to the "free and robust" quality of our national public discourse. On the fiftieth anniversary of the ruling, the *New York Times* editorial board characterized the decision as one that not only "instantly changed libel law in the United States" but served as "the clearest and most forceful defense of press freedom in American history."[5] What follows is a history of the landmark case.

·   ·   ·   ·   ·

Under the rule of *New York Times v. Sullivan*, a public official must show that a defamatory statement was false and made with "actual malice"— that the publisher issued the statement knowing that it was false, or with "reckless disregard of whether it was false or not." The "actual malice" requirement sets high bar, making it extremely difficult for a public official to win a libel suit over statements concerning his or her official conduct. Without this protection, the Court feared, libel law would "chill" the press, as the *Times* had been chilled. Less robust protections would cause speakers to hold back issuing critical comments, even true statements, for fear of being sued and held liable for libel. Freedoms of expression must have the "breathing space" they "need to survive," Brennan wrote.[6] Subsequent rulings known as *Sullivan*'s "progeny" extended constitutional protections to speakers commenting on public figures, with "public figure" defined expansively as anyone who voluntarily engaged in a public controversy or even was drawn into such a controversy.[7] *Sullivan* has protected the right of citizens to speak out on public affairs and has prevented officials and others in power from using libel law as a form of censorship to suppress criticism and dissent.

The *Sullivan* standard is not ideal, as critics have noted over the years. For one, it protects false statements. Under *Sullivan*, innocent persons must suffer harms caused by speakers who got the facts wrong because of carelessness, so long as they did not "recklessly disregard" the truth. Under *Sullivan*, it's better for journalists not to investigate—the more a reporter uncovers, the more likely it is that they will discover facts that call into question the truth of the story, making them more likely to be held liable for acting with actual malice. Today, damaging falsehoods can be spread online with a click, and reputations destroyed instantly. Our unhappy experiences with social media have cast doubt on the virtues of uninhibited and robust discourse. Increasingly, critics are calling for the overruling or modification of *Sullivan* and its extensions, raising the once-heretical question, "Was *New York Times v. Sullivan* wrong?"[8]

Politics are also behind recent calls to overrule *Sullivan*. Donald Trump, as candidate and president, was vocal about his desire to eliminate *Sullivan* (presumably to make it easier to sue his liberal enemies in the press) and brought a spree of unsuccessful libel suits against the news media, as if *Sullivan* didn't exist.[9] Trump's attack generated further criticism of *Sullivan*. In March 2021, Laurence Silberman, a conservative judge on the U.S. Circuit Court of Appeals for the District of Columbia, wrote a dissenting opinion in which he expressed sentiments similar to those of U.S. Supreme Court justice Clarence Thomas, who argued that the actual malice rule has no "relation to the text, history, or structure of the Constitution" and should be struck down on that basis.[10] In July 2021, Justices Thomas and Neil Gorsuch, in separate opinions dissenting from the Court's decision not to hear a libel case, suggested that the Court revisit, and potentially overrule, *Sullivan* and the extension cases.[11] As of this writing, the constitutional protections offered by *New York Times v. Sullivan* may be in peril.

This work does not address technical debates over the merits of the *Sullivan* rule, which have been discussed extensively in the legal literature. Through a narration of the history of *Sullivan*, I make a few points that are pertinent to the scholarship and public debate over the case.

New York Times v. Sullivan has been memorialized in legal doctrine, history, and scholarship as a case primarily about the First Amendment. Yet the decision was as much about civil rights and the civil rights movement as it was about freedom of speech and press.

The Warren Court was keenly aware that the struggle for racial justice in the South depended on robust enforcement of First Amendment guarantees. In aid of the civil rights movement, the Court wrote an opinion that revolutionized free speech law. As this work demonstrates—drawing on archival sources, including the records of the New York Times Company and its personnel, Martin Luther King Jr., and the Southern Christian Leadership Conference—the crusade for civil rights in the 1960s, and the backlash against that struggle, produced one of the most important articulations of the meaning of freedom of speech in American history.[12]

The *Sullivan* decision was driven by First Amendment principles and at the same time by its unusual facts. The Supreme Court was determined to turn back the segregationists' "libel attack." The extreme circumstances of the case produced a sweeping set of rules that was carefully crafted to extricate the *New York Times* and the civil rights leaders from their dire situation, facing millions of dollars in damages. Some have argued that the unusual circumstances of the case may not have provided the Court with an ideal opportunity to engage in a nuanced consideration of the balance of interests between freedom of speech and reputation that would have been present in a more typical libel case, in which the plaintiff's reputation had been harmed. For this reason, it has been said, *Sullivan* may be a flawed foundation for modern libel law.[13]

Yet the dramatic story of *Sullivan* underscores the need for *Sullivan's* speech-protective rules. Libel laws, as they existed before *Sullivan*, imperiled the ability of newspapers to hold officials accountable and to inform the public about critical issues of the day. Libel law had a "chilling effect" on citizens seeking to use freedom of expression to effect social change. The Supreme Court's decision in *Sullivan* marked a courageous and much-needed iteration of the centrality of freedom of speech to democracy, and its rules and constitutional vision remain essential to the pursuit of social justice and authentic public debate.

1 All The News That's Fit to Print

In 1960, there was no American newspaper more acclaimed or prestigious than the *New York Times*. The *Times* was America's "newspaper of record," its most influential newspaper, renowned for its thorough reporting and aura of responsibility and credibility.[1] It had the third-largest weekday circulation of any newspaper in the country, around 650,000. It was sold in 12,041 cities and towns, making it the nearest thing to a national daily newspaper.[2]

Dubbed the "gray lady" for its reliance on text rather than pictures, the *Times* was not the easiest to read, best-written, or best-edited newspaper, but it carried more news and won more journalistic prizes than any other news outlet. The president of the United States read it, as did the pope (the international edition), and thousands of officials in Washington and around the world. It had the largest staff of any newspaper in the world, including the largest Washington news bureau and the largest foreign staff.[3] Each morning, the *Times* "emerg[ed] with a view of life that thousands of readers accepted as reality," observed journalist Gay Talese. For thousands of Americans, "the *New York Times* was the bible."[4]

.   .   .   .   .   .

The *New York Times* started in 1896, when a thirty-eight-year-old publisher from Chattanooga named Adolph Ochs went North to buy a newspaper. Possessed of sharp features and enormous self-confidence, Ochs was the son of a German-born Jew who had emigrated from Bavaria to Tennessee in 1845 and made his way as a peddler. At seventeen, he had started out as a printer's assistant, a so-called "printer's devil," at a Chattanooga newspaper. At twenty, he bought the *Chattanooga Times* and over the next eighteen years built it into a profitable paper.[5]

Ochs intended to purchase the *New York Times*. Started in 1851 by a young politician named Henry Jarvis Raymond, the *Times* initially prospered. It gained acclaim in the 1870s for exposing the corruption of Boss Tweed and his political machine in New York. In 1884, it abandoned its traditional support for Republicans and endorsed Grover Cleveland for president. This move caused Republican readers and advertisers to abandon the *Times*.[6] By 1896, the newspaper had an anemic circulation of 9,000 and was losing $1,000 a day. One contemporary critic described it as "the most picturesque old ruin among the newspapers of America."[7] Bearing a letter of recommendation from President Grover Cleveland (which he had gotten simply by writing the president and asking for it), Ochs offered $75,000 for the paper.[8]

Ochs transformed the *Times*. By cutting its price from two cents to a penny, he tripled its circulation within a year. Seeking to appeal to the city's elite, he announced his intention to run a "decent, dignified, and independent" newspaper, a model of objectivity and impartiality that would give "the news, all the news, in concise and attractive form" "without fear or favor, regardless of any party, sect, or interest involved." The slogan "All the News That's Fit to Print," adopted in 1896, was a jab at competing "yellow" papers, such as Pulitzer's *New York World* and Hearst's *New York Journal*, which were lurid, partisan, and sensational. There would be no comics, no gruesome murders, no screaming headlines in the *Times*; Ochs wanted "a paper that would not dirty the breakfast linen." An early slogan was "Will Not Soil the Breakfast Table."[9]

Headlines were discreet. The editorial page was bland and wholesome. There were few pictures. The *Times*' specialty was breaking news, accurately and thoroughly reported. The paper began covering financial news, the stock market, the real estate market, and court proceedings. In 1914, the *Times* made newspaper history when it was the first to report on the sinking of the *Titanic*. In 1918, it was the only newspaper in the world to publish the entire Treaty of Versailles (83,300 words). The paper detailed every development in World War I, and this cemented the newspaper's reputation for complete and accurate reporting. Never cutting costs when it came to news and putting the profits back into the paper became a hallmark of Ochs's leadership.[10] Politically, the newspaper was moderate, supporting the government and capitalist growth. The *Times* became the newspaper of the Establishment. Ochs had worked hard to bring himself up from impoverished roots and did not want to jeopardize his empire with unconventional views.[11]

When Ochs died in 1935, control of the *Times* passed to his forty-four-year-old son-in-law, Arthur Hays Sulzberger. Sulzberger was very different from Ochs. Unlike Ochs, who pulled himself up from hardscrabble roots, Sulzberger hailed from a wealthy and socially prominent Jewish family that made a fortune in the textile import business. Sulzberger attended the elite Horace Mann School and Columbia University and was permitted to indulge a taste for fine things. While a student at Columbia, Sulzberger met Iphigene Ochs, Adolph Ochs's only child. When Sulzberger married her in 1917, he was asked to join the *Times*. In 1918, he started as assistant treasurer and in 1919 was made vice president. Asked for advice on how to become the publisher of a great paper, he replied: "You work very hard, you never watch the clock, you polish up the handle on the big front door. And you marry the boss's daughter."[12]

Sulzberger vowed to continue Ochs's mission of comprehensive and responsible journalism. At the same time, he expanded the paper's scope and influence. Recognizing the need for interpretation in a world of increasing complexity, he introduced columns labeled "news analysis." News columns were written brightly, clearly, and concisely. The paper acquired a new urbane and sophisticated personality. It printed more and larger photographs, and the layout of the paper became attractive. There was more news on specialized subjects.[13] During World War II, Sulzberger made a crucial decision that turned the *Times* into the preeminent newspaper of the country. He put a sharp limit on advertising and devoted maximum space to news. The *Times'* claim to seriousness was practically unassailable.[14]

Ochs had separated news and opinion in an age of highly partisan journalism, but Sulzberger did not believe that opinions would interfere with the objectivity of the news. To him, an independent newspaper owed the public "responsible opinion."[15] During Sulzberger's tenure, editorials spoke out on major issues with a strong concern for foreign policy. In 1938, an editorial supported U.S. involvement in the war. Under Ochs, the *Times* had described itself politically as "independently democratic." Sulzberger dropped "democratic." The paper supported Republican candidates four times and Democrats three times under his leadership. Editorial opinions came from the editorial board, not from Sulzberger, who had a policy of not injecting his personal views into the paper. Because this policy kept him off the editorial page, he wrote letters to the editor that were published under his pseudonym "A. Aitchess" [AHS].[16]

Sulzberger was a handsome, well-dressed man, often considered glamorous because of his sophisticated lifestyle and the cachet of the *New York Times*. Trim and square-shouldered, he gave the impression of being tall and dominating, though he was actually of average height. Sulzberger brooded over the paper's day-to-day operations. He carried in his front pocket a small, black, gold-cornered pad on which he scribbled observations about headlines and stories, or if he found a newsstand that didn't sell the *Times*.[17] Daily, he fired off memos he called "blue notes," because they were printed on blue paper. Editors received hundreds of these notes annually, filled with questions, critiques, and story ideas.[18] In his three-story brownstone on the Upper East Side, Sulzberger read the paper in bed each morning in an unusual ritual. Attired in a maroon-and-navy dressing gown, he would tear off the precious front page and editorial page and put them aside on his pillow. He would peruse the least important pages first, then his favorites, making notations and correcting errors with a red pencil.[19]

The *New York Times* was a family empire, but Sulzberger described it as a "public trust." "We tell the public which way the cat is jumping," he would say. "The public will take care of the cat."[20]

In 1960, the *New York Times* occupied a massive structure at 229 West 43rd Street off Broadway. The fourteen-story Gothic gray-stone building, which resembled a French chateau, stretched an entire city block from Forty-third to Forty-fourth Street. It was a news factory amidst a theater district.[21]

A million words flowed into the building daily, from 47 foreign correspondents, 10 domestic bureaus, 158 New York City reporters, 400 domestic correspondents, and several wire services. Editors culled this down into a still-bulky average of 145,000 words in the *Times* daily edition and 450,000 in its Sunday edition. It was the fattest, thickest newspaper in the country. A copy of the Sunday *Times* dropped from a plane for delivery in a rural area accidentally hit an ox and killed it.[22]

Four thousand workers each day walked through the revolving door, where they were greeted in the marble lobby by a sentimental inscription chosen by publisher Arthur Hays Sulzberger: "Every day is a fresh beginning...every morn the world is made anew."[23] The slogan, "To Give the News Impartially, Without Fear or Favor," was displayed at various places throughout the building.[24] The heart of the building was the third-floor newsroom, a cavernous block-long space so vast that the presiding editor had to use a microphone to page his staff. Each morning three hundred workers seated themselves behind rows of gray metal desks.[25] When news came in, it was fed into typewriters, edited by graphite pencils, and swirled through purple-inked mimeograph machines. The staccato clacking of the manual typewriters was so loud that it created a seeming bubble of privacy around each writer.[26]

At four each afternoon, the tapping of typewriters stopped, and copy was stuffed into pneumatic cylinders and whooshed through tubes down to the composing room on the fourth floor, where it was hand-set into page forms. After a few hours, molds of the pages were sent down chutes to the press room in the basement and used to cast printing plates. When the "let go" order was given, the presses began warming up, and newsprint was sent up from the subbasement to be put through the presses with such force and speed that the fifteen-story building shook.[27] Finished papers were whisked from the loading platform to waiting planes at LaGuardia, or put onto trucks, to be dropped in piles at newsstands in the city and remote suburban locales.[28]

The *New York Times* was the product of an army of reporters, managers, accountants, typists, editors, copyreaders, and fact-checkers. It was the work of desk clerks, critics, news assistants, typesetters, truck drivers, printers, and delivery boys. Lawyers also toiled quietly and unglamorously behind the scenes.

Until the mid-1960s, the *New York Times* didn't have a legal department—somewhat surprising, given the scope of the newspaper's operations. Since Ochs's tenure, the paper had relied on a small, outside law firm for advice on legal matters. Alfred Cook, of the law firm of Cook, Nathan, and Lehman, one of the leading Jewish law firms in the city, represented Ochs when he bought the *Times* in 1896 and remained counsel to the paper until the 1940s. At the time, Jews were not accepted into mainstream law firms and were effectively segregated into their own legal practices.[29]

Louis Loeb, a lawyer for the Cook firm and Cook's son-in-law, began handling the *Times'* legal affairs in the 1930s. Loeb became a revered figure at the paper, known to every executive. Loeb was such an important voice at the *Times* that he was even asked to write editorials from time to time. From 1948 to 1968, Loeb served as *Times* general counsel. In his words, he "specialized in the *New York Times*."[30]

Loeb stood at around six feet tall and weighed a little over two hundred pounds. He was physically imposing but not fearsome. A gregarious, affable conversationalist, Loeb was in high demand as a master of ceremonies, especially at the prestigious New York Bar Association, which he led for many years. Loeb dressed flashily in brightly colored striped suits with pearl stickpins at the collar. Albinism, a lifelong condition, gave him lustrous white hair and nearly translucent skin. Because he had very weak eye muscles, all his life he wore thick, black-framed glasses that lent him a myopic and slightly confused expression.[31]

Loeb, like Sulzberger, hailed from a prosperous family of German Jewish immigrants. Loeb's father had started out as a dry goods peddler in Alabama and went on to start a Birmingham department store. When Loeb was a child, the family moved to New York, where Loeb attended fine schools—Philips Exeter, Yale University, and Columbia Law School. As a senior at Yale, Loeb gained renown as an actor when he mastered more than four hundred lines of blank verse for a single performance in the title role of *Tamburlaine the Great*.[32]

Loeb went to work for Cook, Nathan, and Lehman after law school. Soon afterward, he married Cook's daughter, Janet. Before long, Loeb was assigned to handle legal matters for the *Times*. Like the paper itself, the *Times*' legal representation was a family affair, passed on to the son-in-law.[33] Loeb became close to Sulzberger and worked with him in difficult negotiations with the American Newspaper Guild in the 1930s. Loeb sustained Sulzberger's position that the guild, which was under strong Communist Party influence, should not win control of the *Times*' editorial staff.[34] Loeb was held in high regard by his colleagues on the management side and also by union negotiators. He was said to be a man of such judicial temperament that his clients were tempted to ask him if he was sure which side had retained him.[35]

In 1940, Sulzberger asked Loeb if he would work more regularly as legal adviser to the *Times*. Loeb suggested to Sulzberger that he come up to the *Times* office half a day each day. He would maintain his partnership with the Cook firm. By 1941, he was spending four hours a day at the *Times* and four at his law office. In 1947, when Cook retired, Loeb needed to find another firm. A Yale classmate invited him to join the firm of Lord Day & Lord. After Loeb agreed, he went to see Sulzberger, who said that he had been concerned about what would happen when Cook retired and that he believed the *Times* should be represented by a firm that had continuity. Sulzberger decided that the *Times* would follow Loeb to Lord Day & Lord. Loeb called it "one of the greatest thrills of my professional career."[36]

Lord Day & Lord, established in 1845, was one of the city's oldest and most prestigious law firms. It was known as a "carriage trade" and "admiralty house," meaning that it represented shipping companies and wealthy private clients. The firm, at 25 Broadway, had a nineteenth-century aura about it. Many of the paintings in its office were of hunting horses and tall ships or photographs of partners in mutton chops and Civil War uniforms. By the 1950s, it was the epitome of stuffy, proper, "white shoe" practice.[37] Herbert Brownell, who had been attorney general under Eisenhower, was the most prominent member of the firm. Not surprisingly, the firm was conservative both in politics and in matters of legal strategy. Lord Day

& Lord would represent the *Times* until 1971, when they split over the paper's decision to publish the Pentagon Papers. Arthur Ochs Sulzberger, Arthur Hays Sulzberger's son, *Times* publisher from 1963 to 1992, once remarked that it "was a well-established firm numbering among its clients the Cunard Line." "Whether they were traumatized by the loss of the Titanic, I really can't say. But they certainly were cautious."[38]

Loeb came up to the *Times* building most working days, had an office and a secretary, and talked regularly with the top editors and managers. When he first started, his office was on the fourteenth floor. The desk he used was the original desk that Ochs had when he first came to the *Times*. He then moved to the tenth floor near the editorial board. A private phone connected Loeb's office on Lower Broadway with the *Times'* executive suite, bypassing two switchboards.[39]

Loeb's work centered on the business activities of the *Times*. Loeb drew up employment contracts, contracts for paper and ink, and negotiated building leases and advertising deals. Libel suits were only a minor portion of his responsibilities. Contrary to what is often assumed, libel was not a major liability for the *Times* before 1960. Loeb boasted that, excepting one judgment for around $25,000, the paper never paid more than a dollar in judgments in a libel suit in the years that Lord Day & Lord represented the *New York Times*.[40]

. . . .

Libel is a civil cause of action that protects personal reputation against false and defamatory statements. A defamatory statement is one that seriously lowers a person's reputation; it exposes a person "to hatred, shame, obloquy, contumely, odium, contempt, ridicule, aversion, ostracism, degradation or disgrace [and] deprives one of their confidence and friendly intercourse in society."[41] It "injures [a person] in his profession or trade, [and] causes him to be shunned or avoided by his neighbors."[42] According to an authoritative legal treatise, the *Second Restatement of Torts*, "a communication is defamatory if it tends to so harm the reputation of another as to lower him in the estimation of the community or to deter third persons from associating or dealing with him."[43] Historically, defamation had a moral dimension. Accusations of having committed a crime, engaging in professional incompetence, having a promiscuous tendency, or a "loath-some illness"—a venereal disease—were considered defamatory *per se*, meaning that the plaintiff didn't have to introduce evidence as to why the charge would damage their reputation. [44]

The law of libel is ancient. Libel dates to the Middle Ages when the king's courts intervened in verbal arguments between men of great wealth and power. Because disputes over the reputations of magnates of the realm often resulted in violence, the creation of new criminal penalties for defamation was one way of halting breaches of the peace.[45] When civil actions became increasingly common around 1600, the tort of defamation came into being. The civil action, for which the remedy is the payment of money damages, became the most popular method of dealing with defamation between individuals. Libel laws, both civil and criminal, were transplanted to the United States with the rest of the English common law. Criminal libel was rarely employed in the United States and fell almost entirely out of use by the twentieth century.[46] The tort of libel, by contrast, was commonly used (*New York Times v. Sullivan* was a civil libel case).

With its antiquated and convoluted terminology, libel was—and still is—one of the most complex areas of law. Libel has been described as "perplexed with minute and barren distinctions," "a mausoleum of antiquities peculiar to the common law and unknown elsewhere in the civilized world."[47] Before 1964, a person who sued for libel didn't have to prove the statement in question to be false; its falsity was presumed. The presumption of falsity reflected the old English notion that it didn't matter whether a statement was true or false since it harmed a person's reputation either way. The plaintiff didn't have to show actual injury to their reputation, only that the statement had the potential to harm their reputation. Libel was judged under the rule of strict liability, meaning that the publisher was responsible for its statements regardless of their intent or state of mind at the time of publishing. A careless mistake, or one made in good faith, would subject a newspaper to liability no less than an error made with ill will, or malice. The only way a publisher could defend itself was by proving that the statement fell into one of a few narrow categories of statements that were "privileged," legally justified or excused, or more commonly, by proving the truth of the statement, "in all its particulars."

Truth was a complete defense to libel, but as a practical matter, proving the truth of a statement "in all its particulars" was difficult even if the statement was in fact true.[48]

These stringent laws reflected the high value placed on reputation. Reputation is defined in the law as "the estimate in which [a person] is held by the public in the place [one] is known."[49] Reputation was often regarded as a form of property, generated by one's efforts, "slowly built up by integrity, honorable conduct, and right living."[50] For businessmen and professionals, a good reputation was essential to career and commercial success. Historically, a woman's reputation for chastity determined her marriageability. A good reputation "makes friends...creates funds... draws around [one] patronage and support and opens...a sure and easy way to wealth, to honor, and happiness," it was said.[51] A good reputation was often described as a person's most prized possession—one's "greatest pride" and "choicest treasure." One was thought to "own" one's reputation, like one owned the fruits of one's labor. An injury to reputation created "far more pain and unhappiness...than any physical injury could possibly occasion." To rob a man of his reputation was "a crime against the community as well as against the individual," and it was "the duty of the community to punish it."[52]

Like most major newspapers, the *New York Times* had an elaborate system to prevent and defeat libel claims. It was structured around the newspaper's advantages as a well-funded corporate institution with well-trained, highly paid attorneys. The *Times* used its financial and legal muscle to intimidate, frustrate, and wear down libel plaintiffs and convince them to abandon their claims.

Each year dozens of individuals sent angry letters to the *Times* threatening to sue for libel. Sometimes the claims were valid; the allegations were indeed false. More often, the threats were baseless and mere harassment. Some saw filing a libel claim as a way to vent their anger over an unflattering statement. According to one *Times* attorney, in nine times out of ten, starting a lawsuit was "the safety valve blowing off," and the case never went to trial.[53]

When the *Times* received one of these threats, the lawyers used a standard procedure. First, they fired off a sternly worded response denying liability or error. "Although the *New York Times* is always ready to correct any error in its columns which is called to its attention, we must advise you that our attorneys have informed us that the article of which you complain was a true, correct and fair report... and that it was published as a matter of news and in good faith, and there is nothing for us to do other than to await the presentation of your attorneys," read the letter.[54] If the plaintiff asked for a retraction or correction, they warned them that the initial charge would be repeated with the correction, scandalizing them all over again. If the complainant persisted, the attorneys would try to get them to back down. If the alleged libel was based on an official or public hearing, the lawyers would inform them that such reports were privileged and could not be the basis of a libel action.[55]

Intimidation was one strategy, and stalling was another. The *Times* lawyers would drag out libel suits through motion after motion and intentional delays. The *Times* was famous for its "no-settlement" policy. Unlike many newspapers, which would settle to get rid of a case, the *Times* always made the plaintiff go before the highest court it could get to before paying anything. This policy, developed by Adolph Ochs, was known as the "Ochs policy" on libel. Ochs felt that this approach would discourage "nuisance suits" and dissuade lawyers from taking libel suits against newspapers.[56] Ochs wrote to Alfred Cook in 1922, "You know my views about settling libel suits. No need repeating them. I would never settle a libel suit to save a little money. If we have damaged a person we are prepared to pay all he can get the final court to award, and we accept the decision as part of the exigencies of our business. I am aware that in some cases this may cost us more than necessary, but in the long run I think it is a wise policy."[57] The *Times* could afford to pay its lawyers during this process, while most plaintiffs were unable to withstand the burdens of a lengthy lawsuit and eventually relented and abandoned their claims.

George Norris, an eccentric, bespectacled Columbia Law School graduate, was the *Times* in-house "libel expert," assigned to investigate libel cases full-time. Norris, who had worked at the *Times* since 1916, was utterly devoted to the *Times* and to preserving the paper's stellar record on libel. He was a feared figure on the third floor. Whenever he went to the newsroom and approached a member of the news staff with a libel complaint, they would nervously insist, "I was off that day." No editor or reporter wanted to admit that they had been responsible for a story accused of libel. But their disinclination to have their record tarnished by a libel action motivated them to cooperate with Norris to show that the plaintiff had no case.[58]

Norris checked facts, tracked down witnesses, and got statements from them. He worked closely with the Lord Day & Lord lawyers handling the litigation. Norris also supervised the "libel detectives." The *Times* employed private investigators who did nothing but work on libel actions. The detectives were assigned to confirm charges on which libel actions had been brought and to "dig up dirt" on claimants. If the plaintiff already had a bad reputation, it would be difficult for them to say that their reputation had been harmed. Plaintiffs would often desist when these investigations turned up unsavory facts, as such details would come out at trial. "It is said that when a person begins a suit for libel, he is inviting an investigation into his past life—maybe, beginning with his birth," Norris quipped. "Much has been spent for such investigations. We think that they pay off, for it seems that sometimes the knowledge of someone's asking questions about him is enough for him to call it quits."[59]

A Midwestern pastor sued the *Times* for libel. Norris sent a detective to Chicago to investigate his record. The detective contacted his parishioners, the minister's university, and even streetcar drivers who knew him. When the detective discovered "discreditable information," the pastor dropped his complaint. Norris observed, "After thirty-five years on the defending end of libel suits, my advice to prospective plaintiffs is—don't bring your linen suit to court unless it's spotless."[60]

The *Times* also took measures to avoid publishing defamatory statements. Education in libel law was offered to staff, there were regular lectures on libel, and libel treatises and handbooks were placed in the newsroom. Copy editors were charged with special responsibility, as many libels stemmed from typographical errors. Lawyers conducted "prepublication review," vetting text for possible libels.[61]

As a result of its aggressive tactics and well-trained lawyers, the *Times* rarely paid out judgments in libel cases. Of the $16,344,284 sought in libel claims from January 1923 to October 1949, it paid only $43,987. Aside from two large judgments, one for $25,000 and one for $8,000, only $10,000 was paid for twenty-seven judgments.[62]

"It would seem," quipped Norris, "that if anyone had an idea of getting rich quick, he would be better off looking for uranium than suing the *New York Times* for libel."[63] That would soon change.

2 Libel and the Press

The *New York Times* had to live with the law of libel because the law seemingly wasn't going to change. While freedom of the press was a legally protected interest, courts had said repeatedly before 1964 that it was not valued more highly than the right to protect one's good name. As such, newspapers like the *Times* creatively adapted their operations and methods to enable them to publish, and even to flourish, despite strict libel laws. Libel nevertheless remained a formidable latent threat for the press, as the *Times* discovered when it was sued for millions of dollars by Alabama officials in 1960.

. . . . .

Although libel law existed since the nation's founding, the history of the American press and libel is surprisingly short. When a lawyer wrote a treatise on libel law for newspapers in the 1880s, he had relatively few cases to draw from.[1] There were more immediate and satisfying means of retribution for defamatory statements. Journalists were "sometimes killed, sometimes horsewhipped, or submitted to other indignities," recalled publisher E.W. Scripps.[2]

Yet in the latter part of the nineteenth century, the press experienced an unprecedented surge of libel cases. A newspaper publishing boom, the result of new printing technologies and an expanding urban population, was one cause of the increase in libel suits. Libel suits also rose because of the sensationalism of the press. "Yellow" journalism—news that was exaggerated or even downright fictionized—became a popular and lucrative trend for publishers.[3]

It wasn't long before people from all walks of life began suing the press for libel. Many who sued were ordinary citizens alleging that newspapers had falsely accused them of crimes or other improprieties. Politicians and public officials were frequent litigants against the press. Newspapers of the time were active and unrestrained critics of government. Attacks on officials were often laden with epithets like "rascal," "demon," and "knave." Sometimes the accusations were false, and the libel claim had merit. But often the allegations were true, and the politician sued merely to harass and to intimidate the newspaper. Politicians and public officials sought high damage awards for maximum intimidation. Railroad magnate James Fisk sued the *Springfield Republican* for $100,000, then followed it up with two more lawsuits against two other newspapers for the same sum, then another for a million.[4]

Winning a libel case wasn't difficult, as the law was weighted heavily against the defendant. Given public animus toward the sensationalistic press, jurors were "disposed to make a newspaper pay heavy damages in libel cases on almost any sort of pretext," one editor observed in 1901.[5] Juries tended to be more skeptical of claims brought by public officials, but even they recovered when allegations appeared to be outrageous and intentionally false. In 1897, for example, the mayor of Philadelphia won $45,000 against the *Philadelphia Times* for headlines reading: "The Dandy Mayor Skips. Col. William B. Smith Shakes Philadelphia Dust from His Feet. A Sudden Flight to the West. His Legacy of Bogus Checks, Protested Notes and Bad Debts."[6]

Publishers sought leniency from courts in cases of "honest mistake," where they claimed that false statements had arisen from careless errors. Most false and defamatory statements weren't intentional and malicious, they argued, but rather the product of "the hurry of getting up a large newspaper."[7] They claimed that a legal privilege to make "honest mistakes" was essential to protecting the freedom of the press to report the news without fear of being sued for libel.[8]

A few states recognized the "honest mistake" privilege or "good faith" privilege, which would play an important role in the *New York Times v. Sullivan* case. In *Coleman v. MacLennan* (1908), the Kansas Supreme Court applied the privilege to statements about public officials and candidates for office, and all "matters of public concern": to "the management of all public institutions...the conduct of all corporate enterprises affected with a public interest...and innumerable other subjects involving the public welfare." In his decision in favor of the newspaper, Judge Rousseau Burch opined, "The importance to the state and to society of such discussions is so vast and the advantages derived are so great that they more than counterbalance the inconvenience of private persons whose conduct may be involved, and occasional injury to the reputations of individuals must yield to the public welfare, although at times such injury may be great." The plaintiff could defeat the privilege by showing that the defendant published the statement with "malice," defined as spite or ill will.[9]

This "conditional privilege," recognized by less than half the states by 1950, and thus known as the "minority" rule of privilege, proved to be controversial because it seemed to encourage the dissemination of falsehoods and to provide insufficient protection for reputation. Henry Schofield, a law professor at Northwestern University, condemned it as "unauthorized judicial legislation destructive of men's reputations and property, inviting and encouraging the owners and editors of newspapers and periodicals to found their educational power on falsehood."[10] The privilege, it was feared, would "create a disinclination for public life on the part of honorable men by making them feel that it was incompatible with wholesome self-respect and decent reputation; it would...leave public employment to callous and self-seeking adventurers."[11]

The rule used in most states, the "majority rule," or so-called "strict rule" of privilege, was known as "fair comment." Under fair comment, if a newspaper reported facts accurately, a wide range of commentary on it was permitted, but if it reported false facts, even in good faith belief in their truthfulness, it could be liable. "What the interest of private citizens in public affairs requires is freedom of discussion rather than of statement," opined the Massachusetts Supreme Court in 1891, in a leading case on the fair comment rule.[12] The controversy between the majority and minority rules of privilege was the most contested issue in libel law until it was at last resolved in *New York Times v. Sullivan* in 1964.

The "libel crisis" peaked during the first two decades of the twentieth century. There was an "astonishing epidemic of libel," reported *Printers' Ink*, the trade journal of the newspaper industry, in 1909. Just as "debonair, touchy patriots" once took out "their pistols and side swords at slight provocation," politicians were "press[ing] the push button for their libel lawyers."[13]

One of the most spectacular libel cases involved Henry Ford, who sued the *Chicago Tribune* in 1916 for having called him an "ignorant idealist" and an "anarchist."[14] Former president Theodore Roosevelt brought claims against a Michigan newspaper that accused him of being a drunk. Roosevelt and Ford both won their suits, having technically met the legal requirements. But each recovered only six cents, an indication of what juries thought of their cases.[15] Ford and Roosevelt knew well that even if their claims didn't result in damage awards, there were benefits merely to suing. A libel suit could serve as effective publicity—a way to shape one's public image by openly denying accusations against them—and a way of inflicting pain and suffering on one's critics by forcing them into costly defenses.

The threat of libel led the press down a path of self-reform that transformed journalism and ultimately ended the "libel crisis." In the attempt to avoid libel suits, journalism professionalized, adopting fairness, truthfulness, objectivity, and accuracy as ideals.[16] By 1920, most newspapers had eliminated extreme sensationalism. Publishers adopted the mantle of "civic responsibility." Newspapers performed a public function, they claimed, exposing official wrongdoing and providing readers with facts they needed to make informed decisions as citizens of a democracy. Newly formed professional associations such as the American Society of Newspaper Editors invoked historic metaphors of the "fourth estate" in an effort to change the public image of the press from gadfly and rumormonger to guardian of democracy and venerable "watchdog" of the public.

Exhorted by the new demands of professionalism, as well as their business departments, newspapers instituted "libel vetting" programs to avoid publishing defamatory material and bringing their publications into costly litigation. Under these programs, fact-checkers and copy editors reviewed all articles. Reporters were exhorted to take precautions in newsgathering. When columnist H.L. Mencken started out as a reporter at the *New York Herald* in the early 1900s, the management told him to "verify reports whenever possible, be careful about names, ages, addresses, and figures, [and] keep in mind the dangers of libel."[17] Lawyers scrutinized copy and made corrections or deletions. Large newspapers reported that they often managed to keep out of libel trouble through only slight changes in style—eliminating inflammatory language and the intermingling of news and opinion, for example. Small newspapers that didn't have resources to engage in libel vetting were more likely to experience libel's "chilling effects" and to suppress reports on public officials and public figures who might retaliate with libel suits.[18]

"Libel vetting" yielded greater accuracy in news content, a reduction in libel suits, and public confidence in the press. By 1922, libel actions had become "rare things" at newspapers, a publishing trade journal announced triumphantly.[19] The *New York World* was sued for libel an average of only ten times a year between 1913 and 1931. The tabloid the *New York Evening Graphic* paid less than $6,000 to plaintiffs in the 1920s and '30s.[20] In 1942, the law firm for the *New Yorker* noted that in the ten years it represented the magazine it had been taken to court for libel just a handful of times.[21]

The reduction of libel suits, and more favorable outcomes for the press, also reflected changing attitudes toward freedom of speech. The populist upheavals of the Great Depression in the 1930s had produced greater tolerance for dissenting views.[22] The use of libel suits in politics waned, as Americans became cynical about the "phenomenon of a maligned politician publicly announcing that he is consulting his lawyers and that he is filing a libel suit asking for six or seven figures in damages," in the words of law professor David Riesman. There was a feeling that public officials should have a thick skin and "dish it out" in reply, rather than running to the courts for relief, Riesman observed in 1942.[23]

Although libel law "looks bad on paper," one editor observed in 1947, "no newspaper editor has just cause for complaint."[24] Yet libel suits and the possibility of large damage awards remained an underlying hazard for newspapers, especially since they could take no refuge in the First Amendment's guarantees of freedom of speech and press.

The First Amendment commands that "Congress shall make no law … abridging the freedom of speech, or of the press." Libel law clearly limited speech, yet prior to 1964, the Supreme Court insisted that the punishment of libelous statements didn't abridge constitutionally protected expression. Defamatory speech was deemed to be "outside" the First Amendment, and its regulation could be left wholly to the states.

Before the 1930s, the First Amendment did little to curb the government's broad powers to restrict freedom of speech in the name of the common good. The dominant rule of constitutional free speech was that prior restraints (gag orders, or the suppression of speech before publication) were prohibited, but punishment of speakers for utterances that had a "bad tendency"—that offended the sensibilities of "right-thinking" persons or had a "tendency" to create individual or social harm, including harm to reputation—was considered to be a legitimate exercise of the state's police powers, its capacity to regulate behavior and enforce order in the interest of public safety, health, and morals.[25]

The "bad tendency" rule, which determined "badness" based on the views of "right-thinking" people, was used to quash unpopular ideas and to legitimate the status quo. World War I saw the widespread suppression of dissent based on its purported "bad tendency." The hyperpatriotic mood of the country led Congress to pass a sweeping Espionage Act in 1917, making it a crime to "cause or attempt to cause insubordination" or to "willfully obstruct the recruiting or enlistment service." Hundreds who opposed the war were prosecuted for merely writing about the government in negative terms. The Sedition Act of 1918 extended the Espionage Act to cover expressions of opinion that cast the government or the war effort in a negative light.[26] Cases challenging convictions came up before the U.S. Supreme Court, free speech arguments were made, and the claims were sustained under the "bad tendency" rule.

This repression of dissent birthed a new era of freedom and a new

paradigm for judging First Amendment claims. In his dissenting opinion in *Abrams v. U.S.* (1919), voting to invalidate a conviction of Socialist
protesters under the Sedition Act of 1918, Justice Oliver Wendell Holmes
invented the "clear and present danger" test. The remote "tendency" of
speech was not enough to justify punishment; instead, courts should ask
"whether the words used are used in such circumstances and are of such a
nature as to create a clear and present danger that they will bring about the
substantive evil that Congress has a right to prevent," Holmes explained.
"Only the emergency that makes it immediately dangerous to leave the
correction of evil counsels to time warrants making any exception to the
sweeping command, 'Congress shall make no law abridging the freedom
of speech.'" The best way to eradicate noxious ideas, Holmes believed, was
through testing and discrediting them in the "marketplace" of ideas: "But
when men have realized that time has upset many fighting faiths, they
may come to believe even more than they believe the very foundations of
their own conduct that the ultimate good desired is better reached by free
trade in ideas—that the best test of truth is the power of the thought to get
itself accepted in the competition of the market."[27]

Justice Louis Brandeis, in his concurring opinion in *Whitney v. California* (1927), one of the most eloquent tributes to free speech in history,
established a variation of "clear and present danger" known as the "time to
answer" test. *Whitney* considered the constitutionality of a woman's conviction under a California anti-syndicalism statute for helping to establish
the Communist Labor Party of America. No danger flowing from speech
could be considered "clear and present" if there was full opportunity for
"public discussion" of it, Brandeis wrote. "Fear of serious injury alone
cannot justify suppression of free speech and assembly...there must be
reasonable ground to believe that the danger apprehended is imminent.
Those who won our independence believed that...freedom to think as
you will and to speak as you think are means indispensable to the discov-
ery and spread of political truth; that without free speech and assembly,
discussion would be futile; that with them, discussion affords ordinarily
adequate protection against the dissemination of noxious doctrine."[28]

Before long, Holmes and Brandeis's views became the law of the land,
expressed in the majority opinions of the Supreme Court. This was facili-
tated by the ruling in *Gitlow v. New York* (1925). The First Amendment

had been intended as a check on the federal government, but *Gitlow* "incorporated" the First Amendment, applying it to the states through the Fourteenth Amendment.[29]

Starting in the 1930s, the Supreme Court afforded unprecedented protection for dissenting views. Decisions upheld the right of labor unionists to picket, and of Communists, Jehovah's Witnesses, and other unpopular speakers to hold meetings, to proselytize, and to distribute literature. "The maintenance of the opportunity for free political discussion to the end that government may be responsive to the will of the people and that changes may be obtained by lawful means, an opportunity essential to the security of the Republic,... is a fundamental principle of our constitutional system," stated a majority of the Court in *Stromberg v. California* (1931), striking down a law that prohibited the display of a red flag as a symbol of Communism.[30] Because free expression was "the matrix, the indispensable condition, of nearly every... form of freedom," state actions restricting speech would be forbidden unless justified by a compelling government interest beyond disagreement with the views espoused, wrote the majority in *Palko v. Connecticut* (1937), instituting the practice of heightened judicial scrutiny for claims involving First Amendment rights.[31]

Although there was no separate jurisprudence for the press, which received the same protections as other speakers, the Court nevertheless recognized the important role of newspapers in facilitating "public discussion." *Near v. Minnesota* (1931) struck down a gag law banning tabloid newspapers and in so doing constitutionalized the law against prior restraints.[32] In *Grosjean v. American Press Co.* (1936), invalidating a state income tax levied on newspapers with large circulations, Justice Sutherland observed the value of a free press in enabling the public to "unite... for [its] common good" as "members of an organized society," observing that "the newspapers, magazines, and other journals of the country, it is safe to say, have shed and continue to shed more light on the public and business affairs of the nation than any other instrumentality of publicity."[33]

In a series of cases in the 1930s and '40s, the Supreme Court held that the "clear and present danger" rule limited state laws prohibiting contempt of court, insurrection, and breach of the peace.[34] Yet the First Amendment didn't restrict libel law, the Court made clear. Under its emerging categorical theory of the First Amendment or "two level theory," there were certain categories of speech, "low value speech," that were unprotected because they had no redeeming social value. These categories included obscenity, "fighting words"—words that would incite violence—and defamatory or libelous speech.[35]

The theory of "low value" speech, which would play a role in the *Sullivan* case, first appeared in *Chaplinsky v. New Hampshire* (1942), known for the "fighting words" doctrine. Chaplinsky, a Jehovah's Witness, had accused a police marshal of being a "god damned fascist" and was convicted under a New Hampshire law that prohibited the use of "offensive" or "annoying" words. He appealed unsuccessfully on First Amendment grounds. Wrote Justice Murphy in the majority opinion: "It is well understood that the right of free speech is not absolute at all times and under all circumstances. There are certain well-defined and narrowly limited classes of speech, the prevention and punishment of which has never been thought to raise any constitutional problem." "These include the lewd and obscene, the profane, the libelous, and the insulting or fighting words.... It has been well observed that such utterances are no essential part of the exposition of ideas, and are of such slight social value as a step to truth that the benefit that may be derived from them is clearly outweighed by the social interest in order and morality."[36]

The "two level theory" was formally enshrined as First Amendment doctrine in the "group libel" case of *Beauharnais v. Illinois* (1952). Joseph Beauharnais, president of a white supremacist group called the White Circle League of America, had circulated leaflets petitioning Chicago officials to halt the alleged "encroachment and invasion" of white neighborhoods by African Americans. Beauharnais was convicted under a state statute that prohibited libels against any racial or religious group if it might cause unrest or breach of the peace. The Court affirmed the conviction over arguments that it violated his First Amendment rights. "Libelous utterances not being within the area of constitutionally protected speech, it is unnecessary, either for us or for the State courts, to consider the issues behind the phrase 'clear and present danger,'" wrote Justice Felix Frankfurter for the majority. "Certainly no one would contend that obscene speech, for example, may be punished only upon a showing of such circumstances. Libel, as we have seen, is in the same class."[37]

The Supreme Court never ruled directly on the constitutionality of state libel laws before *New York Times v. Sullivan,* despite explicit invitations to do so. Between 1951 and 1963, the Supreme Court declined to review forty-four libel cases coming from the state and federal courts, implying that the issue of the First Amendment and libel had been settled.[38] As First Amendment scholar Harry Kalven Jr. observed in 1952, even among civil libertarians there was a "general agreement" that the "core of defamation law" as it then existed was "indubitably constitutional."[39] The law of libel stood here on the eve of *New York Times v. Sullivan.*

3 The Paper Curtain

In 1947, the *New York Times* began its historic coverage of the civil rights movement. That year, Turner Catledge, managing editor of the *Times*, asked publisher Art Sulzberger to come to his daily happy hour to talk with him about a "pressing matter." Catledge had a practice of inviting *Times* executives to gather around a bucket of ice and a bottle in a small room behind his office, which he called his "branch water and bourbon nook."[1]

Catledge wanted to discuss with Sulzberger a new "sociological trend," as he put it—the stirrings of civil rights sentiment in the South. There was going to be a social "revolution" below the Mason-Dixon line, he told the publisher, and it deserved the newspaper's utmost attention. "Being a Southerner, loving the South, I had a special feeling for and concern about the unfolding racial drama," Catledge recalled in his memoir. "I saw it as my job to ensure that the *Times* printed the fullest possible presentation of the facts about the racial situation in America."[2]

The *New York Times* building on West 43rd Street was a long way from rural Choctaw County, Mississippi, where Catledge was born at the turn of the century. Though Catledge descended from Confederate soldiers, as a young man he became an ardent opponent of segregation, convinced that the separation of races was immoral and unconscionable. Catledge graduated from Mississippi State University in 1922 and reported for the Memphis *Commercial Appeal*. During a Mississippi Valley flood in 1927, Catledge traveled across six states to chronicle the destruction. This act brought him to the attention of Secretary of Commerce Herbert Hoover, who recommended him to Adolph Ochs of the *Times*, who hired him in 1929. At the peak of his career in the 1950s, Catledge lived in a luxury apartment on the East Side, earned $100,000 a year, and was known to every newsroom in America. These worldly trappings notwithstanding, he remained at heart a Southerner with a Mississippi accent that was especially thick when he was drinking, mawkishly sentimental when reminiscing late at night about his youth in the red clay hill country.[3]

Catledge was right—a revolution in civil rights was underway. Civil rights activism wasn't new; forces had been working to end discrimination and segregation since the nineteenth century. Interracial groups in both North and South, including the NAACP, founded in 1908, litigated against segregation in schools and other public places, and initiated campaigns to eliminate lynching. Communist-affiliated unions in the 1930s sought to organize black sharecroppers and industrial workers.

It wasn't until after World War II, however, that public opinion mobilized broadly in favor of civil rights, and the cause won the sympathies of Northern white liberals. In the wake of a global conflict that highlighted Nazi mistreatment of Jews, segregation seemed to be fundamentally at odds with democratic values. The federal government was beginning to oppose segregation openly. In 1947, President Truman created a commission on civil rights to investigate and remedy racial inequality. The following year, Truman desegregated the armed forces, and the Supreme Court, in *Shelley v. Kraemer*, outlawed the enforcement of racially restrictive real estate covenants. Black soldiers who had risked their lives for their country resented their return to second-class citizenship. The rising economic status of African Americans during the war, and their migration to Northern cities, empowered further challenges to segregation.[4]

Catledge's request that the *Times* cover the civil rights movement was by no means radical. Although no national newspaper or magazine before World War II consistently addressed the topic of race or covered African American life in detail, the *Times* had traditionally paid more attention to the South than most Northern news outlets. Chattanooga was Ochs's second home, and the family clung to the *Chattanooga Times* with Ochs's granddaughter Ruth as publisher. In the 1930s, the *Times* sent prizewinning reporters to the South to cover such events as the rise and assassination of Huey Long and the trial of the Scottsboro Boys. Civil rights were an article of faith in the Sulzberger family.[5] In 1946, the *Times* announced a pioneering stance of omitting racial designations in news stories.[6] As victims of antisemitism, the Sulzbergers were sensitive to ethnic labels, and they enforced this policy strictly.[7]

Catledge was certain that the "race story" would best be covered by reporters from the South with Southern accents who would never be suspected of working for the *New York Times*. He called this his "Southern strategy." In 1947, at Catledge's initiative, and with Sulzberger's blessing, the *Times* sent a reporter named John Popham to be based in Chattanooga, making it the first national news outlet with a Southern bureau.[8]

Popham was on the scene of the most dramatic developments in the civil rights movement. In 1954, Popham was the only national reporter covering the South when the Supreme Court issued *Brown v. Board of Education*, striking down segregation in public schools as a violation of the equal protection clause of the Fourteenth Amendment. After *Brown*, the *Times* printed the Supreme Court's opinion in full, and an editorial lauded the Court for reaffirming the "American faith in the equality of all men and all children before the law."[9] The *Times* became the nation's most comprehensive source of civil rights news, and America's conscience on civil rights.[10] The following year, Popham reported from Sumner, Mississippi, on the dramatic trial of the killers of Emmett Till, a fourteen-year-old boy who had been lynched for allegedly flirting with a white woman.[11] The acquittal, and shocking images of Till's mutilated body, published in the black magazine *Jet*, awoke Americans to the brutalities of the South's racial system and catalyzed civil rights activism nationwide.

In 1956, Popham and other *Times* reporters covered the bus boycott in Montgomery, Alabama, the first large-scale, direct-action demonstration against segregation in the South. Jim Crow laws required blacks to ride in the back of the bus and surrender their seats to white passengers. After Rosa Parks refused to give up her seat to a white person, black residents began using carpools or walking to avoid the segregated transportation system.[12] The year-long boycott led to a 1956 Supreme Court decision, *Browder v. Gayle*, invalidating Alabama's segregated seating laws as a violation of the Fourteenth Amendment, and it launched its leader, twenty-seven-year-old minister Martin Luther King Jr., to national fame.

.   .   .   .

Catledge went to visit his Mississippi hometown of Tunica not long after *Brown v. Board of Education*. He found his old friends, surprisingly, to be quite calm about integration. He returned to New York and reported confidently that his native region would accept the Supreme Court's mandate. To confirm this, Catledge dispatched nine reporters to the South to "investigate the Southern mood."[13] The resulting "Report on the South," published in March 1956, concluded optimistically that many Southerners were "resigned" to integration. At the same time, it noted in passing that no black student attended a public school or university with white students in several states and that there was great hostility toward "liberal and moderate voices in much of the Deep South."[14]

Indeed, the mood in the South turned ugly after *Brown* and the *Brown II* decision of 1955, dictating that integration must occur with "all deliberate speed." When the Court in 1955 held that segregated beaches and bathhouses in Baltimore and segregated golf courses in Atlanta were unconstitutional, it was clear that *Brown* was not just about education, and that the Court would likely declare all of Jim Crow unconstitutional. An all-out fight against integration began, dubbed "massive resistance." One hundred and one members of the House and the Senate from the eleven states of the Old Confederacy signed a "Southern Manifesto" denouncing the Supreme Court's "abuse of judicial power" and pledging "all lawful means" of resistance. A columnist for the *Richmond News Leader* named James Kilpatrick popularized the concept of "interposition": the decisions of the Court were not valid unless the affected states agreed to them. By 1956, eleven Southern states had enacted over 140 laws of "interposition" to circumvent *Brown*.[15]

These laws were just one facet of massive resistance. Resistance was also carried out through violence, with knives, guns, billy clubs, and bombs. The KKK gained force in Southern communities. It was accompanied by a new, militant, powerful white supremacist group called the White Citizens' Council. Rather than outright violence, the Citizens' Council used economic coercion to punish blacks who challenged segregation, ensuring that they lost their jobs or couldn't get credit. With doctors, business leaders, lawyers, and educators in its ranks, the Citizens' Council was nicknamed the "country club Klan."[16]

These tensions were hitting close to home for the *Times* in a way that even the optimistic Catledge couldn't ignore. In 1956, a black woman named Autherine Lucy was admitted to the University of Alabama on the order of a federal court. After she was mobbed by students, and whites rioted for three days, the school finally removed her from campus. The *Times* reporter was attacked and pelted with eggs. "Outside agitator!" "Troublemaker!" "Commie!" "Lying Northern newsman!" mobs shouted at him.[17]

Reporters sent to cover the admission of black students to Little Rock's Central High School in September 1957 met a similar fate. Governor Orval Faubus called out the Arkansas National Guard to prevent students from enrolling. His actions prompted President Eisenhower to enforce integration with federal troops, and the armed showdown at the school dominated headlines for weeks. Popham had led the *Times* to believe that Central High's desegregation would proceed peacefully, so it sent its mild-mannered education editor, Benjamin Fine, a Jewish reporter from New York, to cover it. Jeering crowds assaulted him and asked him, "Have you been to Moscow lately?"[18]

It was then that Catledge realized that Southern resistance to integration was far greater than he anticipated and that the *Times* needed someone more aggressive to cover the region. In 1958, Catledge made the historic decision to replace Popham with Claude Sitton, who became the *Times'* one-person regional bureau working out of Atlanta. Born on a Georgia farm, and a veteran of wartime naval service, Sitton was tough and hard-bitten. In nine hundred articles over six and a half years, he would portray vigilant demonstrators, blacks who confronted white mobs, violent police officers, and segregationist public officials.[19] Sitton's hard-hitting articles opened readers' eyes to the violence that met the civil rights movement—beatings, bombings, and church burnings. Sitton endured the equivalent of "guerrilla warfare unscathed, worn to the bone, combat-

wise, building an experience no one in America could match," recalled one
Times reporter. "The South which Sitton was to endure was as dangerous
a place as a reporter could find."[20]

By the time of Sitton's arrival in the South, most of the nation's major
news outlets—including the national newsmagazines *Time, Newsweek,*
and *Life,* and the television networks NBC, ABC, and CBS—had dispatched corps of reporters to the region. So had other prominent Northern newspapers like the *New York Post,* the *New York Daily News,* and
the *Washington Post,* which would establish their own Southern bureaus.
This influx of journalists was greatly resented by the South and likened to
an "invasion." "There are as many Yankee reporters dropping off planes
and trains as there were carpetbaggers in the 1860s," complained a South
Carolina segregationist newspaper editor.[21] Primed by years of regional
tensions, Southerners would wage war on Northern journalists, who were
derided as "propagandists" using "lies" to attack the customs, traditions,
and beliefs of the South.

• • • • •

Segregationists feared the power of the press, its power to sway public
opinion toward civil rights and integration, and with good reason. In the
1950s, the mass media were at the peak of their prestige and influence.
Media consumption reached record highs. More than a third of families
read picture-filled *Life* magazine.[22] The new medium of TV was national-
izing, going straight into Americans' homes. By the end of the decade, 85
percent of the population watched television for more than five hours a
day.[23]

Civil rights leaders also knew the power of the press, and they intently
courted it. Although Martin Luther King Jr. had initially hoped that his
message of peace and nonviolence would awaken a sense of moral shame
among white Southerners, this strategy proved fruitless. King came to
believe that most Americans, if confronted with the reality of Southern
racism, would be appalled by it. The civil rights movement would rely on
sympathetic media coverage to win the allegiance of Northern whites,
who would force Southern compliance with *Brown* through federal legislation and intervention.[24] In a strategy known as "creative tension," civil

rights activists would provoke violence against themselves in the hopes of attracting news attention.[25] Andrew Young, an assistant to King, recalled that "it was no accident that our demonstrations were always in the morning; that we completed them by two o'clock in the afternoon so we could make the evening news, and so that reporters could file their deadlines for the coming day."[26]

The civil rights movement depended on media like NBC, ABC, CBS, the *New York Times*, and *Life* magazine to educate Northern whites, tug at their heartstrings, and convert millions of Americans into supporters of integration and civil rights. In the words of civil rights movement veteran Julian Bond, "Newspaper, radio and television coverage brought the legitimate but previously unheard demands of southern blacks into the homes of Americans far removed from the petty indignities and large cruelties of southern segregation. These racial structures were indefensible; once challenged and exposed, they finally crumbled."[27] Media images of protesters being attacked by cops with billy clubs, of the mutilated body of Emmett Till, and neatly dressed activists ejected from segregated lunch counters would illuminate for the nation the cruelties of the South's racial system and the courage of those who defied it.

This unfavorable media coverage triggered bitter reactions in the South. It provoked the South's long-standing sense of inferiority, its feeling of being maligned, humiliated, and misunderstood. Southerners had long perceived themselves to be indicted by the North, and stereotyped as ignorant, uncultured, and violent. There was a collective chip on the region's shoulder; in the words of one historian, "the overwhelming and crushing defeat of the Confederacy in 1865 left the people of the Southern states with a defeatist attitude, an inferiority complex, a tender skin to criticism, and a fear of ridicule."[28] Many Southerners feared, as a practical matter, that the critical attention would undermine their efforts to promote industrialization and Northern investment in the region.

During massive resistance, segregationists waged a fierce battle against the Northern press. They canceled subscriptions to national magazines and newspapers. Reporters and photographers were beaten and assaulted.[29] Southern officials denounced "indoctrination" and "brainwashing" by the "left-wing liberal press." The White Citizens' Council sought to "nullify" the "propaganda assault being waged against the minds of our young people and our citizens" through the dissemination of "counter-propaganda" promoting segregationist views.[30] Through this attack, segregationists intended to heal long-standing wounds of dignity, to rally the public in defense of segregation, and to quash reporting on civil rights, limiting outside scrutiny of the South's treatment of race.

The Northern press was accused of a multitude of sins, including slanting facts to promote an "anti-South" worldview. Reporters were said to indulge in gross stereotypes, going South with "pre-conceived notions... seemingly derived from *Uncle Tom's Cabin* or abolitionist literature they found in an old trunk," according to the *Montgomery Advertiser*.[31] In a belligerent 1957 article titled "Why Pick on Dixie?" published in the *American Mercury* magazine, journalist Harold Lord Varney denounced the "suffocating fog of indoctrination and propaganda" "blanketing most of the opinion-influencing agencies of the North." The theme of "damn the South" "assails our ears mightily on the airwaves via both radio and television," he wrote. "It comes to us... in the dignified columns of the *New York Times*." [32]

Journalist William Workman, in his 1960 segregationist treatise *The Case for the South*, indicted Northern newspapers for "exploit[ing] every splash—or ripple—on the Southern scene with headlines and editorials which would lead their readers to believe that anarchy reigned in the South," yet minimizing "instances of racial discord" in the North.[33] This "race hypocrisy," as it was called—overplaying Southern racial tensions while ignoring Northern racial problems—was said to cast all news reporting into question. The most egregious offense of the press was its alleged suppression of Southern views on race. The "paper curtain," a reference to the iron curtain around communist countries, was used to describe this purported "media blackout."

"A paper curtain shuts out the Southern side of the race relations story from the rest of the country," wrote Tom Waring, editor of the *Charleston News and Courier*. "Neither metropolitan newspapers nor nationally circulated magazines deal honestly and truthfully" with the subject of race and civil rights. "They publish many distorted articles, and almost anything against the Southern viewpoint. But they refuse to print the other side."[34] "Because no large newspaper is published in the South which permeates other areas of the country, because no national magazines are published and owned in this area... the South has almost no opportunity to get a break in the publicity-propaganda campaign of the moment."[35] The South needed to "pierce the paper curtain of Northern press censorship," it was said, in order to "win its battle to preserve segregation as best for both races."[36]

Publications that had taken strong integrationist positions were deemed "South-hating" and singled out for attack. *Look* magazine was denounced as "the official organ of the National Association for the Protection of Colored People, the Communist Party, and other riff raffs engaged in a determined effort to destroy the Southern way of life."[37] *Time* magazine was a "systematic abolitionist ragpicker."[38]

With its liberal viewpoint, command over public opinion, and well-known Jewish leaders, the *New York Times* was declared to be the worst offender. "For many years the [*New York Times* has] looked down on the South, and with great gusto played up, on every possible opportunity, crime or racial news having origin in the South," opined the Madisonville, Kentucky *Messenger* in 1959. "This practice grew so prevalent... that the phrase Paper Curtain was coined to describe it."[39] In the view of the Talladega, Alabama *Daily Home News*, "the smallest, lamest Alabama weekly with the least circulation" told "the truth and the whole truth" while "the *Times* lies, directly or by suppression."[40]

Segregationists devised another means to attack the "paper curtain" press—high-value libel suits.

Even before the *Brown* decision, segregationists realized that libel law, with its plaintiff-friendly rules, could be used to threaten and terrorize the press. Libel suits could be used to harass newspapers that advocated integration, to stop them from criticizing the South, and to send a message that the South wouldn't tolerate insults and slights from the "lying Yankee press."

In 1946, Florida governor Millard Caldwell, an unrepentant segregationist, began this "libel attack" trend when he sued *Collier's*, a respected New York magazine with over three million readers. A gang of white men had taken from jail and shot to death a black Florida sharecropper under indictment for attempted rape. *Collier's* reported that Caldwell said that no lynching occurred and that the murderers "saved the courts considerable trouble."[41] An outraged Caldwell declared that he never made those comments and that *Collier's* falsely accused him of "condoning and approving lax law enforcement and lynch law." He sued for $500,000.[42]

Florida newspapers cheered the governor's efforts to redeem not only his own but also the state's public image. "Governor Caldwell's suit will be a protest against the tendency of many northern magazines and newspapers to picture the South as an area that lynches in wholesale fashion and on the slightest provocation," opined the *Tallahassee Democrat.*[43] Exhorted by Caldwell's lawyers to not "let people sitting up at 250 Park Avenue in New York tell us down here the kind of man we ought to have to run our state," an all-white jury awarded the governor $237,500, the largest libel verdict in the United States to that time.[44] The award was later reduced to $100,000, still regarded as a victory by Floridians.[45]

Alabama governor James "Kissin' Jim" Folsom got on the "libel attack" bandwagon in 1951 when he sued two magazines over an article describing brutal conditions in Alabama's Kilby prison. The article, titled "Devil's Island, USA," which appeared in a pulp magazine called *Front Page Detective*, described such atrocities as "floggings, perversion, and sadism." The piece was reprinted in *Readers' Digest*, with over nine million readers. Folsom and his aides sued each publication for a total of six million dollars. Folsom claimed that the article accused him of "misfeasance" in office and declared that "I and my associates . . . have been smutted and libeled by national publications, in fact all the people of Alabama have been libeled."[46] The magazines settled with the governor and his aides for an undisclosed sum, and another victory over the Yankee press was duly proclaimed.

Ken for Men was a tawdry pulp magazine that in 1957 ran an alleged exposé of Montgomery, Alabama, titled "Kimono Girls Check In Again." The article described copious narcotics, brothels, and "numbers rackets," and called the city a place of "wide open sin and sex." City commissioners W.A. Gayle, Clyde Sellers, and Frank Parks denounced the allegations as "downright lies" and filed libel suits for $250,000 each.[47]

This article was grossly fabricated. *Ken's* writer never visited Montgomery; the magazine published the stories knowing that they were untrue.[48]

The suit was eventually settled for $15,000 and a public apology.[49] By then, libel suits brought by segregationist officials against Northern news media were emerging as a potent weapon. They were so worrisome that they prompted a lawyer writing in one of journalism's revered trade publications to comment that such lawsuits were giving the South an opportunity "to reverse the verdict at Appomattox."[50]

4 Heed Their Rising Voices

On January 30, 1960, a seventeen-year-old black college student named Joseph McNeil launched the sit-in movement in Greensboro, North Carolina. What sparked McNeil's decision to protest the segregated Woolworth's lunch counter was his recent denial of service in the lunchroom of the Greyhound bus terminal. He convinced three of his classmates to join him in a protest of Woolworth's. The students sat down at the lunch counter and were, predictably, refused service.[1]

The students stayed in the Woolworth's until closing. The next day they came back, bringing more students with them. The following day they returned. By the fifth day, there were over three hundred protesters. After forty-five were arrested and charged with trespassing, the students boycotted all the lunch counters in the city. Woolworth's later agreed to integrate its lunch counter.[2]

These dramatic events, which were covered sympathetically in the *New York Times* and other newspapers, ignited one sit-in after another. Within two weeks, protesters demonstrated in several Southern cities including Charlotte, Raleigh, and Nashville.[3] The sit-ins represented the largest mass protest in the United States since the strikes and labor uprisings of 1930s, and they transformed the civil rights movement. After the

Montgomery bus boycott, Martin Luther King and his Southern Christian Leadership Conference had focused heavily on fundraising, and activism lagged. With the sit-ins, students launched a massive direct-action movement that became the focal point of national attention and a catalyst of large-scale change. At the end of February, the sit-ins reached Montgomery, Alabama's capitol, and one of the South's most racially tense cities.

.   .   .   .   .

It was known as the "Cradle of the Confederacy." In 1861, Jefferson Davis had taken command of the secessionist cause in Montgomery and unfurled the Confederate flag. The city clung mightily to this distinction. A hundred years later, a tablet on Commerce Street commemorated the site of the First Confederate Headquarters. [4] The White House that symbolized the Confederate government was still standing, and people still "walk around in those halls and cry," novelist James Baldwin observed in 1961.[5] On the steps of the white-domed state capitol stood an old Confederate cannon and a statue of Jefferson Davis. Dexter Avenue, the city's main thoroughfare, swept down from the capitol toward the city's central plaza, known as Court Square. It wasn't far from the bus stop where Rosa Parks in 1955 had refused to give up her seat to a white passenger.[6]

Montgomery was a bucolic mix of antebellum houses, modern bungalows, hotels, and industrial plants, built on several hills that sloped toward the central business section, which was divided into rectangular grids. Downtown thoroughfares were broad and shaded by old trees. Montgomery had once been a cotton and slave marketplace, and an agricultural hub, but after World War II, local boosters began a systematic campaign to bring industry to the area. By the middle of the 1950s, Montgomery was amidst a manufacturing boom, with dramatic increases in industrial employment. The largest "industry" was Maxwell Air Force Base, which spread out over former farmland onto city limits.[7]

Montgomery's population was 134,000 in 1960, 60 percent white and 40 percent black. Its economic and social structure depended on the cheap service labor of its black residents, who toiled as domestics and manual laborers, and in the city's light industries and commercial establishments. Segregation in the city was total and reinforced by law, custom, and coercion. Violence was considered a normal and expected aspect of race relations.[8]

Montgomery was a stronghold in Alabama's "massive resistance" to integration. Alabama had been the first state to adopt an "interposition" resolution in 1956, deeming the *Brown* decision to be "null, void, and of no effect." That year, Governor Jim Folsom's refusal to follow court orders to integrate the University of Alabama resulted in the deployment of federal troops. State attorney general John Patterson, later elected governor with KKK backing, banned the NAACP from the state with trumped-up charges that it failed to properly register as a business operating within Alabama, an action copied by several other Southern states. The local Montgomery press never tired of telling whites that civil war was still going on in Dixie—a war against "Yankees and race mixing."[9] After the bus boycott in 1956, the Alabama White Citizens' Council moved its headquarters to Montgomery, and the local Citizens' Council chapter flourished. Montgomery, it boasted, was the place where the tide turned in the civil rights battle and "integration efforts were stopped cold."[10]

·   ·   ·   ·   ·

White residents of Montgomery feared that the sit-in movement would arrive in their city. On February 25, 1960, that came to pass. Thirty-five male students from the local black college, Alabama State College, marched into the snack bar in the basement of the Montgomery courthouse and asked to order coffee. The whites in the lunchroom reacted with panic. Staff cut the lights and herded the students into the hallway outside of the lunchroom, where they awaited the arrival of law enforcement. Police arrived and padlocked the grill. The students left the courthouse, promising that they would "be back in larger numbers."[11]

Within hours, officials proceeded to lock down other cafeterias in the area. Public Affairs Commissioner L.B. Sullivan, in charge of the police department, went on television to threaten the "agitators." "We do not intend to permit outside forces to create, provoke, or otherwise incite any racial incident here in our city," he bellowed. "We are prepared to take whatever actions might be necessary to maintain the time-honored tradition and customs of the South."[12] Governor Patterson ordered Alabama

State to expel the protesters and threatened to cut off state funds if it didn't.[13] The routine harassment of black citizens escalated, with police pulling over and harassing drivers around campus and arresting students for pretextual offenses like jaywalking.[14]

The following day, two hundred and fifty students rallied at the courthouse to protest Patterson's threats to expel the students. Twenty-five white men, hearing rumors that students would sit in at lunch counters downtown, took to the streets armed with miniature baseball bats concealed in paper bags, a weapon that was considerably larger and potentially more dangerous than a blackjack. One of them struck a black woman over the head. Sullivan's police witnessed the attack but did nothing to punish it. Sullivan accused the protesters of "causing" the incident and denounced the *Montgomery Advertiser* for reporting it, which resulted in a "stigma" on the city that was "undeserved," he said. The national media had taken an interest in the events in Montgomery, which were reported in a less than favorable light.[15]

Martin Luther King Jr. exhorted the students to protest until they "turned the Cradle of the Confederacy upside down." The following day, March 1, a thousand students gathered on the Alabama State campus and marched to the capitol to demonstrate against the governor's threat to expel the protesters. They lined up on the majestic white marble steps, not far from the spot where Jefferson Davis took the oath of president of the Confederacy a hundred years earlier. They bowed their heads and said the "Lord's Prayer," then sang the "Star-Spangled Banner."[16] Patterson ordered the State Board of Education to expel the "ringleaders" in the lunch counter incident to prevent "bloodshed in this city."[17]

Nine hundred Alabama State students voted to stay away from classes until their classmates were reinstated. Because the beginning of the boycott fell on the first day of winter quarter exams, the students voted to suspend their strike until the end of exams and resolved instead not to register for the next quarter until they were notified by their leaders. To persuade the students to complete registration, the college abandoned its usual procedure of permitting all students to eat at the dining hall during the first week of the new quarter, which was dubbed the "week of grace." The college issued temporary meal tickets given only to those students who had begun the process of registration, which meant that approximately three hundred students were excluded from the dining hall. Within three weeks, virtually everyone reregistered for classes.[18]

Ralph Abernathy, civil rights leader and pastor of Montgomery's First Baptist Church, announced plans to hold a mass prayer meeting at the capitol that Sunday. Sullivan issued a warning over local television. "We have no intention whatsoever of permitting our city to be used as a site for the racial agitators and prejudiced Northern press to further their program of racial strife and exploitation for financial gain and spectacular distorted news coverage," he announced. "If the Negroes persist in flaunting their arrogance and defiance by congregating at the capitol Sunday the police will have no alternative but to take whatever action that might be necessary to disperse them."[19]

Defying Sullivan's orders, a thousand protesters dressed in fine church clothes gathered at the Dexter Avenue Baptist Church, a humble red-brick building with a white steeple across the street from the capitol. An army of law enforcement converged on the lawn in front of the capitol awaiting the demonstrators' arrival.[20] A thousand or more whites, many dressed in rough country garb, milled about in the street discussing "what they would do if the Negroes appeared."[21]

As services ended and the clock struck two, the doors of the Dexter Baptist Church swung open, and two pastors dressed in robes led a line of marchers in the direction of the capitol. The mob lurched forward and knocked several protesters to the ground.[22] It wasn't until the whites had assaulted the blacks that the police acted; Sullivan delayed intervening to allow the mob to have their way with the protesters. Policemen charged toward the crowd, and firemen began coupling their hoses to hydrants. The crowd dispersed, singing the national anthem and the "Battle Hymn of the Republic" while walking back to the church.[23]

The students vowed to continue their protest on campus. The following day they staged a picket line on the Alabama State grounds, holding placards reading "Remember the Nine" and "1960 not 1860." A few got rowdy and began chanting and dancing in conga lines. Sullivan's police, on the request of campus officials, swooped down with billy clubs, tear gas, and machine guns. Thirty-two students were hauled off in paddy wagons.[24] King called President Eisenhower and asked him to restore law and order in Montgomery. "Gestapo-like methods" were being used to intimidate

Figure 1. L. B. Sullivan was elected Montgomery's Commissioner of Public Affairs on a platform of white supremacy and law and order. Alabama Department of Archives and History.

protesters, he said. "We feel this terror which grips a whole community in an American city violating elementary constitutional rights requires immediate federal emergency action."[25]

Sullivan, who had emerged as an informal media spokesman for the city and its face of white resistance and intransigence, proceeded to denounce King as a "rabble-rousing agitator."[26] The sit-ins had "backfired" because "our customs and traditions can't be changed overnight," he told reporters. The whites, he explained, "are more united than ever before."[27]

Lester Bruce "L.B." Sullivan was a stout, moon-faced man of medium height, handsome, well-dressed, and gray-haired. He had the look of a man in his fifties, although he was only thirty-nine at the time of the sit-ins. Heavy smoking and stress had aged him. Though he had been public affairs commissioner for only a few months, he had formidable responsibilities and was now being scrutinized on the national stage.

Sullivan was a child of the poor rural South. He grew up in a family of Baptist fundamentalists in 1923, in Vanceburg, Kentucky, a village of pool rooms, lunch counters, and feed stores that was so small it could be captured in a single photograph. His father, Henry, had been a sheriff and farmer; his mother, Pauline, was a schoolteacher who died when L.B. was eight. As a young man Sullivan worked in construction and butchered pigs in a rural grocery store.[28]

Military service offered Sullivan a ticket out of hardscrabble life in Depression- era Vanceburg. Sullivan enrolled in the Army Air Corps in 1941 and served as a military policeman stationed in Germany. In 1945, he left the military as staff sergeant at Maxwell Air Force Base in Montgomery. Shortly after, he took the position of chief inspector of the Alabama Public Service Commission, an agency charged with regulation of the state's utilities. Gordon Persons, the commission's director, was elected governor in 1950. Persons appointed Sullivan state director of public safety, a position that included direction of the state police. Sullivan gained acclaim for leading the legendary cleanup of Phenix City, Alabama, a notorious haven of crime, gambling, and prostitution. After Persons left office in 1954, Sullivan returned to the private sector, moving through positions of increasing status and responsibility in the fields of public safety and law enforcement, including police consultant with the International Association of Chiefs of Police and safety director of the P.C. White Trucking Line.[29]

Montgomery was run on a commission form of government at the time. Three commissioners led the city—the mayor; a public affairs commissioner, who presided over the city's fire and police departments; and a public works commissioner, who oversaw the operation of parks, libraries, street maintenance, and garbage collection. The public affairs commissioner was responsible for the police department but not for day-to-day police operations, the 175 full-time policemen being under the immediate supervision of Montgomery's chief of police.[30]

Clyde Sellers had been public affairs commissioner during the bus boycott. It was under his leadership that Montgomery's transportation facilities had been integrated by court order. In 1958, Sellers decided to

Figure 2. Sullivan attempting to disperse a civil rights protest in Montgomery. Alabama Department of Archives and History.

pay a fine for Martin Luther King, who had been arrested for criminal loitering, to deprive him of the publicity that would have been generated by his going to jail. This decision made him unpopular with hard-line segregationists, to put it mildly.[31]

Sullivan, who had ties to the Ku Klux Klan, ran against Sellers on a platform of white supremacy and law and order. "L.B. Sullivan Will Not Back Down on the Southern Traditions of Complete Segregation in Schools, In Parks, On Busses," read his campaign advertisements.[32] "No fines paid for 'trouble makers.' No 'kid glove' handling of agitators."[33] In 1959, a constituency of working-class segregationists from Montgomery's east side voted Sullivan public affairs commissioner. A former football coach named Earl James was elected public safety commissioner, which was by custom named the city's mayor, and Frank Parks, a dour, long-faced former interior decorator, was voted public works commissioner. All the commissioners were members of the White Citizens' Council.[34]

Sullivan was arrogant and conceited, yet he projected a cool, polished, family man image. Sullivan was a father of three, a Baptist churchgoer, and an Elk and Mason. He was known for his impeccable dress, his neat daily uniform of suit and tie. Self-conscious about his lack of education, he wrote out his speeches longhand, poring over his words before addressing an audience. Sullivan was "sophisticated for Montgomery," recalled one local resident. He was "no redneck, no clod."[35] Sullivan was a calculated, diligent climber. His position in Montgomery, he hoped, was the stepping-stone to more ambitious endeavors, including statewide elected office.

Martin Luther King Jr. shared one thing with his antagonist L.B. Sullivan, and that was tenacious and formidable drive. King had emerged on the national stage in 1955 with his charismatic and courageous leadership of the Montgomery bus boycott. The *New York Times* had been one the first news outlets to recognize the twenty-seven-year-old divinity school graduate and exponent of Gandhism as an extraordinary leader, a "soft-spoken man with learning and maturity far beyond his years" who spoke "with such passion that it overwhelmed the listener with the depth of his convictions."[36] After a series of favorable press articles in 1957 heralding him as "Alabama's modern Moses," King was anointed leader of the civil rights movement and a *bona fide* cultural icon.[37]

White Alabamians promptly vowed to destroy this "number one Negro agitator," considered the most dangerous man in the state. On the night of December 30, 1956, segregationists bombed his home, causing damage to the property but no injury to King or his family. Authorities arrested him for spurious offenses on several occasions. Officials charged King with violating the state boycott statute and apprehended him for speeding when he was caught driving thirty miles an hour in a twenty-five mile an hour zone. King was later detained on phony charges of "loitering" while attempting to attend the arraignment of a man accused of assaulting Ralph Abernathy.[38]

After the U.S. Supreme Court struck down segregation on Montgomery's buses, Abernathy, King, and Rosa Parks took a historic ride on the front seat of a Montgomery bus. In retaliation, whites opened fire on downtown buses, burned crosses, and raided black neighborhoods. It was during this reign of terror that King recognized the need for an organization that would coordinate the activities of civil rights groups in the South. In a meeting in Atlanta in January 1957, King and 110 civil rights leaders representing ten states formed the Southern Christian Leadership Conference (SCLC), which would become the most consequential organization of the civil rights movement. Through its grassroots organizing and mass demonstrations, the SCLC would convince Americans that federal legislation was necessary to eradicate racial discrimination and effect the "Second Reconstruction."[39]

Unlike the NAACP, which targeted its efforts on litigation to force compliance with *Brown*, the SCLC focused on direct action tactics as a means of drawing national attention to civil rights. The SCLC was composed not of individual members but local "affiliate" organizations such as civic leagues, ministerial alliances, and individual churches. For $25 in dues, each affiliated group received the right to send five delegates to the SCLC's annual convention. Most of the SCLC's founders were ministers, and its operations would be guided by Christian principles. King described the SCLC's purpose as "spread[ing] the philosophy of nonviolence and demonstrat[ing] through action its operational techniques."[40] One of its early efforts was a campaign for voter registration, a "Crusade for Citizenship" that would register two million new black voters before the 1960 presidential election.[41]

Despite its inspiring mission of "redeeming the soul of America" through nonviolent protest, the organization had a less than promising start. Though the SCLC had a central office in Atlanta, there was only one full-time employee. The group had no coordinated fundraising program. In its first year, the SCLC received almost no publicity and made virtually no progress on voter registration. Most board members were too busy to participate. In February 1960, the SCLC faced a crisis that seemed fated to destroy the organization altogether.[42]

．　　．　　．　　．　　．

Earlier in the year, King had moved from Montgomery to Atlanta to devote his energies to the SCLC. Not long after the Greensboro sit-ins, Georgia officials marched into King's Ebenezer Church and arrested him on an

Alabama warrant. They claimed that he falsified tax returns for 1956 and 1958. This was untrue. King had deposited funds that had been donated to the Montgomery Improvement Association, the organization that led the bus boycott, into his personal account. He then transferred the funds to the organization. For this minor lapse, he had agreed to pay $2,100 in back taxes. But Alabama authorities insisted that the issue wasn't settled. King surrendered at the Montgomery County courthouse and was booked and released on a $4,000 bond.[43]

The charges were an obvious frame-up intended to remove King from the movement's leadership and to attempt to bankrupt the SCLC. Tax fraud was usually a misdemeanor. Charges for perjury, a felony, could have sent him to prison for ten years. With the stakes higher, the cost of legal defense would increase, diverting even more funds from the movement. It was part of Governor Patterson's campaign of using the courts to undermine the civil rights movement, as he had done in his battle against the NAACP.[44]

King was distraught by the perjury charges. They attacked his honesty and integrity and threatened his legitimacy as civil rights leader. He felt that a conviction in Alabama would undermine his authority in all the Southern states. He was concerned not only for his reputation but for the survival of his movement. The NAACP assembled a team of lawyers to defend him, but they wouldn't take his case for free.[45]

· · · · · ·

The announcement of the charges alarmed King's followers. On February 22, 1960, sixteen of King's allies convened an "emergency meeting" to plan fundraising for King's defense. The meeting took place in the New York apartment of Harry Belafonte, celebrity singer and longtime civil rights activist. Esteemed figures in the civil rights movement were there that night, including Mordecai Johnson, president of Howard University, prominent liberal minister Harry Emerson Fosdick, and baseball legend Jackie Robinson.[46]

By the end of the evening, the group had resolved to raise $200,000 to pay for King's lawyers, to support the student protest movement, and to back the SCLC's campaign to register black voters in the South. They chose this three-pronged approach at King's behest. He had told them, "I would not be so selfish as to be concerned merely about my defense and not be concerned about the great creative causes that were taking place in the South."[47] The organization was christened, awkwardly, the "Committee to Defend Martin Luther King and the Struggle for Freedom in the South." A. Philip Randolph, a respected labor leader who was president of the Brotherhood of Sleeping Car Porters, the largest black union in the country, was elected chairman. Randolph appointed as executive director Bayard Rustin, a flamboyant man with a national reputation as an organizer of mass movements.

Rustin was tall and thin, with high cheekbones and intense eyes. The press described the fifty-year-old activist as "a tall, greying Negro Quaker."[48] An illegitimate child born to West Indian immigrants, raised by his Quaker grandmother, Rustin had become a radical nonconformist at a young age. In the 1930s, he had joined the Young Communist League. In 1942, Rustin helped set up the Congress on Racial Equality (CORE), which pioneered nonviolent direct action to fight racial discrimination. A leader of the War Resisters' League, during the war Rustin spent twenty-eight months in Lewisburg prison for draft evasion. He later served on a chain gang after participating in bus trips organized by CORE to protest segregation on interstate transportation. Rustin had advised King on the doctrine of nonviolence during the bus boycott and assisted him in forming the SCLC. By 1960, he had participated in over two hundred challenges to segregation and had been arrested more than twenty times.[49]

Not long after the committee's inaugural meeting, Rustin established its headquarters in an office on 125th Street, Harlem's main thoroughfare.[50] Rustin and Stanley Levison brainstormed novel ways to attract publicity. A keen, bespectacled forty-seven-year-old Jewish lawyer from New York, Levison was King's adviser, literary agent, and publicity strategist and had been involved with the formation of the SCLC.

Rustin and Levison proceeded to enlist thirty-eight celebrity endorsers, or "cosponsors" of the committee, including such big names in entertainment as Marlon Brando, Sammy Davis Jr., and Frank Sinatra. They planned fundraising drives in churches, direct mail campaigns, and "star-studded" benefit concerts.[51] In less than three weeks, the committee had netted over $10,000.[52] This was enough to fund their most promising plan to date—a full-page ad in the *New York Times*. The *Times* was the favored publication of liberal Northern whites who might be sympathetic to the appeal and willing to open their pocketbooks for the civil rights cause.[53]

.   .   .   .   .

Rustin sat down at a desk in the headquarters of the committee and began dictating a memo. This was the document, soon to be historic, that would become the template for the committee's fundraising ad in the *New York Times*.

Rustin dictated the memo quickly, keeping in mind that King's trial was coming up soon and that his lawyers needed to be paid. Rustin's memo described King's arrest, the sit-ins in Montgomery and other Southern cities, and the reprisals they generated. Rustin linked these events as part of a concerted attack on the civil rights movement by Southern officials. He based the memo on personal conversations he'd had with Ralph Abernathy and other civil rights leaders.

Rustin called up John Murray, a playwright and screenwriter. Murray was one of several writers who volunteered for the committee; others included Lorraine Hansberry of *Raisin in the Sun* fame. Rustin asked Murray to develop the memo into an advertisement consisting of a few hundred words. The ad needed to convey the issues compellingly, so movingly that readers would reach for their wallets, Rustin explained. Murray agreed to do this, and two days later he returned with ten paragraphs:

> As the whole world knows by now, thousands of Southern Negro students are engaged in widespread non-violent demonstrations in positive affirmation of the right to live in human dignity as guaranteed by the U. S. Constitution and the Bill of Rights. In their efforts to uphold these guarantees, they are being met by an unprecedented wave of terror by those who would deny and negate that document which the whole world looks upon as setting the pattern for modern freedom....
>
> In Orangeburg, South Carolina, when 400 students peacefully sought to buy doughnuts and coffee at lunch counters in the business district, they were forcibly ejected, tear-gassed, soaked to the skin in freezing weather with fire hoses, arrested en masse and herded into an open barbed-wire stockade to stand for hours in the bitter cold.

The third paragraph discussed the events in Montgomery:

In Montgomery, Alabama after students sang "My Country, 'Tis of Thee" on the State Capitol steps, their leaders were expelled from school, and truck-loads of police armed with shotguns and tear-gas ringed the Alabama State College Campus. When the entire student body protested to state authori-ties by refusing to re-register, their dining hall was padlocked in an attempt to starve them into submission.

The fourth and fifth paragraphs focused on other cities:

In Tallahassee, Atlanta, Nashville. . . . and a host of other cities in the South, young American teenagers, in the face of the entire weight of official state apparatus and police power, have boldly stepped forth as protagonists of democracy. Their courage and amazing restraint have inspired millions and given a new dignity to the cause of freedom.

Small wonder that the Southern violators of the Constitution fear this new, non-violent brand of freedom fighter . . . even as they fear the upswell-ing right-to-vote movement. Small wonder that they are determined to destroy the one man who, more than any other, symbolizes the new spirit now sweeping the South—the Rev. Dr. Martin Luther King, Jr., world-famous leader of the Montgomery Bus Protest. For it is his doctrine of non-violence which has inspired and guided the students in their widening wave of sit-ins; and it [is] this same Dr. King who founded and is president of the Southern Christian Leadership Conference—the organization which is spearheading the surging right-to-vote movement. . . .

The sixth paragraph described assaults on civil rights protesters com-mitted by "Southern violators" of the Constitution:

Again and again the Southern violators have answered Dr. King's peace-ful protests with intimidation and violence. They have bombed his home almost killing his wife and child. They have assaulted his person. They have arrested him seven times—for "speeding," "loitering" and similar "offenses." And now they have charged him with "perjury"—a *felony* under which they could imprison him for *ten years*. Obviously, their real purpose is to remove him physically as the leader to whom the students and millions of others—look for guidance and support, and thereby to intimidate *all* leaders who may rise in the South. Their strategy is to behead this affirmative move-ment, and thus to demoralize Negro Americans and weaken their will to struggle. The defense of Martin Luther King, spiritual leader of the student sit-in movement, clearly, therefore, is an integral part of the total struggle for freedom in the South.

The text went on to exhort "decent-minded Americans," "men and women of good will," to do more than "applaud the creative daring and the quiet heroism of Dr. King" by contributing "material help so urgently needed by those who are taking the risks, facing jail, and even death in a glorious affirmation of our Constitution and the Bill of Rights." "We urge you to join hands with our fellow Americans in the South by support- ing, with your dollars, this Combined Appeal for—the defense of Martin Luther King—the support of the embattled students—and the struggle for the right to vote."[54]

Murray's ad evoked arresting images of brutality and oppression—an "unprecedented wave of terror" visited on "American teenagers" by "South- ern violators of the Constitution." "The entire weight of official state appa- ratus and police power" had been brought to bear on young "protagonists of democracy," "freedom fighters," "Southern Upholders of the Constitu- tion." These bold assertions were backed by sixty-four luminaries of poli- tics and the arts who signed onto the ad, including actors Sammy Davis Jr., Marlon Brando, Dorothy Dandridge, Eartha Kitt, and Frank Sinatra, former first lady Eleanor Roosevelt, Socialist leader Norman Thomas, writers Lorraine Hansberry and Langston Hughes, and singers Mahalia Jackson, Harry Belafonte, and Nat King Cole. Volunteer members of the committee had contacted each of the celebrities to confirm their endorse- ment. Their names were listed at the bottom of the text, under the heading "Your Help Is Urgently Needed . . . NOW!!" Underneath, in the lower right corner, was a coupon to be returned with a contribution: "Please mail this coupon TODAY! . . . Please make checks payable to: Committee to Defend Martin Luther King."[55]

Brilliantly, the ad wedded the student protests with King's arrests, the Bill of Rights, prestigious liberal names, and the imprimatur of the *New York Times*. A headline, "HEED THEIR RISING VOICES," ran across the top of the ad. The line had been taken from a *Times* editorial that had run just a few days before, on March 19, titled "Amendment XV," which encouraged voting rights legislation then being debated in Congress, passed later that year as the Civil Rights Act of 1960. The editorial described the "peace- ful mass demonstrations by Negroes" as "something new in the South, something understandable . . . Let Congress heed their rising voices, for they will be heard."[56] This quote would appear in large type as a "kicker" in the top right corner of the ad.

Figure 3. The "Heed Their Rising Voices" ad appeared in the *New York Times* on Tuesday, March 29, 1960.

The ad was emotional and compelling, as Rustin intended. Unfortunately, it was filled with errors. In their zeal to dramatize the events and to publish the ad in a hurry, Rustin and Murray had, intentionally or unintentionally, taken liberties with the facts. There were mistakes about the events in Montgomery contained in the ad's third and sixth paragraphs. Some were minor, and some more significant.

The Montgomery "police" came to Alabama State to prevent demon-strations, but they never circled or "ringed" the campus, as the ad alleged. The expulsion of the student leaders was for their part in the lunch counter sit-ins and not for singing "My Country, 'Tis of Thee" on the capitol steps (and the students actually sang "The Star-Spangled Banner"). Less than the full student body protested by not re-registering for classes. King had been arrested only four times, not seven. Although the police did appear on the Alabama State campus, it wasn't in connection with the protest at the capitol.

The most serious was the statement about authorities padlocking the dining hall. The dining hall wasn't padlocked, and officials never attempted to "starve" the students "into submission."

On the afternoon of March 25, 1960, Murray walked down to the *New York Times* building to put the error-laden ad in the newspaper.

Through the revolving doors and marble lobby, Murray was directed to the National Advertising Department on the second floor. There, he was greeted by a sixty-three-year-old advertising salesman named Gershon Aronson. Aronson specialized in "editorial advertisements," advertise-ments for organizations that advocated a cause rather than tried to sell a product.[57]

Murray took from his briefcase six typewritten pages containing the text of the ad and identified himself as a member of the "Committee to Defend Martin Luther King." Murray explained that he needed the ad to run quickly, "just as soon as it could be done." Clipped to the ad was a one-page letter of endorsement from the committee's head, A. Philip Ran-dolph. "This will certify that the names included on the enclosed list are all signed members of the Committee to Defend Martin Luther King and the Struggle for Freedom in the South. Please be assured that they have all given us permission to use their names in furthering the work of our Committee," it read. It was standard policy at the *Times* to accept letters from responsible persons attesting that individuals' names weren't used in ads without consent.[58]

When Murray got to the advertising office it was 4:30 p.m., "wrap up time" at the end of the day. Aronson scanned the ad and Randolph's letter quickly. One of Aronson's main responsibilities in the Advertising Department was to check all incoming ads for fraud, smut, and "attacks on personal character." Aronson was impressed by the prominent members of the committee and assured that the organization was worthy and legitimate. Aronson told Murray that everything "looked fine" and that the *Times* would publish the ad within the week. After Murray left, Aronson made two copies of the ad and sent one to the Union Advertising Agency, a respected advertising firm that would coordinate the ad's layout.[59]

The next morning, Aronson sent the other copy of the ad to the Advertising Acceptability Department. Advertising Acceptability was a five-person office separate from the Advertising Department, charged with vetting all advertisements offered to the newspaper and excluding those that seemed "misleading, inaccurate, and fraudulent." [60] The *Times* had a vigorous practice of "advertising censorship," as it was dubbed at the paper. "The chief purpose" of this practice, according to the *Times*, was "to protect the reader and to maintain the high standards of decency and dignity in . . . advertising columns which the *Times* has developed over the years."[61]

This strict advertising policy had been created by Adolph Ochs, who believed that "a newspaper fit for the home is the best sort of newspaper." The *Times* rejected fraudulent or deceptive advertisements, "vulgar" advertisements, matrimonial offers, "medical advertising of dangerous drugs," and "any other advertising which is regarded by the *New York Times* as unworthy." The *Times* did not accept entire categories of advertising such as "unwarranted promises of employment in school advertising" or claims that any "cosmetic will cure wrinkles or banish freckles." It rejected advertisements that it had reason to believe came from "individuals or firms of an undesirable character."[62]

All ads were checked for accuracy and conformity with the department's policies. When the department discovered statements that should be eliminated or changed, the advertiser was notified. Advertising Acceptability made investigations to determine the truthfulness of advertisements. Ads were reworded to avoid overstatement—"the finest coat we have ever seen" became "the finest coat we have ever sold." In 1959, Advertising Acceptability made 900 changes to advertisements and declined almost 18,000 lines of advertisements.[63] The *Times'* advertising rules were considered stricter than any newspaper in the country.

The head of Advertising Acceptability, a fifty-year-old former journalist named D. Vincent Redding, looked over the "Heed Their Rising Voices" ad. Like Aronson, he was impressed by the high-profile signatories and the letter from A. Philip Randolph. He was so impressed that he never attempted to fact-check the ad, which would have been easy, as the *Times* published sixteen news stories on the events in Montgomery. Copies of these articles were contained in files in the newspaper's library or "morgue," which was one flight upstairs from the Advertising Acceptability Department. This careless treatment of the committee's ad violated the *Times'* well-established advertising policy.[64]

Three days before the ad was to run, Rustin had a change of heart. He worried that the ad wasn't persuasive enough, that it might not recoup the cost of running it. He summoned Murray to his office. Rustin pulled from a file cabinet a list of Southern black ministers associated with the SCLC and chose twenty names to be included in the ad as endorsers. The names would be prefaced with this introduction: "We in the south who are struggling daily for dignity and freedom warmly endorse this appeal." Rustin explained to Murray that the addition of these "voices from the South" would strengthen the committee's plea—they would "round out the appeal."[65]

Was it all right to use the ministers' names? Murray asked. There was no time to check with the ministers, as the ad was to run immediately, Rustin said. Plus, since the SCLC was King's organization, the clergymen would surely approve. Rustin called his connections at the Union Advertising Agency, which added the ministers' names to the ad without having to go back through the *Times* advertising department. Rustin added the names on Saturday night, got the ad redrawn on Sunday, and the advertising agency sent it to the *Times* on Monday, March 28. The "Heed Their Rising Voices" ad appeared on page 25 of the *New York Times* on Tuesday, March 29, 1960.[66]

Within days, contributions flooded the offices of the Committee to Defend Martin Luther King. Some donors sent large checks. Some envelopes contained dimes and crumpled-up dollar bills with handwritten notes from teenagers.[67] In the short term, the ad was a success, generating far more than the $4,800 it cost to put it in the newspaper.

Montgomery v. The New York Times

Only 394 copies of the *New York Times* went to Alabama, so it was remarkable that anyone in the state saw the "Heed Their Rising Voices" ad.[1]

The only copies of the *Times* that were sent to Alabama went to newspaper offices, "to eccentrics . . . a couple of Harvard graduates, a Yale man, a Princeton dropout, and the like—and a few libraries, where the newspapers were largely unread until tucked away on some obscure shelf," in the words of one local editor.[2] In Montgomery, the staff of the morning and afternoon papers, the *Montgomery Advertiser* and *Alabama Journal*, which shared a newsroom, received copies. The editors read the *Times* daily to see what was newsworthy in national and international affairs.

On April 3, 1960, Ray Jenkins, city editor of the *Alabama Journal*, was eating a homemade sandwich for lunch, as he usually did. Jenkins worked through his bologna on white bread as he went through the three-day-old newsroom copy of the *Times*.[3]

Jenkins spotted the ad on the twenty-fifth page of the first section. Here was something newsworthy—the publication of the ad by the Committee to Defend Martin Luther King was a potential story for the *Journal*, given King's notoriety and the upcoming trial. Jenkins had a feeling that the facts in the ad weren't completely accurate, and when he made a few phone calls, he found that to be the case. Within thirty minutes, he had typed out thirteen paragraphs.[4]

Jenkins's article, which ran under the headline "Liberals Appeal for Funds to Defend M.L. King," listed the endorsers of the ad and quoted language from the ad, including the passage about "an unprecedented wave of terror." Jenkins noted that the statement that student leaders at Alabama State were expelled after students sang "My Country 'Tis of Thee" on the capitol steps was incorrect. "Actually," Jenkins wrote, "the students were expelled for leading a sit-down strike at the courthouse grill." He went on to explain how the ad falsely claimed that the dining hall had been padlocked to starve the students into submission.[5]

Jenkins finished writing the article and threw the copy of the newspaper into the wastebasket. Grover Hall Jr., the *Advertiser*'s editor, read the article, stormed into the newsroom, and demanded to see the ad. Jenkins fished the paper out of the trash can.[6] Had the trash been taken out earlier that day, the constitutional law of freedom of the press would have been much different.

The *Advertiser* was the most influential organ of public opinion in Montgomery. The newspaper reflected the larger-than-life personality of editor Hall, who was grumpy, arrogant, puckish, and confrontational. On the *Advertiser*'s lively editorial page, Hall offered tart verbal flourishes on everything from post office pens to segregation to foreign policy, in the fashion of his journalistic hero, H.L. Mencken. In a fit of pique, he once described Alabama governor James Folsom as an "untaught knave . . . [who] lacks the grace and prudence to keep zippered his flapping mandible to conceal his void."[7] Hall cultivated his eccentricity to extreme proportions, going as far as to decorate his home with large stands of camellias. He trained his mynah bird, named Mute, to say "hello fat ass" to anyone who came through the door. Colored dress shirts, suspenders, and porkpie hats contributed to his aura of pomp and insouciance. The forty-five-year-old bachelor reveled in his image as a contrarian, swashbuckler, and wit.[8]

Hall appeared to be the epitome of swagger and ebullience, but the man was deeply insecure. Hall descended from an esteemed family of Alabama newspaper publishers. In 1948, after working as a police reporter, then as a capital correspondent and columnist for the *Advertiser*, Hall inherited the editorship from his father, Grover Hall Sr., who had won a Pulitzer Prize in 1928 for editorials condemning the Ku Klux Klan. The younger Hall, who never attended college and was a less gifted writer, knew he would never attain his father's status and sought renown through other means. If nothing else, Hall knew how to get attention.[9]

But Hall was more complex than that. At the same time he was preening his dandified image, he was injecting a thoughtful voice into local affairs. Hall was a political moderate who approved of segregation but opposed the violent steps that hard-line segregationists like L.B. Sullivan were taking to enforce it. Hall's editorials on race took a sophisticated and thoughtful tone that made many in Montgomery uneasy. Hall had denounced the White Citizens' Councils as "manicured Kluxers" and supported the bus boycott editorially, a move that cost the *Advertiser* subscription revenues. In his 1958 memoir *Stride Toward Freedom*, Martin Luther King Jr. described Hall as a "brilliant but complex man who claimed to be a supporter of segregation but could not stomach the excesses performed in its name."[10]

What Hall did share with most Montgomery residents was hostility toward the Northern press. Hall was convinced that the press was suppressing the South's perspectives on race and concealing the North's own racial problems in a "conspiracy of silence." This animus intensified in 1956, when Hall found himself host to more than a hundred reporters from "up Nawth" who descended on the city to cover the bus boycott and used the *Advertiser* office as their headquarters.[11] The *New York Post*'s star reporter Murray Kempton took out a red pencil and drew a map showing how school districts in New York were gerrymandered to achieve segregation. When Hall heard this, he sprang to his feet and volunteered to do an expose of racism in New York for the *Post*.

The *Post*'s editor declined his offer, and Hall set out to do the job himself. Hall's staffers made phone calls to editors, judges, and police in Northern cities.[12] Racial conflict in the North was ignored by its press, they concluded, but "a bus station arrest anywhere in the Deep South was always good for page one in those same papers."[13]

In the "Askelon series"—thirty articles published in the spring of 1956 under the dramatic title "TELL IT NOT IN GATH, PUBLISH IT NOT IN

THE STREETS OF ASKELON"—the *Advertiser* unfolded an encyclopedia of Northern racial sins and the alleged failure of its press to report those sins.[14] The mayor of Dearborn, Michigan, once said, "I am for complete segregation, one million percent, on all levels," the *Advertiser* reported. Hall found parts of Detroit where blacks were unable to buy or rent living quarters, and fiery crosses in Ohio. "Anything like that happening in Montgomery would have made the lead story in all of those [Northern] papers. Yet they ignore their own dirty wash. It makes me mad," he wrote. "Discrimination is discrimination everywhere, not just when it happens under a Southern magnolia."[15]

For the "Askelon series," Hall was celebrated as a hero in the region. The Alabama House of Representatives passed a resolution praising the *Advertiser* for defending the South from attacks on the "Southern way of life."[16] Grover Hall "possessed both the courage and the ability to rip the veil of hypocrisy from these Northern publications," gushed the *Clarke County Democrat* of Grove Hill, Alabama.[17] Hall's thorough and hard-hitting reporting was acclaimed in national publications like *Newsweek* and even nominated for the Pulitzer Prize. "Askelon" did impact Northern press coverage of race relations. As a result of Hall's series, the *New York Post* did a series on discrimination in New York, and the *New York Times* ran a four-part sequence on racial tensions in the North.[18]

Yet Askelon didn't free Hall of his rage toward the "paper curtain press"; it only convinced him of the rightness of his position. Hall maintained that Northern newspapers and magazines had caricatured the South, held it up to ridicule, and failed to appreciate how the South was dealing with its racial issues on its own terms.[19] He denounced the editors and reporters of the *New York Times* as "deluded racists" that "pompously droned" that the South must obey the law of the land yet concealed how schools in their region were "buckets of scorpions," with girls "raped and stabbed on schoolhouse stairways."[20]

With its melodramatic and stereotypical portrayal of the South, and Montgomery in particular, as violent and racist, the "Heed Their Rising Voices" ad outraged Hall and drove him straight to his typewriter. In less than forty minutes, he fired off a pungent editorial titled "Will They Purge Themselves?" that appeared on the second page of the *Advertiser* on April 7, 1960:

There are voluntary liars, there are involuntary liars.

Both kinds of liars contributed to the crude slander against Montgomery broadcast in a full-page advertisement in the *New York Times* March 29.

And its [*sic*] up to the *New York Times* and the involuntary liars to purge themselves of their false witness.

The *Times* boasts that it screens advertisements to eliminate what is indelicate or in bad taste. Perhaps demonstrable lies will at some future time be screened and found unfit for print.

Hall printed the statement in the ad about Montgomery police padlocking the Alabama State dining hall and ringing the college campus. Those statements were "lies, lies, lies—and possibly willful ones on the part of the fund-raising novelist who wrote those lines to prey on the credulity, self-righteousness, and misinformation of northern citizens."[21]

Hall noted that esteemed liberal figures signed onto the ad, including Harry Emerson Fosdick, Eleanor Roosevelt, and Norman Thomas, longtime leader of the Socialist Party—all detested names in the South. "Such ones were victimized and we should think they will deem it a duty to their own honor to test *The Advertiser*'s perjury charges and cleanse their names." Hall described others on the committee, the actors and entertainers, as "corner pick-ups from the Broadway marquees." "They, of course, just came along for the ride and it probably is not possible to excite their interest in a thing so homely as the truth." "But the *Advertiser* is going to have to revise some estimates if committeemen such as Dr. Fosdick, Rice, and Thomas and *The New York Times* do not feel called upon to ascertain whether *The Advertiser* is correct in asserting their names are married to a slanderous lie."[22]

•   •   •   •   •

The morning after his editorial came out, Hall was standing outside the *Advertiser* office, as he usually did. He had a daily habit of standing on the steps and shooting the breeze with passersby, hoping to rope them into chitchat on one of his pet causes or editorial topics. Calvin Whitesell, an ambitious thirty-one-year-old who litigated cases for the city, was coming up the street. It was a good coincidence, as the night before Hall had been thinking about libel.

"Hey, come here," Hall shouted. He waved the copy of the *New York Times* at Whitesell. "I know you don't have sense enough to read the *New York Times.*"

"You better take this thing and show it to City Hall" because it "libeled every one of them," he said, handing Whitesell the paper.[23] Hall was referring to city commissioners James, Parks, and Sullivan. Hall knew that it would be useless to sue the Committee to Defend Martin Luther King, which was practically insolvent. But under the libel laws of Alabama and most states, the *Times*, as the publisher of the ad, was just as responsible for its contents as the ad's creators.

Later that morning, Whitesell put the dog-eared copy of the *Times* on the desk of Mayor Earl James and told him what Hall had said about a libel suit. James brought Sullivan and commissioner Frank Parks to his office on the second floor of the Montgomery city hall. The three men hovered over James's glass-topped desk, reading the ad intently.

What troubled them, as it had disturbed Hall, wasn't the minor errors, such as the mistaken names of the songs that had been sung by the student protesters on the capitol steps. Rather, it was the allegation that the police had "padlocked" the Alabama State dining hall to starve the students, which was false. They also resented the melodramatic language that villainized the South and its officials, which seemed to them another example of "paper curtain" coverage that belittled and ridiculed the region.

In its overall gist, of course, the statements were true. The Montgomery officials had abetted and committed violence against the civil rights protesters, although perhaps not the specific acts of which they were accused. The reputations of the commissioners were certainly not harmed in Montgomery—inflicting brutality on civil rights "agitators" would enhance one's reputation among local whites—although their images were arguably lowered among audiences above the Mason-Dixon line.[24]

There was another, more inviting reason to sue, apart from injury to reputation. Here was a brilliant opportunity to sink the *New York Times*. A large damage award would injure the *Times* financially and send a powerful message that the South wouldn't tolerate insults and slights from the "lying Yankee press." A massive libel judgment would intimidate Northern media outlets, deterring them from covering civil rights activities and portraying the South in an unfavorable light. The 1957 *Ken* case brought by the Montgomery commissioners had shown that libel suits against Northern media could be easily won before local juries and were lucrative.

James picked up the phone and called the lawyer, Whitesell. "Hall says that this is libel? What are the damages?" he asked.

"The damages," Whitesell replied, are "whatever the jury thinks you're entitled to."

Whitesell warned the commissioners that when they sued the *Times*, it would "come down and hire the local counselors for the newspapers." The elite law firm Steiner, Crum, and Baker represented the *Advertiser* and the *Journal*. Whitesell wanted to get the firm on the city's side so the *Times* couldn't use it.[25]

Whitesell walked down to the First National Bank Building, the prestigious office building where Steiner, Crum, and Baker had their headquarters. Baker and Steiner told Whitesell that it was a "super, wonderful case" and that they were happy to get involved.[26] Grover Hall gave his permission for the officials to employ the firm, violating the unspoken rule in journalism that newspapers didn't cooperate in libel suits against other newspapers. The case was assigned to M. Roland "Rod" Nachman Jr., a thirty-seven-year-old lawyer at the firm who had brought the *Ken* case, defended the *Montgomery Advertiser* in libel suits, and was an obvious choice for this task.

.   .   .   .   .

It's often been assumed that the lawyer for the Montgomery commissioners was a die-hard segregationist, but that wasn't the case. Nachman was cosmopolitan, Harvard-educated, and Jewish—an unusual figure in Montgomery.

Nachman was born in Montgomery in 1923 to a German Jewish family that ran an upscale department store called Nachman and Mertief. Jews were a minority in Alabama and subject to discrimination, but they didn't experience the same persecution as blacks. Jewish merchants and bankers were needed in Montgomery and thus welcomed into the community.[27]

The Nachman family enjoyed a privileged and cultured lifestyle. Rod, a wunderkind of sorts, graduated at the age of sixteen from Sidney Lanier High School, Montgomery's white high school, then went to Harvard.

After his second year at Harvard, at the height of World War II, Nachman enlisted in the Navy and served as an intelligence officer stationed in Hawaii for three years. He then went to Harvard Law School, graduating in only two years. Although he was offered a prestigious job in the state government of California, Nachman accepted an offer to serve as Alabama's assistant attorney general and returned to his hometown. By the time he was thirty, he had argued several cases for the state before the U.S. Supreme Court.[28]

Nachman was tall and scholarly-looking, with a receding hairline, thick, black-rimmed glasses, and a mischievous smile. He was bright, hard-working, witty, and temperamental, and despite his liberal leanings, respected in the Montgomery community for his intelligence and professionalism. Nachman and his wife, Louise, were part of Montgomery's small intellectual community and were known for the lively cocktail parties and salons they held in their elegant Tudor home.[29]

Politically, Nachman was a moderate Democrat who had supported Harry Truman in the 1948 election and worked on Adlai Stevenson's 1956 presidential campaign. Nachman was hardly a segregationist. His travels, family background, and elite education had given him a cosmopolitan outlook on race. As a Jew, he had his own experiences with discrimination. In the 1950s, as antisemitism crested in Alabama alongside white supremacy and Southern xenophobia, Nachman was forbidden to join the Montgomery Country Club.[30]

In 1954, Nachman left government service and entered private practice with Walter Knabe, former city attorney. Two years later, he left Montgomery for Washington to work as an assistant to Democratic senator John Sparkman. In 1959, he returned to Montgomery and joined the firm of Steiner, Crum, and Baker. The firm was general counsel for the First National Bank, the Western Railway of Alabama, and several other railroads, banks, and newspapers. With three generations of Harvard graduates in its ranks, it was considered a "white shoe" firm, one of the most prestigious in the city.[31]

Nachman was known for his tenacious, shrewd, and spirited representation of an array of clients, from the city government to local newspapers to residents who sued the press for libel. Nachman liked to win, so he was inclined to take anyone's case as long as it had merit. In 1959, he represented a black Montgomery citizen named Edward Davis, who had been charged with assaulting civil rights leader Ralph Abernathy but was acquitted. *Jet* magazine alleged, incorrectly, that he was the same Davis who had been expelled from his teaching job for making sexual advances on students. A jury awarded him $67,500. It was the largest libel award in the state to that time.[32]

Like Grover Hall and the commissioners, Nachman was irked by the "Heed Their Rising Voices" ad. "Some of the things were absolutely false and some of the charges were grossly exaggerated to the point of bullshit," he believed—in particular, the charge about police padlocking the dining hall.[33]

But it wasn't outrage that got him into the case. It wasn't animus against the *New York Times*, or a desire to enforce segregation. It was old-fashioned competitiveness, tinged with regional pride. Here was a case that was almost impossible to lose. Under existing libel law, all the plaintiff had to demonstrate was that the statements were defamatory and "of and concerning" him—that they referred to the plaintiff. The statements were presumed to be false; the only way the *Times* could defend itself was by demonstrating the truth of the statements "in all their particulars."[34]

Within a day, Nachman had drawn up letters on behalf of Parks, James, and Sullivan demanding retractions of the allegedly false and defamatory statements.[35] The letters called on the addressee to "publish in as prominent and as public a manner as the foregoing false and defamatory material contained in the foregoing publication ... a full and fair retraction of the entire false and defamatory matter so far as the same relates to me and to my conduct and acts as a public official of the City of Montgomery, Alabama."[36] The demand for a retraction was a prerequisite to filing a libel suit and a requirement for the plaintiff to receive punitive damages, damages to punish the defendant for reprehensible conduct and to deter similar conduct by other defendants. Under Title 7, Section 913 of the State Code, if the defendants didn't publish a "full and fair" retraction within five days, "offering amends before suit by publishing an apology in a newspaper ... in a prominent position," the plaintiffs could recover punitive damages.[37] The failure to retract was said to be evidence that the defendant had published the libel spitefully or maliciously. Punitive damages were important; a large punitive damage award could seriously injure the *Times*.

Nachman's letters alleged that the "Heed Their Rising Voices" ad contained falsehoods that imputed to the commissioners "grave misconduct and improper actions and omissions as an official of the city of Montgomery." Nachman identified two paragraphs of the ad as false and defamatory, the third paragraph and a portion of the sixth:

> In Montgomery, after students sang "My Country, 'Tis of Thee" on the State Capitol steps, their leaders were expelled from school, and truckloads of police armed with shotguns and tear-gas ringed the Alabama State College Campus. When the entire student body protested to state authorities by refusing to re-register, their dining hall was padlocked in an attempt to starve them into submission. . . .
>
> Again and again the Southern violators have answered Dr. King's peaceful protests with intimidation and violence. They have bombed his home almost killing his wife and child. They have assaulted his person. They have arrested him seven times—for "speeding," "loitering" and similar "offenses." And now they have charged him with "perjury"—a felony under which they could imprison him for ten years.[38]

Even though the ad didn't identify the commissioners by name, the passages implicitly accused them (as the "police" and "Southern violators") of ringing the campus with armed police, arresting King for spurious offenses, padlocking the dining room and starving the students, bombing the King home, assaulting King, and charging him with perjury, according to Nachman. The commissioners claimed that the allegations, to use a libel law technicality, were "of and concerning" them; that is, they impliedly referred to the commissioners such that their reputations would be impugned.

Nachman sent the retraction letters to the *Times* and to four Alabama ministers whose names had been added to the ad by Bayard Rustin at the last minute: Ralph Abernathy, Solomon Seay, Joseph Lowery, and Fred Shuttlesworth. Under existing libel laws, these men were just as responsible for the ad's content as the *New York Times*. They were said to have endorsed or "ratified" the ad by allowing their names to appear on it. The four ministers were leaders of the SCLC but were not connected with the Committee to Defend Martin Luther King. Nachman had brought them into the lawsuit because they were Alabama residents. He knew that the *Times* would try to remove the case to the federal courts in Alabama, which were far more sympathetic on racial issues than the state courts, but that this would be blocked under jurisdictional laws if residents of the state were parties in the case. The four ministers were sued to prevent, under formal legal terminology, "complete diversity," so that the *Times* could be sued in Alabama. Nachman wanted the case to be heard in state court by a local judge and jury. Suing the ministers would also undermine the SCLC by forcing its leaders into a costly defense.

.   .   .   .   .

Roland Nachman wasn't the only one preparing to take legal action against the *New York Times* over the "Heed Their Rising Voices" ad. Grover Hall's editorial had put the entire state on notice. Alabama authorities began gearing up the state's machinery to "prosecute" the *Times* and the Committee to Defend Martin Luther King for the purported offense of "slandering the South."

Alabama secretary of state Bettye Frink sent a letter to the Associated Press, printed in newspapers nationwide, announcing that she intended to bring charges against the *Times* and the Committee to Defend Martin Luther King for "using the mails to defraud," by circulating false statements. Attorney General McDonald Gallion was reportedly considering actions against the *Times* on behalf of the state of Alabama for "circulating lies."[39] "We are sick and tired of warped and slanted attacks on Alabama and the South and it is particularly reprehensible to be the subject of this lie attack," he announced.[40] It was explained to him that only individuals could sue for libel. Gallion advised the members of the State Board of Education, of which Patterson was a member, to file a "multi-million-dollar lawsuit."[41]

The Montgomery City Commission then published an "official resolution": "Each of the city commissioners of Montgomery today, by registered mail, demanded that the New York Times and certain other individuals publish a retraction of the defamatory material that was published in The

New York Times recently. We demanded that a full and fair retraction be published in as prominent and public a manner as the false and defamatory material was published. We await their retraction."[42] By now, the *Times* was aware of the libel suits, having received the retraction letters as well as the *Advertiser* editorial, which Hall mailed to the newspaper himself.

Alabamians were being rallied by these official pronouncements, backed by zealous editorials in the state's press. Opined the *Alabama Journal*:

> Now that Montgomery is once again the victim of wholly false stories published by a group of Negroes and Mrs. Roosevelt in the *New York Times*, we must remember the trials our forefathers endured years ago.... there is nothing new when the South is traduced and misrepresented. Unfortunately there is nothing we can do about it. Even a war did not stop the lies about the South.... It must be very disappointing to regular readers of the *New York Times*, one of the world's really great newspapers, to find it has been willing to lend its columns for such a page of falsehood as that published the other day and signed by money beggars who want to defend such a despicable character as Martin Luther King in the courts and to save him from the penalties of his derelictions.[43]

The libel suits were uniting segregationists, energizing them, convincing them of the rightness of their efforts.

. . . . . .

Louis Loeb was unfazed. As counsel for the *Times*, he had received hundreds of similar letters before. Loeb nonetheless took Nachman's letter seriously and set out to determine if the statements in the ad were true.

Loeb called Robert Garst, assistant managing editor, and asked him to have someone in Montgomery fact-check the ad. Garst wired Don McKee, a reporter for the *Advertiser* who was a "stringer" for the *Times*. A stringer was a writer for another newspaper whom the *Times* called for news on an as-needed basis. The *Times* had three stringers in Alabama.[44]

Shortly after, McKee called Garst with bad news: some of the statements in the ad were, in fact, false. McKee interviewed officials at Alabama State and found that there was "absolutely no truth" to the allegation that the dining hall was padlocked and that the "entire student body refused to re-register." The police didn't ring the campus. Almost all the 1,900 students had re-registered, meal service was furnished to all the students, Montgomery police entered the campus upon request of the college officials, the students sang the national anthem, not "My Country 'Tis of Thee," and King was arrested only four times.[45]

Loeb—overconfidently, in retrospect—sent a letter to Nachman informing him that the *Times* refused to retract any of the statements. Most of the statements were substantially true, he said—perhaps not true in all details, but in their overall meaning—and moreover, none of the statements referred specifically to any of the commissioners, so none of them could have been libeled:

> Dear Mr. Commissioner: Your letter of April 8 sent by registered mail to The New York Times Company has been referred for attention to us as general counsel. You will appreciate, we feel sure, that the statements to which you object were not made by the New York Times but were contained in an advertisement proffered to the Times by responsible persons. We have been investigating the matter and are somewhat puzzled as to how you think the statements in any way reflect on you. So far, our investigation would seem to indicate that the statements are substantially correct with the sole exception that we find no justification for the statement that the dining hall in the state college was "padlocked in an attempt to starve them into submission."
>
> We shall continue to look into the subject matter because our client . . . is always desirous of correcting any statements which appear in its paper and which turn out to be erroneous.
>
> In the meanwhile you might, if you desire, let us know in what respect you claim that the statements in the advertisement reflect on you. Very truly yours, Lord Day & Lord.[46]

The threatened lawsuits quickly materialized. On April 19, without answering Loeb's letter, Nachman filed libel suits in the circuit court of Montgomery County against the *Times* and the four Alabama ministers.[47] The libel action was formally commenced on April 21, when the sheriff of Montgomery, Mac Sim Butler, served a summons and complaint on the stringer, McKee.[48]

The commissioners sought $500,000 each in damages "for false and defamatory matter or charges reflecting upon the conduct of the plaintiff as a member of the Board of Commissioners and imputing improper conduct to him, and subjecting him to public contempt, ridicule, and shame, and prejudicing the plaintiff in his office, profession, trade, or business." Under the law in Alabama and most states, a libel plaintiff did not have to show specific economic loss caused by the alleged libel. They could receive "general damages" for emotional and reputational harm without calculating the precise worth of the loss. The sum of $500,000 was arbitrary. In the first iteration of Nachman's complaint, the plea was for one million dollars, which Nachman cut down to $750,000, then to half a million for each commissioner.[49]

The *Times* did very little business in Alabama and hadn't designated anyone to accept service of process there. Nachman relied on Sections 188 and 199(1) of Title 7 of the Alabama Code to commence the lawsuit. Section 188 provides that process may be served on a corporation by delivering a copy of the summons and complaint upon officers or employees of the corporation, including "any agent thereof." Papers were served on McKee, whom Nachman alleged was an "agent" of the *Times*. In addition, Nachman served process on the secretary of state under Section 199(1), the state's so-called long-arm statute. Under the statute, "any nonresident person, firm,... or any corporation not qualified as doing business herein, who shall do any business or perform any character of work or service in this state shall be deemed to have appointed the secretary of state ... their agent."[50] A long-arm statute allows a court to obtain personal jurisdiction over an out-of-state defendant on the basis of certain acts committed by the defendant, provided that the defendant has a sufficient connection with the state.[51] Such statutes are known by lawyers as "one-act statutes" and were at the time used primarily in cases involving auto accidents. The *Times* would contest the service of process on both McKee and the secretary of state.

The libel suits were clearly being used to punish the *Times* for its civil rights coverage and its liberal, pro-integration stance, and to stifle that reporting by intimidating and burdening the paper financially. Through the lawsuits, the Montgomery officials intended to let not only the *Times* but the entire Northern press know that they faced libel suits if they covered civil rights sympathetically, supported integration, ran King's advertisements, or published any criticism of Alabama. The Montgomery officials also intended to quash the SCLC and to inform the civil rights movement that it would be destroyed and its leaders persecuted if it con-tinued to challenge the racial status quo.[52]

This purpose was made crystal clear by editorial commentary in Ala-bama newspapers not long after the lawsuits were filed. "One Southern community, long a target of journalistic abuse and integrationist pro-paganda in the Northern press, apparently has reached the end of its patience and is striking back," observed the outspoken segregationist journalist William Workman.[53] "You would think that a newspaper as old as the *New York Times* would recognize anything so maliciously written," opined a columnist in rural Florala, Alabama. "Apparently they didn't even bother to learn if the malicious statements were truth or if it could be that they don't give the people of the South enough credit for having enough sense, or perhaps guts, to file a libel suit against them. But the peoples of the South can take just so much malicious activities of the Northern press. Eventually the people of the South will have swallowed just as much 'untruth' as they can and will resist. The South has now been pushed to that point."[54]

Whenever it was sued outside New York, the *Times* relied on out-of-state lawyers for routine litigation work. Like banks, lawyers had "correspon-dent" firms in other cities to whom they turned for collaboration on local cases, with the idea that local lawyers were friendlier with the local bench and more familiar with their home state's laws.

Loeb called up a prestigious law firm in Birmingham that had handled other matters for Lord Day & Lord. The partners, to his surprise, told him that they couldn't get involved, saying that there was a "conflict of inter-est." Loeb tried two more top firms in the city, which both said the same thing. It was clear that no one in Alabama wanted anything to do with the *New York Times*.[55]

In the end, a Birmingham firm called Embry & Beddow stepped up. They were a small practice, specializing in litigation. Despite a reputation as a maverick for their defense of labor unions and poor black criminal defendants, the firm maintained the high regard of the Alabama bar and bench. The senior partner, Roderick Beddow, one of the state's most respected criminal lawyers, was nicknamed the "Perry Mason of Birmingham." He had unsuccessfully represented the Scottsboro boys, the nine young black men falsely accused of rape in the infamous case of the 1930s—a most unpopular cause in Alabama, if there ever was one.[56]

The junior partner Thomas Eric Embry, who went by Eric, was a bespectacled, dark-haired, overweight six-footer. The foul-mouthed and cantankerous thirty-nine-year-old with a defiant sneer had served as a captain in the U.S. infantry during the war and had turned down a professional baseball contract to study law at the University of Alabama. Embry descended from a long and distinguished line of Alabama lawyers and jurists. He had a thriving practice representing plaintiffs in personal injury cases when the *Times* came calling.[57] To be clear, Embry and Beddow didn't take the *Times* case because they cared about freedom of the press. It was clear that with the newspaper paying the bills, the cases would be lucrative, and that was worth being shunned in Alabama.

Embry and Beddow flew to New York and met with *Times* officials. The newspaper executives explained how the *Times* was put together and how the ads were placed. They said that the *Times* had a stellar record on libel and they weren't about to lose it. "They told me they didn't care what it cost to defend the case, they wouldn't pay anything voluntarily," Embry recalled. Per the "Ochs policy," the *Times* refused to settle.[58]

6 Birmingham v. The New York Times

The *New York Times*' troubles in Alabama were just beginning. When the sit-in movement spread, Catledge had to assign more staff to cover it. One of them was Harrison Salisbury, among the newspaper's most intrepid correspondents. Salisbury's scathing indictment of race relations in Birmingham would trigger another round of libel suits.

.   .   .   .   .

Harrison Salisbury could never be mistaken for a Southerner. A native of Minnesota, Salisbury was tall and lanky with broad shoulders and an angular face and spoke in a nasal, flat-toned voice. His hair was gray and combed sharply across his forehead. He had a drooping mustache and a severe and stoic expression. Salisbury wore tweedy suits and wire-rimmed glasses that framed intense, pale blue eyes.[1]

Salisbury was a living legend in journalism, renowned for his lucid writing, deeply researched stories, and talent for making trouble for the powerful. From the start of his career at the United Press in the 1920s, his work generated intense reactions. Salisbury wrote a harsh account of the Great Depression's impact on Minneapolis that won critical acclaim, as well as a demand from the *Minneapolis Journal* that he be fired from the UP for slandering the city. Salisbury worked for the United Press for eighteen years, moving through increasingly important positions and amassing accolades for his dynamic reporting. A self-described "action addict," possessed of phenomenal energy, he moved swiftly between cities, amidst disasters and deadlines, from St. Paul to Chicago to Washington to London to Cairo and Moscow. His abundant confidence led him to sweeping conclusions that editors were often hesitant to challenge.[2]

In 1949, Salisbury joined the *Times* as its Moscow correspondent, a challenging assignment because of Soviet restrictions on foreign journalists. In 1955, he won the Pulitzer Prize for foreign reporting and later published the uncensored versions of his dispatches in *Moscow Journal: The End of Stalin* (1961). Prevented from entering the Soviet Union after 1955, he reported domestic stories for the *Times*, wrote for magazines like the *Saturday Evening Post*, and expanded a popular story he had written about Brooklyn's teenage gangs into a bestselling book called *The Shook-Up Generation* (1958).[3]

As a foreign correspondent, Salisbury had regularly "parachuted" into unfamiliar territory and wrote quick "overview" stories. Catledge asked him to do the same in the South. A month after the Greensboro sit-in, Salisbury reported from Nashville, then Raleigh and Columbia, South Carolina. Catledge liked Salisbury's dispatches and asked him to pick a few key cities, to go there and "analyze what was happening, and try to figure out what was likely to happen." He chose Birmingham. People warned him about Birmingham, one of the nation's roughest, most segregated cities. It was like "Gibraltar, impenetrable," they told him. "It would take an earthquake to roll over Birmingham."[4]

It had been dubbed "Bombingham" for its racial violence. Since 1940, Birmingham had been the site of more than fifty bombings of black homes and businesses. As civil rights tensions increased in the 1950s, there was a widening spectrum of brutality ranging from muggings to floggings and castrations. In the first months of 1960, a racist and antisemitic branch of the White Citizens' Council had carried out a series of bombing attacks on black churches and homes, as well as several synagogues. Hard-line segregationists dominated politics, and moderate white opinion was almost completely submerged. The KKK, considered "respectable," was more active

Figure 4. Theophilus Eugene "Bull" Connor, a former baseball announcer with a booming voice, used his authority over the police and education departments to enforce segregation in Birmingham. Alabama Department of Archives and History. Donated by Alabama Media Group. Photo by Ed Jones and Robert Adams, *Birmingham News.*

than it had been in twenty years. Salisbury was convinced that much of Birmingham's racial strife was the result of violence-prone public safety commissioner Theophilus Eugene "Bull" Connor, a former baseball announcer with a booming voice who terrorized black residents and used his authority over the police and education departments to enforce segregation.[5]

On his way to Birmingham, Salisbury stopped off in Montgomery. It was the day after the "Heed Their Rising Voices" ad appeared in the *Times.* He bought a batch of Montgomery and Birmingham newspapers and found that officials were talking about libel suits over the ad. "The Alabama press was full of threats and denunciations of the *New York Times*," he recalled. "To me [a libel suit] sounded plain nutty, but I took it as a serious reflection of the feverish temperature of the state, a clear warning to watch my step." But Salisbury didn't think much of the Montgomery controversy because that weekend the sit-in wave hit Birmingham. On Thursday, April 2, ten black students went two-by-two into five downtown

Birmingham stores. They made small purchases and sat at lunch counters. All were arrested on charges of trespassing.[6]

Salisbury drove to Andalusia, in the heart of Alabama's segregationist belt, to report on a speech by minister Truman Douglas asking fellow white clergymen to join black students in their fight against discrimination. He returned to Montgomery, then went to Baton Rouge, where he had been assigned to cover another sit-in, this one at Southern University. The following day, he drove four hundred miles north to Birmingham. The time stamp at the Tutwiler Hotel recorded the time of his arrival: 9:53 a.m., April 6, 1960.[7]

·   ·   ·   ·   ·

A bellboy escorted him through the hotel's ornate halls. The Tutwiler, on Twentieth Street North in downtown Birmingham, built in a grand and opulent style, was a local landmark and considered the embodiment of the Birmingham establishment.

Salisbury was shown to Room 1117. He put down his bags and picked up the phone. Within minutes, a clerk instructed him to move to Room 1060. It wasn't until years later that Salisbury figured out the reason for the change—he had initially been placed in a room without a bug. Connor's men were taping his calls from their command post at an old firehouse nearby. From his new room, unaware of this surveillance, he began calling sources given to him by the *Times*' National Desk. Salisbury had been told to conduct his interviews with extreme care. "Be careful of what you say and whom you mention. Lives are at stake. Birmingham is no place for irresponsible reporting," they warned him.[8]

Times stringer John Chadwick took him on a tour of the city. In Chadwick's beat-up Buick, they drove by the statue of Vulcan atop Red Mountain, symbolizing the steel and coal industry that had led Birmingham to be known as the "Pittsburgh of the South." Salisbury lunched at "the Club," where the city's bankers and businessmen, nicknamed "Big Mules," talked over martinis and king crab salad. They drove through the affluent suburb of Mountain Brook, with its expensive homes adorned with lush flowers and foliage. They toured Honeysuckle Hills, the best black residential district. At the end of the day they went to Bessemer, a tough, grim-looking industrial enclave fifteen miles south of Birmingham, home to the city's steel mills.[9]

When night fell, Salisbury took a cab from the Tutwiler to the home of Reverend Robert Hughes, executive director of an interracial civil rights group called the Alabama Council on Human Relations. The soft-spoken twenty-six-year-old Methodist minister, a tense, slightly built man, had become known as a contact point for out-of-state reporters who found official sources of information closed to them. Hughes had hit upon an expedient mechanism that would expose Birmingham's problems to the nation and in so doing force the city to confront its problems. In 1958, he commenced a systematic program of providing reporters from major publications with information about the extent of Birmingham's racial violence. Hughes's first success came when *Time* magazine in December 1958 published an article warning that "the death of leadership, the silence of fear, the bomb blasts of hatred" contributed to Birmingham's being the "toughest city in the South, and likely to get tougher."[10] Local business leaders, who had embarked on a campaign to reverse Birmingham's economic decline (it was once known as the "Magic City" for its industrial growth), were terrified by this stain on the city's reputation.[11]

Hughes had suffered greatly for this work. Crosses were burned in his lawn. Local tabloids smeared him, and harassers called his phone at night. His wife was assaulted. When Salisbury arrived, Hughes let him in only after peering to see if any cars had followed him. The shades were pulled, and the curtains drawn.[12]

In a soft and quivering voice, Hughes told Salisbury of racial terror—of violence and threats, the KKK, of Bull Connor's police, of wiretapping, beatings, and murders, of racist politicians and the city's intimidated power structure. At midnight, Hughes drove Salisbury back to the Tutwiler. Salisbury got another list of sources from Hughes, including Fred Shuttlesworth, who had just been sued by the Montgomery commissioners over the "Heed Their Rising Voices" ad. Later, Salisbury interviewed Lieutenant Governor Albert Boutwell, discussed with a representative of a local black college student involvement in sit-ins, and met a group of businessmen who said racial tensions in the city were going to "erupt." Milton Grafman of Temple Emanuel led Salisbury into his study, locking the door behind him. Two weeks earlier, a local synagogue had been firebombed by a Nazi sympathizer.[13]

Back at the Tutwiler, Salisbury composed his articles, typing them up on his 1942 Remington portable. Before leaving Birmingham, he dictated his material, two articles' worth, to New York from the airport telephone. Birmingham was gripped by a reign of terror, Salisbury concluded.[14] Salisbury's first article, "Fear and Hatred Grip Birmingham," appeared near the bottom of the *New York Times'* front page on April 12, 1960.

. . . . . .

The articles were classic Salisbury, shrewd reporting wrapped in layers of invective and flair. The "eavesdropper, the informer, the spy have become a fact of life," Salisbury had written. "It is not accidental that the Negro sit-in movement protesting lunch counter segregation has only lightly touched brooding Birmingham. But even those light touches have sent convulsive tremors through the delicately balanced power structure of the community."[15]

> From Red Mountain, where a cast-iron Vulcan looks down 500 feet to the sprawling city, Birmingham seems veiled in the poisonous fumes of distant battles.
>
> On a fine April day, however, it is only the haze of acid fog belched from the stacks of the Tennessee Coal and Iron Company's Fairfield and Ensley works that lies over the city.
>
> But more than a few citizens, both white and Negro, harbor growing fear that the hour will strike when the smoke of civil strife will mingle with that of the hearths and forges....
>
> Whites and blacks still walk the same streets. But the streets, the water supply and the sewer system are about the only public facilities they share. Ball parks and taxicabs are segregated. So are libraries. A book featuring black rabbits and white rabbits was banned. A drive is on to forbid "Negro music" on "white" radio stations....
>
> Every channel of communication, every medium of mutual interest, every reasoned approach, every inch of middle ground has been fragmented by the emotional dynamite of racism, reinforced by the whip, the razor, the gun, the bomb, the torch, the club, the knife, the mob, the police and many branches of the state's apparatus.[16]

"If fear and terror are common in the streets of Birmingham, the atmosphere in Bessemer, the adjacent steel suburb, is even worse," Salisbury continued. He described a band of floggers in Bessemer who beat a white woman who confessed that she was dating black men. Seven carloads of hooded men roared into the street where a civil rights protester lived with his mother and sister. Armed with clubs, iron pipes, and leather black-jacks into which razor blades were sunk, the men attacked the boy and his mother and sister. "The list of beatings and violence could almost go on indefinitely. Birmingham's whites and blacks share a community of fear." He quoted one black resident as saying, "The difference between Johannesburg and Birmingham is that here they have not opened fire with the tanks and big guns." A caption beneath a picture of Connor said he "was elected in 1958 on race hate platform."[17]

A second article, titled "Race Issues Shakes Alabama Structure," appeared the following day. It described how Alabama's political and social structure was developing "symptoms of disintegration" "under the corrosive impact of the segregation issue." Salisbury noted the development of horse patrols—"the rough equivalent of vigilantes of the Wild West days"—in five counties, the expanding activities of the Klan, growing antisemitism, and increasing violence. "The lines between legality and extra-legality are becoming blurred. . . . the distinction between exercise of state power and mob power is being eroded." The article discussed the passage of legislation allowing for the dissolution of the school system should integration be ordered and to dissolve the legislature to prevent the seating of black legislators. It concluded, "In this kind of political atmosphere there is little or no barrier to the growth and influence of organizations and movements dedicated to hate, intolerance, and terror."[18]

Salisbury had written even more that was cut by the editors. "To one long accustomed to the sickening atmosphere of Moscow in the Stalin days the aura of the community which once prided itself as the Magic City of the South is only too familiar. To one who knew Hitler's storm troop Germany it would seem even more familiar." The National Desk thought that the Hitler reference was too strong and deleted it.[19]

•   •   •

Salisbury had gone to Birmingham to report news, but his series became one of the most newsworthy events in the city's history. A *Washington Post* reporter who visited the city after the articles described them as a "bucket of cold water in the face."[20] City boosters had long aspired to diminish the appearance of racial and political tension. With a few thousand words, Salisbury upended that effort. His picture of lawlessness would no doubt dissuade outsiders who might consider locating a branch office or industrial plant in Birmingham.[21] The local white reaction "bypassed shame and went straight to outrage."[22]

Birmingham first learned of "Salisbury's assault" in a news column written by E.L. Holland Jr., editor of the *Birmingham News*. Holland had just arrived in Princeton for a conference when a friend handed him that morning's edition of the *Times*. Holland was floored. "Salisbury may have made this trip. He may have talked with various Birmingham people.... other Northern newsmen have come South in this racial hegira. Virtually all have checked in with local newsmen to discover the sources of information.... We have not seen Salisbury. If he was in Birmingham, he worked quite secretly." His last paragraph set the tone for Birmingham's reaction: "That headline (in the *Times*) says worlds: 'Fear and Hatred Grip Birmingham.' This is the big lie. Perhaps the biggest of all. Salisbury has done his damage, Radio Moscow please copy."[23]

Birmingham's dailies, the *News* and the *Post-Herald*, reprinted the Salisbury articles in full, which is how most residents came across them, since no one got the *New York Times* in Alabama. The *Birmingham News* sprawled the first story over four columns under the headline, "NY Times Slanders Our City—Can This Be Birmingham?" "Fear and hatred do not grip Birmingham," the *News* wrote in what one historian described as the "most outraged editorial ever to grace the paper's pages."[24]

One more asinine "expose" of the South would not seem to matter much. But when *The New York Times*, with a longstanding reputation for respectability and integrity, stoops to journalistic demagoguery and South-baiting a response is required.

We must remember that *The Times* readership is one of the most influential segments of America and that for *The Times* readers this noxious falsehood, couched in the most purple of phrases, is the truth. These readers do not and probably will not know that normally high journalistic standards have not been followed. Interpretation of an isolated incident as typical of the entire region has long been a favorite instrument for libeling the South...

That a shoddy, vicious type of reporting should be resorted to by *The New York Times* makes the articles slandering Birmingham even more shocking for the people of the city.... We believe *The New York Times* has done Birmingham and American journalism a grave disservice.[25]

These reactions continued for days. Editorials reminded readers that the "diabolical reports" in the *New York Times* were just the most recent example of "offenses" against the South by the "outside" press. "Hardened as Alabama newspaper editors are at the journalistic lash of the Northern press,... indignation was running at high tide this past week in the Alabama press as the result of *The New York Times'* Birmingham and Alabama 'expose,'" opined the *Birmingham News*. "Dailies and weeklies have joined in expressions of amazement that the highly-reputed *Times*, unofficially regarded as the nation's newspaper with the greatest integrity and ethics, should resort to bias, prejudice, and shoddy reporting for the sake of a headline."[26]

The *Post-Herald* started a "Write to the Times Campaign," urging Birmingham residents to send hate mail to the *Times*:

To the *New York Times*: We are furious and are planning to retaliate by suing your "newspaper" for an immense sum. I venture to say that beside this, you will and already are suffering damage that the *Times* will never get over. The name of your once respected paper is dirt in the South now and will continue to be just that.

To Arthur Hays Sulzberger: After reading the weird, distorted and ambiguous story one of your reporters wrote of conditions in Birmingham, I am convinced that the only further possible use of your paper could be to the American people is that it be printed on softer paper and sold at a price competitive to toilet tissue.

To the Editor: All the news that's fit to print; Into the gutter this slogan went. All the news that's fit to print, we await Mr. Salisbury's obitument![27]

●   ●   ●   ●

No one was surprised when the libel suits started. On April 16, just a week after the Montgomery lawsuits, the three Birmingham city commissioners, James W. Morgan, Bull Connor, and J. T. "Jabo" Waggoner, announced their intent to sue the *Times* for articles "slandering Birmingham, the Commission, and the state." James Simpson, a corporate lawyer and former Alabama state senator who was Connor's mentor, instigated the lawsuits against the *Times* for their "ruthless attacks on this region and its people." Simpson had been in correspondence with the lawyers in Montgomery. "The article reflects on them [the commissioners] as responsible persons for keeping law, order, and tolerable living conditions in Birmingham," Simpson told the press. He didn't disclose the amount they would seek. "The amount isn't important. It's just high time someone put a stop to irresponsible Yankee journalism."[28] The commissioners sent a retraction letter to the *Times* complaining about nineteen specific statements. They claimed to resent especially the descriptions of bombings of black churches and synagogues, which "invited the false inference that the [commissioners] encouraged or condoned racial hatred or religious intolerance."[29]

The commissioners filed their suits in federal district court in the Northern District of Alabama, asking $500,000 each in damages. The suits had been filed in federal court, Simpson explained, to forestall any charge that the commissioners were "trying to lynch them with local prejudice in state court." Each contended that the April 12 "Fear and Hatred" article was published "with intent to defame" him and that the article had subjected him to "public contempt, ridicule, shame and disgrace."[30]

The Salisbury articles spawned four more libel suits. Three city commissioners of Bessemer filed suits seeking $1,500,000 in damages, alleging that the *Times* had "put them in a bad light throughout the country."[31] A Birmingham city detective named Joe Lindsey brought a libel action for $100,000.[32] The plaintiffs may never "collect one thin dime in those libel suits against the *New York Times*," observed the *Andalusia Star-News*. "But the court actions... will have the effect of slowing the *Times*, one of America's most esteemed journals," in publishing statements that "recklessly condemn the South with facts that are false and untrue."[33]

· · · · ·

The mood at West 43rd Street was grim. The "Alabama cases" were presenting a serious, even existential threat to the paper. The *Times* had been deliberately operated for years by the Sulzberger family on a low profit margin and was barely breaking even in 1960. The international edition of the paper, started in 1949, had drained finances, and there were ongoing labor struggles. The Sulzberger family's lack of concern with financial gain had also contributed to the paper's weak position. The *Times* operated more like a foundation or an educational institution than a business. The Sulzbergers and Dryfoos were "Ochsian fundamentalists," convinced that being financially shrewd, even in the interest of the *Times*, was "corrupting."[34]

The *Times* was at the time defending a handful of libel suits outside the South seeking substantial damage awards.[35] But none of them troubled Loeb as much as the "Alabama cases," which had the potential to seriously injure, even bankrupt the *Times*.[36] It was apparent that the *Times* wasn't dealing with typical players in the libel game. Unlike most who sued for libel, the Alabama officials weren't looking to blow off steam; they were seeking the ruin of the newspaper. Never in the history of the *Times*, and in the history of the American press, had there been a concerted libel attack of the magnitude of Alabama's, effectively a coordinated official conspiracy intended to undermine and destroy a disfavored newspaper.

"In all the years that I have practiced law, nothing had ever arisen that was more worrisome," he recalled. In his more than thirty years of association with the *Times*, "nothing scared me more than this litigation."[37]

In May, Claude Sitton went to cover King's perjury trial in Montgomery. Rex Thomas, the Associated Press bureau manager, came up to him when Sitton was in the newsroom of the *Advertiser*, where out-of-town reporters congregated.

"I hear they're looking for you. A process server is trying to find out whether you're in town," he said. The Montgomery commissioners were trying to strengthen their case by serving process directly on a *Times* reporter.

Shortly after, Sitton got a call from Roderick McLeod, one of the attorneys representing the *Times* in the libel cases. McLeod told him to get out of Alabama immediately. Sitton called the bellhop at the Thomas Jefferson Hotel, where he had just checked in, and asked him to bring his bag across the street to the Hertz rental car office. Sitton ran through the back alleys, hopped into a rental car, and took the back roads to the Georgia line.[38]

Loeb then made a historic decision, ordering all *Times* personnel to stay out of Alabama.[39] For two and a half years, the *Times* barred its reporters from Alabama and relied on stories from the major wire services, the Associated Press and the United Press International, for coverage of civil rights events in the state. The *Times* discontinued the employment of its two "stringers" in Alabama and forbade anyone associated with the *Times* from setting foot in Alabama. They would call this the "iron curtain" at the *Times*. One reason for the "iron curtain" policy was that the presence of *Times* personnel in Alabama, even in Alabama airspace, would undermine the argument that Alabama did not have personal jurisdiction over the *Times*.[40] The *Times* also feared, more generally, that reporting on Alabama would invite further libel trouble.[41] As a result of the libel suits, reporters for the *New York Times* would remain out of Alabama, the site of the most contentious events of the civil rights movement, during crucial years of the desegregation struggle.

7 Doing Business in Alabama

> The *New York Times* boasts of printing all the news that's fit
> to print. From the number of libel suits that the paper is
> now defending in Alabama, it seems that the paper also
> prints some news that is unfit to print, especially about
> Alabama.
>
> —"Some Is Unfit," *Alabama Journal*, September 5, 1960

The stakes were raised when another Alabama official got on the "libel attack" bandwagon and sued over the "Heed Their Rising Voices" ad. In May, Governor John Patterson announced that he would join the Montgomery officials in bringing lawsuits against the *Times* and the ministers.[1] This marked the second time in ten years that a governor of Alabama had sued a Northern news publication over an alleged libel of himself and the "people of the state of Alabama."[2]

The handsome, square-jawed, thirty-eight-year-old Patterson, who had been elected in 1958 with KKK backing, was a hero to Alabama segregationists. During his term as the state's attorney general, Patterson had fought the Montgomery bus boycott and obtained a restraining order against the NAACP that barred the "race agitators" from operating in the state.[3] He had promised in his inaugural address, "I will oppose with every ounce of energy I possess and will use every power at my command to prevent any mixing of white and Negro races in the classrooms of this state."[4] Patterson's decision to sue the *Times* and the ministers made clear that the lawsuits were official, state-sponsored attacks on the press in the guise of private lawsuits.

At a press conference, Patterson alleged that the "Heed Their Rising Voices" ad was "inflammatory, malicious in its entirety, and grossly misleading."[5] Like the Montgomery commissioners, Patterson demanded a retraction of the allegedly false paragraphs stating that "truckloads of police" armed with shotguns ringed the Alabama State campus, that the dining hall was padlocked, and those containing allegations of "Southern violators" answering peaceful protests with "intimidation and violence." He demanded the retraction from the *Times*, the ministers, and from King.[6] King had nothing to do with the ad, but Patterson sued him for maximum intimidation.

Around the same time as Patterson's announcement, Loeb received a disappointing telegram from Claude Sitton. Loeb had charged Sitton with doing another investigation of the "Heed Their Rising Voices" ad. Sitton reported to Loeb that the third paragraph of the ad was "virtually without foundation." The students sang the National Anthem, the police didn't ring the campus, the dining hall wasn't padlocked, and even those taking part in the strike were admitted to the dining hall.[7]

Loeb saw dollar signs and there was no question that Patterson's retraction had to be granted. Even though nothing in the ad referred to the governor, Loeb knew that the failure to retract, given the falsity of some of the statements, could be used as evidence of malice, which could justify a punitive damage award. He called up the *Times* editors and told them to write a retraction and to publish it immediately as a "statement by *The New York Times*."

The advertisement containing the statements to which Governor Patterson objects was received by The *Times* in the regular course of business from and paid for by a recognized advertising agency in behalf of a group which included among its subscribers well-known citizens.

The publication of an advertisement does not constitute a factual news report by The *Times* nor does it reflect the judgment or the opinion of the editors of The *Times*. Since publication of the advertisement, The *Times* made an investigation and consistent with its policy of retracting and correcting any errors or misstatements which may appear in its columns, herewith retracts the two paragraphs complained of by the Governor.

The *New York Times* never intended to suggest by the publication of the advertisement that the Honorable John Patterson, either in his capacity as Governor or as ex-officio chairman of the Board of Education of the State of Alabama, or otherwise, was guilty of "grave misconduct or improper actions and omission." To the extent that anyone can fairly conclude from the statements in the advertisement that any such charge was made, The *New York Times* hereby apologizes to the Honorable John Patterson therefor.[8]

The real reason for the retraction was obvious to many, including not-so-naive readers of the *Times*. As one commented in a letter to the editor, "Your apology and retraction troubled me. I can understand you feared that a white jury in Alabama would probably be apt to award [Patterson] thundering big damages in a lawsuit."[9] Journalist Nat Hentoff, a member of the Committee to Defend Martin Luther King, wrote an article for the *Village Voice* titled "The Soft Decay of the New York Times" in which he denounced the paper's "pusillanimous yielding to the governor of Alabama" and "extraordinary—and shameful—display of cowardice."[10] This prompted an angry letter from *Times* lawyers to Hentoff stating that the accusation of "pusillanimity" was "not fair."[11]

The historic retraction made headlines and signaled the level of panic at the *Times*. The *Chicago Daily News* noted that the *Times* almost never published retractions and that it had never retracted a paid advertisement. Segregationist editors rejoiced. "We hope that the *Times'* experience will not be lost on other publications all too prone to believe anything about the South so long as it is bad," wrote the editor of the Greenville, Mississippi *News*.[12] The retraction, said Grover Hall in the *Advertiser*, proved "the discreditable, fictional character of the *Times* content." "It hurt the state to be misused in the *Times*, but the proof and acknowledgement of misrepresentation are many times more conspicuous than would be in any other publication."[13] "The *Advertiser* has no doubt that the recent checkmating of the *Times* in Alabama will impose a restraint upon other publications."[14]

The retraction notwithstanding, Patterson initiated his lawsuit by serving papers on the *Times'* stringer, Don McKee, and sending letters to the four clergymen. He asked for one million dollars in damages, twice as much as each of the commissioners in Montgomery and Birmingham. His lawyer filed the complaint on the Monday after King was acquitted of the perjury charges by an all-white jury, sending a message to anyone who may have wondered whether the state's pride had been hurt by the outcome.[15]

·   ·   ·

Not long after Patterson filed his papers, Fred Gray received letters from Joseph Lowery and Solomon Seay. Gray, a thirty-year-old black attorney in Montgomery, was one of the leading civil rights attorneys in the South. Gray knew both of those men, having represented them in various civil rights matters. The letters said something about a libel case and an advertisement in the *New York Times*.

Shortly after, he got a letter from Ralph Abernathy, stating that he had been served with papers in a libel suit. Then, he received a letter from Fred Shuttlesworth and a copy of the libel complaints from the Montgomery city commissioners and Patterson. Gray figured out that the ministers were being sued by the Montgomery officials, saw the implications for the civil rights movement, and agreed to take their cases.[16]

Gray was, in King's words, "the brilliant young Negro who... became chief counsel for the protest movement."[17] A Montgomery native who grew up in a poor black neighborhood on a street named after Jefferson Davis, Gray graduated from Alabama State College in 1951. Because of the state's strict segregation laws, he was forbidden from getting a legal education in Alabama. Gray earned a law degree from Case Western Reserve University in Cleveland in 1954, then returned to Montgomery determined to "destroy everything segregated."[18]

When he was only twenty-four, Gray represented Rosa Parks in litigation stemming from the bus boycott. While the case worked its way through the Alabama court system, he filed a separate lawsuit in federal court directly challenging the constitutionality of the Montgomery ordinance that required segregation on buses. Gray represented King in the tax evasion case and was local counsel to the NAACP as it fought the state's effort to prevent it from operating in Alabama. For this work, he was subjected to harassment and death threats.[19]

It was obvious to Gray that the Alabama officials had targeted the most respected figures in the civil rights movement. Ralph Abernathy, regarded as second in command of the movement, was King's closest confidante. The soft-spoken, solidly built, thirty-four-year-old served as pastor of Montgomery's First Baptist Church, one of the largest black churches in the nation. Abernathy had attended Alabama State College and served overseas in the Army during the war, then was ordained a minister in 1948. In 1956, Abernathy and King created the Montgomery Improvement

Association (MIA) to guide the bus boycott. Not long after Abernathy's home and church were bombed in 1957, Abernathy joined King and other civil rights leaders to form the SCLC. Abernathy was the organization's first secretary and treasurer.[20]

Solomon Seay, in his sixties at the time of the libel cases, was the outspoken, rotund leader of the Mount Zion AME Church in Montgomery, whom King described as the "spiritual father" of the civil rights movement. Seay had been involved in grassroots civil rights activities since the 1930s, when he helped blacks in Montgomery register to vote. In 1949, Seay helped lead a campaign to represent Gertrude Perkins, a black woman who had been abducted and raped by two white policemen. The campaign exposed the long-standing practice of white police officers sexually assaulting black women in Montgomery and forced a grand jury hearing. Seay worked with the MIA to lead the bus boycott and advised King on the SCLC.[21] "Seay's was one of the few clerical voices that, in the years preceding the protest, had lashed out against the injustices heaped on the Negro and urged his people to a greater appreciation of their own worth. A dynamic preacher, his addresses from time to time at the weekly mass meetings raised the spirit of all who heard him," King had written in *Stride Toward Freedom*.[22]

Joseph Lowery, quiet and scholarly, was known as "dean of the civil rights movement." Born in Huntsville in 1921, he held a doctorate in theology and since 1952 had served as pastor of the Warren Street Methodist Church in Mobile. Lowery helped lead the Montgomery bus boycott and was later involved in efforts to desegregate Mobile's buses. In 1957, King invited Lowery to become a co-founder of the SCLC, and Lowery served as vice president of the organization until 1967.[23]

Fred Shuttlesworth—a rough-cut, fast-talking, and confident man with a prickly personality—was one of the "big three" of the civil rights movement, with Abernathy and King. Shuttlesworth was pastor of the small Bethel Baptist Church in Birmingham and head of the Alabama Christian Movement for Human Rights (ACMHR), which took up the work of the NAACP after it was banned from the state. Shuttlesworth "could play on the emotions of a meeting like Heifetz bowing and fingering the strings of a violin," noted the *New York Times*.[24] Shuttlesworth believed that blacks must fight for their equality rather than wait for whites to make the first move, and for this he struck terror in the hearts of segregationists.[25]

For his efforts to desegregate Birmingham, Shuttlesworth was beaten by mobs, imprisoned, and attacked. He held the record as the "most jailed civil rights leader." When he announced that the ACMHR would hold a bus boycott in Birmingham on the day before Christmas 1956, someone planted twelve sticks of dynamite that blew his house down with him in it, and he escaped without a scratch.[26] When Shuttlesworth tried to enroll his children in an all-white school the following year, he was attacked by Klansmen wielding bicycle chains and brass knuckles. The doctor was amazed that he hadn't suffered a concussion. "Doctor," he replied, "the Lord knew I lived in a hard town, so he gave me a hard head."[27]

The ministers were astonished when they received the retraction letters. They hadn't heard about the "Heed Their Rising Voices" ad before, much less that their names were in it. The ministers complained to King about Rustin's use of their names and demanded that he be fired from the Committee to Defend Martin Luther King. Rustin insisted that the statements weren't defamatory and that the ministers would have protested as members of the SCLC board if they hadn't been listed in the ad. Writes historian Taylor Branch, "In its preliminary stages of bluster and petty bickering, *Sullivan v. New York Times* showed little promise of a landmark Supreme Court case."[28]

Gray put together a team of attorneys to work on the cases. They included Solomon Seay Jr., Reverend Seay's son, who had just started his practice in Gray's office, and Vernon Crawford, an acquaintance of Lowery's from Mobile. A fee was arranged for the team of three lawyers. The Committee to Defend Martin Luther King promised to pay the expenses. Ultimately, they couldn't, and the SCLC shouldered the costs. Gray knew that defending the libel cases wasn't going to be easy; in part, because none of the lawyers had any experience with libel law, with its dizzying array of technicalities. Gray was already stretched thin with civil rights cases. He was representing the students involved in the Montgomery lunch counter sit-in and involved in the litigation surrounding the state's ban on the NAACP.[29]

The ministers didn't reply to the retraction letters from Patterson and the commissioners because they felt they couldn't retract something they'd never said. Plus, retraction would have required them to publish an ad in the *Times* denying the statements, which would have been impossible as a practical matter. This failure to retract would be cited by Patterson and the Montgomery commissioners as evidence of an "admission" to the ad's statements. Gray unsuccessfully filed a motion before the Montgomery court, asking it to dismiss the case on the grounds that the ministers had no connection to the ad, that they didn't authorize the ad, and had been joined fraudulently to the lawsuit.[30]

King was facing a million-dollar lawsuit against him by the governor of Alabama but didn't even know it. It took seven months for him to forward the complaint and summons to Gray. "Frankly, I did not pay any real attention to this complaint when it was received for two reasons," he reported to Gray. He had been told that couldn't be served with process since he lived outside the state. "Second, I knew that I had not signed the ad in the *Times*, and therefore felt that the whole thing was a mistake. If I had known that the papers constituted a legitimate service, I would have immediately sought legal advice," he wrote.[31] Gray responded that he was sorry King didn't send the complaint to him earlier and advised him not to set foot in the state.[32]

· · · · ·

That summer, the lawyers for the *Times* began planning their defense. The legal team included Embry and Beddow, Louis Loeb, and Tom Daly, an aristocratic-looking, gray-haired lawyer who was considered Lord Day & Lord's "libel expert."

From the start of the litigation, a few things were clear. First, the *Times* had to distance itself from the ministers and avoid any mention of racial inequality if it wanted even the slightest chance of winning the case. It was also obvious that truth couldn't be a defense, since there were errors in the ad. The *Times* could claim that the statements didn't refer to any of the authorities—they weren't "of and concerning" the Alabama officials— though this became more difficult when the *Times* admitted that the ad statements could reflect on Patterson. The *Times* could also argue that the officials weren't defamed—that their credibility in Montgomery had been enhanced by statements accusing them of violence against civil rights protesters.

But the easiest tactic was a jurisdictional strategy that would avoid these issues. The *Times* would argue that the paper wasn't an Alabama company and did no business in the state, other than to send reporters in when news was stirring, and therefore the courts of Alabama couldn't hear it.

Since 1945, the constitutional test for determining the limits of state court power to assert jurisdiction over "nonresident corporations" was known as "minimum contacts." In *International Shoe Co. v. Washington*, the Supreme Court stated that a corporation could be sued in a state so long as it had "minimum contacts" there.[33] Since then, courts had been working out the definition of "minimum contacts." Some interpreted the test narrowly, to require continuous and substantial contact between a defendant and a state. Other courts interpreted "minimum contacts" to be just that—minimum. In 1960, the Supreme Court ruled against Scripto, the pencil manufacturer with headquarters in Georgia, stating that it did business in Florida by selling its pens and pencils there. The Court ruled that even though the Scripto products were sold by independent contractors, the company still had "minimum contacts."[34]

Newspapers argued that this interpretation of "minimum contacts" put undue burdens on freedom of the press. Forcing out-of-state publishers to defend themselves in distant and hostile jurisdictions with which they had only minimal contacts posed a threat to news reporting, they had asserted. In libel cases arising out of reporting on controversial issues, judges could manipulate the law to a newspaper's disadvantage and the jury could make findings of fact against the paper solely because it outraged the local population. The exercise of jurisdiction, in other words, had First Amendment implications.[35]

Roland Nachman brought L.B. Sullivan's case before the court in Montgomery first, since he thought it was the strongest. Because the ad referred to the activities of the police, it more clearly referenced Sullivan as police commissioner than the other city commissioners. Under the libel law of Alabama, as in most states, if a group was defamed, and the group was small enough, any member of the group could recover damages on the grounds that their reputations had been impugned. The libelous statement was said to be "of and concerning" them.[36] The *Times* moved immediately to quash or dismiss Sullivan's lawsuit, alleging that the *Times* didn't do enough business in Alabama to come within the jurisdiction of its courts.[37]

Was the *Times* "doing business" in Alabama? It was a good question. Between 1956 and 1960, nine *New York Times* correspondents made visits to Alabama totaling 153 days. In the first five months of 1960, there were three visits, two by Claude Sitton and one by Harrison Salisbury. The *Times* had three stringers in the state, including two in Montgomery, but they only sold two stories to the *Times* in 1960. The newspaper accepted a small amount of advertising from Alabama sources and circulated only around four hundred daily and Sunday issues in the state.

Nachman asked the judge to require the *Times* to produce for the court thousands of pages of documents, including news articles and business records. The purpose of this exercise was to illustrate that the *Times* sold newspapers, gathered news, and solicited advertising in the state. This was a shrewd tactic on Nachman's part. Nachman knew that forcing the *Times* to assemble this trove of documents would saddle it with a huge financial burden—thousands of dollars in attorneys' fees.

The *Times'* lawyers challenged this. They argued before Montgomery Circuit Court judge Walter B. Jones that the attorneys could consult copies of the *Times* at the local library and that the paper was not doing business in Alabama merely by issuing news stories from the state. Jones ruled in favor of Nachman, and the junior lawyers of Lord Day & Lord toiled hundreds of hours over the next few months compiling the records. Recalled Embry, "Compliance would require untold manhours of tedious work and that thousands of pages of the newspaper be produced. But comply we did, for our instructions from the client were: 'any amount for defense, not a penny for tribute by way of settlement.'"[38] The *Times* was paying Lord Day & Lord for their work on the libel cases and for all their travel expenses, in addition to its normal retainer, as well as fees for Embry and Beddow. Massive legal bills were mounting, and the libel suits were just beginning.

The *Times'* motion to quash Sullivan's lawsuit was heard by Judge Jones in a three-day hearing that started on July 25, 1960. *Times* attorneys contended that the newspaper didn't do business in the state, either through soliciting advertising, gathering news, or selling newspapers. John McCabe, assistant to the *Times'* controller, and Harold Faber, assistant national news editor, attested that no one in Alabama was on the regular payroll of the *Times*. The *Times* had no office, bank account, or property in the state. String correspondents were not on the *Times* payroll. Loeb told the judge, "Your honor, I don't see for the life of me how the fact that the *New York Times* carries news items originating in Alabama makes the *New York Times* doing business in that state any more than we are doing business in the Belgian Congo today because we have a correspondent out there reporting the details of what is going on" (in a revolution taking place in the Congo in 1960). Jones denied the motion in a ten-page decree.[39]

Embry used forms in Judge Jones's legal treatise, *Alabama Pleading and Practice at Law*, in his pleading to the court. He believed, based on Jones's treatise, that he was making a "special appearance," made for only for the purpose of raising the jurisdictional question, and did not concede to the court's jurisdiction. Jones, however, took the position that Embry made a "general appearance," not a "special appearance," and thus consented to the court's jurisdiction over the *Times*. Jones, disingenuously, repudiated the form in his own book.[40]

In addition, Jones ruled that the *Times* did enough business in the state to be subject to the jurisdiction of its courts. The *Times* gathered news in Alabama, both through regular reporters and part-time correspondents, and solicited ads in Alabama and sold newspapers in the state. This was an extensive and continuous course of business activity, he believed. Jones cited a string of court decisions which held that very little contact is necessary to constitute "doing business" in a state.[41]

Jones added that he had been a "staunch advocate and defender of freedom of the press." He wrote a weekly column in the *Advertiser* and was one of the first judges to allow news photographs to be taken in his courtroom. But the city commissioners should not be compelled to travel across the country to sue the *Times*, he declared. Freedom of the press "does not command injured parties to carry his witnesses, his evidence, his counsel, and himself more than 1,000 miles to a distant forum to bring his action for alleged damages to his reputation and to try his case."[42]

The *Times*' lawyers made the same arguments in the first of the Birmingham cases to be heard, *Connor v. New York Times*. Before federal district judge H. Hobart Grooms of Birmingham, they argued that the newspaper didn't do business in Alabama, and that the two correspondents served with process weren't agents of the *Times* upon whom service would be valid.[43] They contended that any libelous action was committed when the stories were published in New York and not because of work done by Salisbury in Alabama.[44] Quipped the *Birmingham News*, "The *New York Times* and Harrison Salisbury are asking a federal court to dismiss suits against them by our city commissioners. The legal claim is that the *Times* 'has not done any business or performed any service...in Alabama.' Well, it hasn't performed any service, right enough. But, man, did it give us the business!"[45]

Grooms concluded that the two stringers, Chadwick and McKee, weren't agents of the *Times* upon whom process could be served. However, he said that the articles were "incident to work or service" performed by Salisbury when he was in Alabama gathering the information, which validated the service of process through the secretary of state's office on both the *Times* and Salisbury. As such, the suits could be tried in Alabama.[46]

The *Times* appealed the ruling to the New Orleans–based Fifth Circuit Court of Appeals, asserting that it would curtail newsgathering activities, thereby impinging on freedom of the press. If the decision were allowed to stand, it would "open the floodgates" of lawsuits against the press. The *Times* argued that if the Alabama federal court was right, "newspaper editors generally fear they will be subjected to suits designed to harass them wherever they send reporters to cover a story."[47] As the *Times* filed its appeal, an extraordinary act of harassment was taking place.

•   •   •

While the *Times* was waiting on the appeals court to rule in the Birmingham cases, the town of Bessemer launched a new tactic in the attack on the press—prosecuting reporters for criminal libel. A grand jury indicted Harrison Salisbury on criminal charges for his "Fear and Hatred" article. This illustrated vividly the state-sponsored nature of the "libel attack." Reporters were now facing loss of their liberty for writing critically about segregationist brutality in the South.

Criminal libel laws are of old English vintage, dating back to the sixteenth century. The premise of the crime of libel was that, in an age when dueling was used to resolve disputes over reputation, libels caused violence and could therefore be punished by the state: "Libels may be penalized by the state because they tend to create breaches of the peace when the defamed or his friends undertake to revenge themselves on the defamer."[48] While the action for civil libel was based upon the damage done to an individual, the basis for criminal libel was the injury done to society. A criminally libelous publication need not actually result in a breach of the peace; it could be criminal if it had a "tendency" to cause a person or group who was libeled to breach the peace.[49]

By the 1960s, criminal libel was practically defunct in the United States. One reason for its decline was that civil actions had largely replaced physical violence as a remedy for defamation. "Preference for the civil remedy, which enabled the frustrated victim to trade chivalrous satisfaction for damages," had eroded the "breach of peace" justification.[50] Criminal libel was also disfavored as officials recognized its possible conflict with freedom of the press. As First Amendment scholar Zechariah Chafee wrote in 1947, criminal libel was a pretty "loose kind of crime."[51] "A publisher never knows when the law may be applied to him; arbitrary and discriminatory prosecutions are encouraged by such an unclear... rule."[52]

Bessemer's use of the state's criminal libel law was remarkable, as the criminal libel statute had been deployed only one time in the previous thirty years. Since 1936, only one person had ever been convicted for criminal libel in Alabama. Alabama's criminal libel law subjected to misdemeanor prosecution "any person who speaks, writes, or prints of and concerning another any accusation falsely and maliciously importing the commission by such person of a felony, or any other indictable offense involving moral turpitude." A defamatory publication was presumed to be false and malicious if no "justifiable motive" for publishing it could be shown.[53] The punishment for criminal libel was a fine up to $500 or a prison sentence of six months.[54]

Knowing that libel was not an extraditable offense under New York law, Bessemer officials asked Salisbury to appear voluntarily before the grand jury.[55] Lord Day & Lord curtly declined. When Salisbury was asked to turn over the names of his sources to the grand jury, he defended his refusal under an Alabama law that shields reporters from having to reveal their news sources. Bessemer officials proceeded to subpoena the Tutwiler Hotel for a list of telephone calls Salisbury made while he was there, revealing the identity of his informants.[56]

Everyone Salisbury spoke to in Birmingham was called to testify. A subpoena *duces tecum* was served on minister Robert Hughes, requiring him to bring before the grand jury records of the Alabama Council on Human Relations. This was intended to undermine the organization by forcing exposure of its members' identities. Hughes refused and was jailed for contempt of court. Several of Salisbury's other sources were harassed.[57]

In September, the Bessemer grand jury indicted Salisbury on forty-two counts of criminal libel, for a possible total of $21,000 in fines and twenty-one years in jail.[58] The charges put the *Times* and Salisbury in an impossible position. The *Times* would need Salisbury's testimony to defend the civil libel suits. But if he appeared to testify, he would be subject to arrest and trial on the criminal indictment. As Salisbury put it, "the Bessemer action had a scissors effect."[59]

The Salisbury indictments sent shockwaves throughout journalism, just as the Birmingham commissioners had intended. The press was beginning to grasp the magnitude of Alabama's "libel attack." On September 25, 1960, the Associated Press news syndicate issued an article about the indictments, which was reprinted in newspapers across the country. The piece appeared under different headlines, such as "Suits in Alabama Raise Press Issue: Implications Believed Wide for Out-of-State Reporting of Racial Developments," "Out of State Newspapers Hard Hit by Court Ruling," and "Libel Suit Against New York Times Gives Concern to Press in Race Incidents."

> A state court judge at Montgomery and a Federal judge at Birmingham have ruled that The New York Times can be sued in Alabama courts. And a Grand Jury at Bessemer, near Birmingham, indicted a Times reporter, Harrison E. Salisbury, on forty-two counts of criminal libel for a series of stories he wrote on racial conditions. The two court decisions, and the grand jury action, dealt only with The Times and Salisbury. But they could apply to other newspapers as well. Another paper could be sued for libel—as The Times has been—in Alabama courts. And another reporter could be indicted for criminal libel if a Grand Jury concluded—as the jury at Bessemer did—that his writing "may tend to provoke a breach of the peace."

The *Montgomery Advertiser* ran the article under the heading "State Finds Formidable Club to Swing at Out of State Press."[60]

The *Washington Post's* legal reporter, James Clayton, visited Birmingham intending to follow up on Salisbury's expose. He found that conditions were as crude as Salisbury reported, and segregationists were eager to keep it that way. "Every newspaperman without a Southern accent who goes to Birmingham and asks about the race question [is] suspect," Clayton observed. "In newspaper circles, the word is being spread that Birmingham intends to take into court any reporter who writes and any newspaper which prints stories that Birmingham's leaders think are biased and unfair. A reporter who goes to Birmingham these days is quickly given to understand that Birmingham's city officials would just as soon sue his paper as the *New York Times*."[61]

At least one other newspaper followed the lead of the *Times* and removed its reporters from Alabama.[62] The libel suits were having a "chilling effect" on the press, and the chill was just beginning.

8 "This New Weapon of Intimidation"

On November 1, 1960, the residents of Montgomery convened in the courtroom of Walter Burgwyn Jones to take part in the ceremonial shaming of the *New York Times*.

The Sons of the Confederate Veterans, coincidentally, had held a ceremony in downtown Montgomery the day before, temporarily changing the name of Courthouse Square for the Civil War centennial year of 1961. Brass blared as men in gray uniforms congregated around the fountain and the area was rechristened "Confederate Square."[1]

Senator Lister Hill called attention to the dramatic history that had taken place there one hundred years earlier. Governor Patterson and Mayor Earl James addressed the crowd, and Attorney General MacDonald Gallion saluted the Confederate flag. Judge Jones, dressed in nineteenth-century garb, reenacted the swearing-in of Jefferson Davis as president of the Confederacy.[2] The following day, some of the participants, still clad in Confederate uniform, went to Jones's courtroom to watch the trial of Sullivan's case, the first of the Montgomery libel suits to go to trial.

•   •   •   •   •

From Montgomery's perspective, no one was better suited to hear Sullivan's lawsuit than Walter Burgwyn Jones. Seventy-two-year-old Jones, presiding judge of the Montgomery circuit court, dubbed "dean of the Alabama bar and bench," was the state's most long-serving and revered jurist.[3] He was a dramatic, and at times eccentric, defender of the South, segregation, white supremacy, and states' rights.

Jones was six foot five, solidly built, bald and bespectacled with a stern gaze. Formal and stately, Jones insisted on wearing robes in the courtroom at a time when most Alabama judges didn't. He spoke in hushed, raspy tones: *why don't you meet me back in the chamber and we'll have a little scotch sometime,* he'd whisper in his low, gravelly voice.[4]

Jones hailed from an esteemed Montgomery lineage. Thomas Goode Jones, his father, had fought for the Confederacy and carried the flag of truce that went from Lee to Grant in 1865. The elder Jones was governor from 1890 to 1894 and a federal district judge for thirteen years. In 1928, Walter Jones started a law school in his father's honor, the Thomas Goode Jones Law School, which still exists to this day as part of Faulkner University.[5]

Judge Jones was obsessed with the Confederacy. He penned odes with titles like the "Confederate Creed" and "Alabama Secedes from the Union" and edited the *Alabama Lawyer,* the state bar's official publication, which featured tributes to the "Southland," racist screeds, and militant denunciations of the Supreme Court's "communistic, atheistic, nihilistic destruction of the Constitution," in pages crackling with italics, exclamation points, and capital letters.[6]

Jones was a key figure in the state's efforts to resist desegregation. In 1956, Jones issued the injunction that put a halt to the operations of the NAACP in Alabama. "I intend to deal the NAACP a mortal blow from which they shall never recover," he declared.[7] Montgomery city officials had sought Judge Jones's assistance in enforcing segregation of the bus lines during the bus boycott. Jones ruled that the transit company must carry out city and state laws, alleging that there was no Supreme Court decision that banned racial separation in intrastate travel. He felt obliged in his opinion gratuitously to issue his thoughts on states' rights. "Where," he asked, "in the federal constitution is there one word, one sentence, one

Figure 5. Seventy-two-year-old Walter Burgwyn Jones, presiding judge of the Montgomery circuit court, was an ardent defender of the South, segregation, white supremacy, and states' rights. Alabama Department of Archives and History.

paragraph, saying that the sovereign states of this union ... are prohibited from making reasonable rules for the separation of the races?"[8]

Jones's weekly column in the *Montgomery Advertiser*, titled "Off the Bench," was another platform for his noxious views on race. In a 1957 column titled "I Speak for the White Race," he declared that "the white race shall remain forever white." The "real and final goal" of the integrationists was "intermarriage and mongrelization of the American people.... We shall never submit to the demands of integrationists."[9] Jones railed against the "lying Yankee press," which were "unwilling to report, without misrepresenting ... news items which relate to our wonderful section of the country" and "distort[ed] anything related to the South."[10] The "white race" was being "unjustly assailed all over the world," subjected to "assaults by radical newspapers and magazines," "communists and the federal judiciary," he believed. "Columnists and photographers have been sent to the South to take back to the people of the North untrue and slanted campaigns about the South. Truly a massive campaign is now being directed against the white race, particularly by those who envy its glory and greatness."[11]

A lifelong bachelor, Jones lived with his sister in an inherited mansion in downtown Montgomery. At his 680-acre summer estate called Jonesboro, he ran a camp for boys he had purportedly "rescued" from the juvenile courts. The walls of his study were said to be covered from ceiling to floor with photographs of these young men, many of them nude. The gavel he used in his courtroom had small inset photographs on its ends depicting an angelic-looking boy, upon which he gazed during court proceedings. Jones had once been arrested for molesting a boy in the YMCA. He fired the director, and L.B. Sullivan hid the arrest report so it wouldn't be mentioned in the local press.[12]

The courthouse in downtown Montgomery was a source of great pride for the community. The square, blocky concrete building was ugly and anti-septic by today's standards but considered fashionable and "ultra-modern" at the time. Opened in July 1958, it was said to exemplify the "modern, progressive spirit of growth in our community." It was not the "cold and ... inferno type courthouse of yesterday." "The courthouse says to Alabama ... that this county has prospered and grown in step with the New South."[13]

Jones was known for his strict and orderly courtroom. "It is the rule of this Court that during its sessions, when the Judge is on the bench, there will be no smoking in the courtroom," he insisted. "Nor is it permitted to bring and drink in this courtroom all sorts and kinds of soft drinks, bottled or otherwise. Nor will witnesses be permitted to go on the witness stand and testify with their mouths filled with tobacco or gum.... Motions and requests for judicial action must be clothed in the proper language of the law and not in the jargon and slang of the street.... Judges who allow the atmosphere of a three-ring circus to fill their court rooms in the belief that the people approve of clowning and buffoonery in their court rooms mistake the temper of their people."[14]

Despite these admonitions, the trial was nevertheless a three-ring circus. Jones permitted news cameras in the courtroom and was the only judge in the area to do so.[15] News photographers and television cameramen swarmed into the courtroom on the morning of the trial. A large crowd showed up, having been lured to the proceedings by numerous articles about the case in the *Montgomery Advertiser*, all of them highly derogatory of the *Times*.[16]

The ugliest manifestations of old-fashioned white supremacy suffused this "ultra-modern" courtroom. Black citizens, it was well known, were underrepresented or entirely excluded from jury panels. Only two of the thirty-seven potential jurors were black. One was a local barber, and the other was a former president of the state NAACP. Sullivan's lawyers struck them. Women were barred from jury service by law. Twelve white men were chosen for the jury after two hours. The *Advertiser* and *Journal* published pictures of them on its front page with their names and addresses so that the community could "get at them." Montgomery residents would accost jurors on the streets during the trial and tell them to "stick it to the *Times*."[17]

The black lawyers for the ministers and the white lawyers sat at separate tables. Deputies with pistols in their belts "protected" the table where the white lawyers sat. Armed guards with pistols at their belts removed black spectators who had tried to sit in the white section of the courtroom.[18] Abernathy, Shuttlesworth, Lowery, and Seay sat at the defense table near witnesses for the *New York Times*. Defense attorneys, fearing that King's presence would prejudice the jurors, had forbidden him from being in the courtroom or in Montgomery. Throughout the trial, Jones referred to the white lawyers as "Mr." but dropped the "Mr." when referring to the lawyers for the ministers.[19]

Calvin Whitesell, one of Sullivan's lawyers, began the case by reading aloud the "Heed Their Rising Voices" ad. Vernon Crawford, representing the ministers, jumped up to object to Whitesell's various racist pronunciations of the word "Negro."

JONES (TO WHITESELL): Read it just like it is.

WHITESELL: Your Honor, I am.

JONES: You are not interpolating anything.

WHITESELL: No, sir ... I have been pronouncing it that way all my life.

"Go ahead and read it," Judge Jones urged him.[20]

• • ⁄ • • •

The *New York Times* lawyers were astonished by the unfolding spectacle—Judge Jones with his lecherous gavel, the armed guards, and several of the prospective jurors garbed in Confederate uniforms with pistols for the Civil War celebrations. Loeb hoped the guns were just replicas—they weren't. By contrast, Nachman, who had argued many cases before Jones before, was relaxed and in his element.[21]

Since the *Times* was conceding that parts of the ad were false, since the words were said to be defamatory by law, and since Jones declared that the court had jurisdiction over the *Times*, Nachman needed only to show one thing: that the statements in the ad were "of and concerning" Sullivan—that readers of the ad would think of Sullivan when they read about "police" and "Southern violators" inflicting violence on civil rights protesters.

Sullivan had been defamed, even though the ad didn't mention him by name, Nachman argued. It wasn't necessary that the ad name Sullivan. The ad was clearly talking about Sullivan, because who else would be responsible for the actions of the police? asked Nachman. The *Times* lawyers insisted that nothing in the ad could possibly be associated with Sullivan.

Nachman also tried to demonstrate that the *Times* published the ad recklessly or maliciously. This was a requirement for Sullivan to receive punitive damages. Nachman would need to show that the *Times* failed to check statements in the ad and the authenticity of the signatories, in flagrant disregard of their own fact-checking policy, and that they failed to retract the statements as they allegedly pertained to Sullivan, even after they knew of their falsity and had retracted the statements for Governor Patterson.

Even though there was no question as to how the case would be decided, Nachman came to court prepared with outlines, lists, and memoranda, which he piled on the table before him and peered at through his thick, dark-rimmed spectacles. Ever the diligent Harvard researcher, he had conducted extensive investigations into virtually every aspect of the *New York Times* and the civil rights demonstrations in Montgomery. He studied the business operations of the *Times* and the newspaper's presence in Alabama. He interviewed local officials about the events in the "Heed Their Rising Voices" ad—the bombing of King's home, the sit-ins, and the expulsion of the students.[22]

Nachman began his presentation by calling Montgomery residents to testify that they thought of L.B. Sullivan as police commissioner when they read the "Heed Their Rising Voices" ad. Grover Hall took the stand first. The third paragraph, about padlocking the dining hall, called to mind "the City government—the Commissioners," Hall attested, cracking his knuckles and pushing up his starched shirt sleeves. He would "naturally think a little more about the police Commissioner because his responsibility is exclusively with the constabulary," he claimed. The statement about padlocking was defamatory, because "starvation is an instrument of reprisal and would certainly be indefensible in my mind in any case."[23]

Six witnesses, Sullivan's friends, followed Hall to the stand. Arthur Blackwell, a member of the city's Water Works Board, appointed by the commissioners, said that if he had believed the statement about padlocking the dining hall, he would have thought "the people on our police force or the heads of our police force were acting without their jurisdiction and would not be competent for the position." Harry Kaminsky, sales manager of a local clothing store, associated the statement about "truckloads of police" with Sullivan "because he is the Police Commissioner."[24]

H.M. Price, owner of a small food equipment business, stated that he associated the first sentence of the third paragraph with Sullivan because "I would just automatically consider that the Police Commissioner in Montgomery would have to put his approval on those kind of things as an individual." Sullivan's friend William Parker Jr. linked the statements in the two paragraphs with the commissioners. Horace W. White, proprietor of Sullivan's former employer, the P.C. White Truck Line, alleged that he wouldn't have reemployed Sullivan if he believed "that he allowed the Police Department to do the things that the paper says he did." White said he thought of Sullivan when he read about the police ringing the campus and having shotguns and teargas. Nachman had made his point.[25]

Yet on cross-examination, all the witnesses confessed that the first time they saw the publication was when Nachman showed it to them in his office three weeks before the trial. They also admitted that they didn't believe any of the statements in the ad. Sullivan's reputation hadn't fallen in their eyes whatsoever.[26]

Sullivan testified on the second day as Nachman's witness. In tones that were measured but indignant, he told the jury how he had been grievously wronged by the allegations in the "Heed Their Rising Voices" ad.

"What is your full name?" Nachman asked.

"L.B. Sullivan," he replied with a straight face.[27]

Though it wasn't legally necessary for him to show that he had been injured, since harm was a presumed consequence of a statement that was considered defamatory *per se*, Sullivan nevertheless explained to the jury how the "Heed Their Rising Voices" ad had defamed him. He considered the ad a "reflection on [his] ability and...integrity." "The statements concerning arrests of people and truckloads of police...are associated with me." The allegations were false and "I resented it very much."[28]

Although they didn't need to, as a defamatory allegation was presumed to be false under the law, Sullivan's lawyers tried to show that the statements were untrue. The *Times* was arguing that the ad had nothing to do with Sullivan, but Sullivan's lawyers were acting as if the statements were "of and concerning" him and that the commissioner had been accused of crimes of which he was innocent. This tactic was a circular one: they would argue that the statement referred to Sullivan, and that it falsely ascribed to him something he didn't do, which was easy to prove false because it didn't refer to him in the first place.

Nachman handed Sullivan a copy of the ad. Was the third paragraph, the one involving truckloads of police ringing the campus, true? Sullivan denied it. Did the police department have anything to do with bombing King's home? Because it was white vigilantes and not the police who bombed King's home, Sullivan could say confidently that "there has never been any incident of bombing or assaulting any person by the police."

"Was King arrested seven times?"

"That is false."

"Did you have anything to do with procuring the indictment of King?"

"Nothing whatever."

As to whether the college lunchroom had been padlocked, he said, "It has never happened in the city of Montgomery."[29]

To show that the description of events at Alabama State was inaccurate, including ringing the campus and padlocking the dining hall, Nachman introduced a story by Claude Sitton about the events in Montgomery published in the *Times*, the report requested by Loeb from stringer Don McKee, and a later report from Sitton to Loeb. Dr. Frank Stewart, state superintendent of education, told the jury that the students had been expelled for the lunch counter protest and not for singing on the capitol steps.

Embry aggressively cross-examined Sullivan to show that the allegations didn't harm his reputation. How could a circulation of thirty-five copies in Montgomery make him feel injured? Embry asked. "Wasn't it your feeling that the ad reflected on the community rather than on you personally that incensed you?" "When it describes police action, certainly I feel it reflects on me as an individual," Sullivan replied. But he conceded that his reputation hadn't been injured.

EMBRY: Have you felt ridiculed since the publication of this article? Do you feel ill-at-ease in walking around the streets of Montgomery...?...

SULLIVAN: I haven't had anyone come up to me personally and say they held me in ridicule on account of it.

EMBRY: If anything...since the publication of this advertisement on March 29th and the thirty-five copies of that newspaper that came into this county—you are not thought any less of and as matter of fact, your reputation has been enhanced, has it not?...

SULLIVAN: I don't know. There has been no contest of popularity and I haven't endeavored to conduct one.[30]

"Mr. Sullivan, do you consider your police force to be Southern law violators?" asked Vernon Crawford, one of the attorneys for the ministers.

SULLIVAN: I certainly do not.

CRAWFORD: Then, Mr. Sullivan, do you consider yourself as police commissioner a Southern law violator?...

SULLIVAN: I don't consider myself a violator period. Southern or otherwise.[31]

"Mr. Sullivan, as a result of your not being harmed, as you testified to, you are not held up in public contempt, you are not being ridiculed, and you are not ashamed," Crawford continued. "The purpose of this lawsuit is the basis for statewide publicity for running for another office. Is that not correct?" Nachman objected to the question, and the judge sustained the objection.[32]

Nachman's cross-examination of the *Times* employees, called as defense witnesses, damned the newspaper's case. The witnesses made clear that the *Times* had published the ad without attempting to confirm its accuracy and did far more for Sullivan's case than for the defense.

Advertising salesman Gershon Aronson revealed that it was the *Times'* policy to review ads carefully and that he violated the policy when he "scanned [the ad] very hurriedly."[33] Vincent Redding, manager of the Advertising Acceptability Department, also crumbled on cross-examination. Redding said that he had no reason to question the ad and had relied on the good reputations of the endorsers, "people who are well-known and whose reputation I had no reason to question." Nachman got Redding to admit that he knew nothing about the incidents in Montgomery and hadn't bothered to verify the facts or to read about the events, even though there were sixteen news stories about the sit-ins before the ad's publication.

NACHMAN: Now, Mr. Redding, wouldn't it be a fair statement to say that you really didn't check this ad at all for accuracy?

REDDING: That's a fair statement, yes.[34]

Under questioning by Fred Gray, Redding admitted that the Advertising Acceptability Department hadn't checked to see if the ministers agreed to the use of their names. The lawyers for the ministers were in the uncomfortable position of trying to show the negligence of their co-defendant—that the *Times* had published the ad without obtaining the consent of their clients.[35] The *New York Times'* lawyers scarcely associated with the ministers' counsel during the trial.

John Murray, the playwright who drafted the ad, testified that the names of the ministers weren't included in the letter from A. Philip Randolph and that they had been added by Rustin at the last minute. He and Rustin wrote the advertisement to "get money," he admitted, and tried to "project the ad in the most appealing form from the material we were getting." As to the accuracy of the advertisement, Murray said: "Well—it did not enter into consideration at all except we took it for granted that it was accurate. . . . We had every reason to believe it."[36]

Harding Bancroft, secretary of the *Times* company, the only official of the paper to testify, said that the *Times* hadn't published a retraction at

Sullivan's request because "we didn't see how the ad reflected on him in any way or how he could be identified with the ad." Bancroft inflamed the jury when he insisted that the statements in the ad were "substantially correct." This assertion would be used by the lawyers for Sullivan as evidence of the newspaper's recklessness in publishing false statements.[37]

The attorneys for the ministers called their clients to the stand. One by one, the clergymen insisted that they hadn't authorized the use of their names, that they knew nothing about the ad when it came out, and they had never given permission to use their names as sponsors. Throughout the trial, Gray was baited with the argument that the ministers must have been complicit in the libel because they refused to retract their statements. Gray declared that they couldn't "retract that which they had not tracted." This elicited a laugh from the judge and assembled spectators. The ministers, he said, were the "forgotten defendants" who had "no business in the case."[38]

.   .   .   .

By the end of the second day, Nachman could hardly conceal his exuberance at his obvious victory and was grinning like a boy. "When you write about a citizen of this town, Mr. *New York Times*," he said to the jury in his closing argument, "you tell the truth—the whole truth—and you won't have to face suit in this county."[39]

The *Times* hadn't even attempted to show the truth of the statements, "the one thing in the world that would have been a complete defense," he explained. "We want you to show how you resent this slur on the reputation of this man you have elected police commissioner.... We don't ask you to punish the *New York Times* out of hate, but that is the only way they can be told that when they write about citizens of this community, they have to tell the truth."[40]

Nachman's co-counsel Robert Steiner stood up and pointed at the *Times'* lawyers. "The *New York Times*, that great newspaper, who in their masthead say 'we print all the news that's fit to print,' published a pack of lies about this man right here." "They couldn't even get the song right." "All of these things that happened didn't happen in Russia where the police run everything; they didn't happen in the Congo where they still eat 'em;

they happened in Montgomery, Alabama, a law-abiding community." At the time, there was a civil war in the Congo and newspaper articles about that unrest and how the Congolese allegedly mistreated whites. "Newspapers are very fine things," Steiner said, "but newspapers have got to tell the truth. One way to get their attention and the attention of everybody else who publishes newspapers is to hit them in the pocketbook."[41]

Embry sprang from his seat. "Where is the evidence that . . . Mr. Sullivan suffered any injury?" "Has possibly . . . his standing in the community been enhanced?"[42] He accused Steiner of "appealing to every base motive in man by making snide references to people living in other parts of the country."[43] Embry had thrown his all into the case, and when it was obvious that he had lost, he was crestfallen.

. . . .

When the lawyers sat down, Jones banged his dubious gavel. He then delivered his charge to the jury, going out of his way to make clear that the trial had nothing to do with race or civil rights, to forestall an appeal on the basis of racial discrimination:

> One of the defendants in this case is a corporate defendant and some of the others belong to various races, and in your deliberation in arriving at your verdict, all of these defendants, whether they be corporate or individuals or whether they belong to this race or that, doesn't have a thing on earth to do with this case, but let the evidence and the law be the two pole stars that will guide you and try to do justice in fairness to all of these parties here. . . . Please remember, gentlemen of the jury, that all of the parties that stand here stand before you on equal footing and all are equal at the Bar of Justice.[44]

Jones explained to the jury the rules of libel in Alabama, which were similar to those in most states. Jones emphasized that the statements were "libelous per se," meaning that they were defamatory on their face, insofar as they accused Sullivan of professional incompetence. No evidence was needed to show that they would or did harm Sullivan's reputation. Once libel per se was established, there was no defense unless the defendant persuaded the jury that the statements were true "in all their particulars." Under Alabama law, the statements in question were presumed to be false, and the *Times* hadn't offered any evidence to counter that presumption. Jones went on to explain that the facts as proven were sufficient to establish liability if the jury was satisfied that the statements were "of and concerning" Sullivan, that they referred to him. When the plaintiff was a public official, he said, an attack on the agency that he led would by inference impugn his reputation.

Jones went on to state the rule on compensatory damages—that "the law implies legal injury from the bare fact of the publication itself." Sullivan did not have to show any tangible loss, such as loss to his earnings or prospective earnings; damages were presumed and did not need to be proven. Punitive damages could be awarded with a finding of malice. Malice was generally defined in the law as acting with "ill will." Jones said that malice could be inferred from the *Times*' failure to retract the statements as they allegedly pertained to Sullivan.[45]

This was an ordinary, typical, and fair jury instruction. The jury could punish the *Times* and the ministers with a legitimate and direct application of Alabama's libel law.

The jurors went into the jury room with a copy of the "Heed Their Rising Voices" ad and reporters and television cameramen trailing behind them. Two hours later they filed out, and the foreman announced that the allegations were "of and concerning" Sullivan and that they would award him all that he asked for. It wasn't clear how much of the judgment was in punitive damages. The spurious harm to Sullivan's reputation had netted half a million dollars.[46]

The liability was "joint and several." This meant that Sullivan could collect the entire award from the *Times* or any of the four ministers. The *Times* would be the obvious source of the funds, but the ministers could also be harassed.

"Naturally, I am very pleased," Sullivan told reporters, smugly. "The case was tried by 12 outstanding jurors."[47]

The lawyers for the ministers issued a statement: "This is evidently one of the trials and tribulations we must endure as we continue the struggle for freedom and human dignity for all Americans without regard to race or color." The *Times*' lawyers announced that they would appeal through the state court system, arguing that the trial judgment was invalid because the *Times* couldn't be sued in Alabama, the ad didn't refer to Sullivan, and the award was excessive based on the evidence before the court. They did not plan any arguments based on freedom of speech.[48]

The enormity of the judgment was breathtaking. Alabama's libel attack had brought forth the largest libel award in Alabama history.[49] "Even the most intrepid publisher," the *Chicago Tribune* noted, "must be intimidated into silence."[50]

Alabama newspapers celebrated the spectacular victory in their war against the civil rights movement and the "paper curtain" press. Crooned the *Alabama Journal*, "The half-million dollar judgment imposed on the *New York Times* et al by a Montgomery jury could have the effect of causing reckless publishers of the North . . . to make a re-survey of their habit of permitting anything detrimental to the South and its people to appear in their columns":

> That the South and the people of the South are individually and collectively are being libeled every day by Northern newspapers, magazines, and their special correspondents is known by all men. Heretofore they have regarded themselves as safe from prosecution for their offenses because they were far off, and under the impression that they could be sued for their derelictions only in the courts of their home cities. The Alabama courts have declared that newspapers like the *New York Times* are doing business in Alabama, and hence are responsible for their actions affecting Alabama and Alabama citizens. Half a million dollars is a mere fraction of what is required to repair the damage to the South, Alabama, and their people inflicted by the New York Times and other newspapers.
>
> Montgomery especially has suffered from their libels and has tried to take it in stride. But the effect of the constant news media misrepresentations of what goes on in Montgomery and in Alabama has been of great damage to the region. So that this verdict—large by normal standards in damage suits—is a mere bagatelle when compared with the total injury to Montgomery caused by wild stories, untrue dispatches, and deliberately false advertisements appearing in the eastern newspapers and magazines. . . . If the Montgomery verdict has the effect of causing an inventory, a resurvey of policy, and study of the violations of law and decency they and their correspondents have been committing, the verdict will have served a good purpose not only to the *New York Times* but to all others who have been even more offensive offenders than the *Times*.[51]

The *Times* ran a modestly billed story about the Sullivan verdict, head-lined "Times, 4 Clerics Lose Libel Case." The three-paragraph article, bur-ied deep on the front page, was relatively insignificant.[52] The concern at the *Times* over the verdict was anything but minor.

The "Alabama cases" were the top item on the agenda at the board of directors' meeting in December 1960. Sulzberger had asked Tom Daly of Lord Day & Lord to write a memo on the litigation. It was the first time in the newspaper's history that a libel case was discussed at a board of directors meeting.

"As you know the Sullivan case was tried and judgment rendered against the *Times* and other defendants in the amount of $500,000," explained Daly's memo. "We are now in the process of making a motion before the trial judge to set aside the verdict as against the weight of the evidence." "We do not expect to be successful. ... The other cases in the Montgomery state court will proceed to trial in the latter part of January. As you will realize, the chances are that verdicts will likewise be rendered against the *Times* in these actions in substantial amounts." Daly also mentioned the Birmingham cases. If those cases went to trial, there was a "grave possibil-ity" of adverse verdicts as well.[53]

Alerted to this impending crisis, *Times* executives held an "emergency meeting" in Orvil Dryfoos's office on January 24, 1961. At the end of two hours, they concluded that the "iron curtain" must stay down—all *New York Times* personnel had to remain out of Alabama.[54]

The libel cases troubled Turner Catledge. He thought about them on the job, drinking with his colleagues, even vacationing in Europe. More than anyone else on the *Times*, he saw Alabama's libel attack as a dire threat to journalism and freedom of the press.

Catledge was more disturbed by the Birmingham cases than the Mont-gomery cases. The Montgomery libel suits dealt with an advertisement, but the Birmingham cases implicated news reporting and the editorial mission of the paper. If those cases resulted in large judgments, no news-paper would feel safe sending reporters into Southern states to cover controversial stories, especially those that criticized segregation.[55] Catledge saw a dangerous precedent, and he set out to make sure that his colleagues—if not at the *Times*, then at other newspapers—felt as he did.

This wasn't difficult, as Catledge was one of the most influential men in journalism. In addition to serving as *Times* managing editor, Catledge was president of the American Society of Newspaper Editors. The venerable society, composed of elite editors at the nation's top newspapers, had been founded in 1922 to defend journalism from its critics and to promulgate and enforce professional codes of ethics. The ASNE lobbied for legal changes that would benefit journalism, particularly in the area of freedom of information, and had occasionally signed on as *amicus curiae* in important freedom of the press cases.[56]

National news outlets had been vocal in condemning Salisbury's criminal libel indictment. So Catledge was surprised when he faced resistance in trying to get the ASNE involved in the Birmingham libel cases against the *Times*. At the meeting of the ASNE board in November, Catledge asked Eugene S. Pulliam, managing editor of the *Indianapolis Star* and chairman of the ASNE Freedom of Information Committee, if the committee would consider filing *amicus curiae* briefs on behalf of the *Times*. Pulliam was initially inclined to assist, but soon after reported to Catledge that he believed the issue fell outside the purview of the Freedom of Information Committee because it didn't involve access to public records or proceedings.[57]

In reality, the editors were afraid of being sued. Southern newspaper editors on the ASNE committee had frowned upon the organization's intervention in the libel cases. The Birmingham newspapers, which were owned by the powerful Newhouse chain, had allies across the country.[58] Catledge was also disappointed when he made an all-out effort to get major news outlets, including the *Atlanta Constitution*, the *Washington Post*, and *Newsweek*, to file *amicus curiae* briefs on behalf of the *Times* in the Birmingham cases. They declined, fearing reprisals from the South.[59]

Catledge couldn't stop thinking about the libel suits and the chilly response of his colleagues. When he was in Paris in December, working on the *Times'* International Edition, he took impulsive action. On the last day of the year, he got out his typewriter and went on a letter-writing spree. His correspondence explained to some of the nation's top editors the importance of lending their support to the *Times*. To Lee Hills, head of the Knight newspaper chain and vice president of the ASNE, he explained that he was "frightened as hell at this new weapon of intimidation which seems in the making."

> What I want to take up with you earnestly at this juncture, however, is whether one or more of the Knight papers, especially the *Miami Herald*, might want to consider filing an amicus brief in the appeal now pending in New Orleans. I leave it to the facts to make their own appeal, but I am sure that after examining them, you will agree with me that here is an issue of the utmost importance to newspapers who are trying to do an honest, wide-ranging job of reporting and commenting on the news...
>
> It certainly seems to me that the court should be informed of the deep concern the whole American newspaper profession, not alone the *New York Times*, feel in this issue.... And I write to you in this manner, Lee, not pri-marily as a representative of the *New York Times* or as a personal friend, but as a professional who is frightened as hell at this new weapon of intimida-tion which seems in the making.[60]

Catledge dashed off letters to editors of the *New Orleans Times-Picayune*, *Atlanta Constitution*, and *Washington Post*. To Felix McKnight of the *Dallas Times-Herald*, he wrote, "You realize, I know, my own reluc-tance personally to urge action by the ASNE or any of my friends. But... I regard this as a matter of such supreme importance that I owe it to the newspaper profession to call earnest attention to it. The basic issue here is one of freedom of inquiry—freedom from the threat of virtual lynch-law damage suits away from your home base." "I think you might well want to consider...whether this is not a case of such importance to the newspaper business that you would want to file an amicus brief in the appeal now pending and soon to be argued before the Fifth Circuit Court of Appeals."[61] But none of the news entities intervened with the exception of the Atlanta Newspapers, publisher of the *Atlanta Constitution* and the *Atlanta Journal*, and the *Chicago Tribune*, a long-standing defender of freedom of the press, which filed amicus briefs before the Fifth Circuit Court of Appeals, urging the court to reverse the decision that the *Times* could be sued in Alabama.[62] For the next three years, as the cases wound their way through the courts, Catledge remained frustrated with the timidity of his colleagues in journalism.

The venerable American Civil Liberties Union wouldn't get involved, either. Since 1920, the nation's preeminent civil liberties organization had been on the front lines of the battle for civil liberties. The ACLU had litigated some of the most important free speech cases heard by the Supreme Court and had been actively involved in assisting the NAACP's civil rights litigation. The ACLU saw the ominous implications of the libel cases for the press and for the civil rights movement, but it was hesitant to assist because it had a long-standing policy of not getting involved in libel cases. ACLU leaders believed that libel cases weren't in the organization's purview since, under existing Supreme Court rulings, there was no constitutional issue at stake.[63]

.   .   .   .   .

The second of the Montgomery libel trials, that of Mayor Earl James, was scheduled for late January 1961, in the week leading up to Montgomery's big Confederacy celebration. The festivities scheduled that week included torchlight parades, historical reenactments, pageants, and fireworks. Men in long beards and women in hoop skirts and bonnets came to the courtroom directly from the festivities. Five of the jurors, and Mayor James himself, sported Confederate-style whiskers.[64]

Before trial, Embry and the lawyers for the ministers had filed a motion asking to postpone the proceedings, arguing that the *Times* couldn't get a fair hearing before an impartial jury because of the Confederacy celebration, the "relation between the nature of the subject matter of this action and certain issues of the war between the states," and the "the revival of such issues in the minds of the community and the emotions and feelings of sectionalism."[65] Jones, naturally, rejected the motion.

The four ministers were represented by Charles Swinger Conley, a forty-year-old black civil rights attorney from Montgomery, a graduate of New York University's law school who represented the SCLC in litigation.[66] Conley asked Jones to dismiss the jury panel, alleging that it excluded black citizens in violation of the Fourteenth Amendment.[67] For the first time, racial discrimination became an issue in the case; Conley was clearly planning an appeal on this basis. Predictably, Jones denied this motion as well.

The trial was essentially a replay of the Sullivan trial. Nachman accused the *Times* of "maliciously" publishing a full-page advertisement designed to bring about "public shame and hatred." The ad was a "slur on the city of Montgomery and on Mayor James who is responsible for police action in the city." Statements in the advertisement referring to "shotguns and teargas" and authorities padlocking the dining hall were "nothing but lies." The *Times* attorneys insisted that "the statements are not directed at the Mayor in any way, shape, or form." The mayor's lawyer pronounced Negro as "Nigra" when reading the ad. Conley objected, and Jones overruled. "I'll leave the pronunciation to him," he said.[68]

New York Times employees tried to convince the jury that the ad was published with good faith belief in the truthfulness of the statements. They insisted that they hadn't intended for the statements to reflect on the mayor. Advertising salesman Gershon Aronson said he had no reason to believe that the ad statements were false but admitted that the *Times* hadn't checked the accuracy of the ad. Vincent Redding, head of the Advertising Acceptability Department, was forced to admit on cross-examination that he hadn't fact-checked the ad or bothered to see if the ministers authorized the use of their names. James testified that the ad criticized his ability to maintain law and order in Montgomery and to "administer the functions of municipal government in an orderly fashion." But he admitted that he still enjoyed a good reputation in Montgomery, and "I trust it will always be that way."[69]

On the first day of the trial, the lawyers for the ministers had asked Jones to integrate the courtroom. They argued that the segregation of the courtroom constituted a violation of the due process and equal protection clauses of the Fourteenth Amendment. The judge summoned the clerk of court, who testified that any segregation that took place was customary and informal; neither the rules nor regulations of the court required the courtroom to be segregated. Shuttlesworth was in town for the trial. That evening, he led a rousing sermon at the Dexter Avenue Baptist Church in which he exhorted the parishioners to test Jones's ruling that there would be no legally enforced segregation.[70]

Black spectators filed into the courtroom the following morning and sat in the white section. The court's deputies were visibly rattled. In plain sight of the jury, bailiffs directed the black attendees to relocate to one side of the courtroom, to "get up and move." The ministers argued that they were being denied their rights and made a motion for a mistrial. Jones ordered the trial to continue.[71]

When spectators tried to integrate the courtroom again the next morning, Jones decided that he wouldn't stand for it. Enraged, he read from the bench a memo he had prepared the day before. Accepting what he called the "challenge of the Negro defendants"—meaning that he was prepared to have his ruling contested in federal court—Jones insisted that the Fourteenth Amendment had "no place" in his courtroom and that his court would be ruled by "white man's justice":

> A number of persons descended on the courtroom to such an extent as to impede the orderly progress of the trial. From what the Presiding Judge saw... from the bench with his own eyes, there was a studied effort by friends of the four individual negro defendants to pack the courtroom with members of their race. It would appear that there has been a planned effort to drum up members of the negro race to take up the seating capacity of the courtroom.
>
> As far as the Court can determine, after study and investigation, the large and unusual in-pouring of negro spectators was not due to any desire on their part as interested citizens to witness the orderly administration of justice and the proper conduct of a trial at law. The presence of this crowd of negro spectators, occupying every seat from the front to the back row of the courtroom, is to test and challenge the right and power of the Presiding Judge to direct the seating of spectators in the courtroom...
>
> The judge... is ready for his judicial power and authority to be tested. He accepts the challenge of counsel for the four negro defendants, that under the XIV Amendment, he is without authority, and powerless, to direct how a trial shall be conducted. The trial judge is willing to meet this challenge. He accepts it. He puts the laws of Alabama against the wishes and whims of the lawyers for the four negro defendants.
>
> From this hour forward, in keeping with the common law of Alabama and in observing the time-honored customs and usages of our people, both white and black, which have done so much for the good of the races and the peace of the state, there will be no integrated seating in the courtroom. Spectators will be seated in the courtroom according to their race, and this for the orderly administration of justice and the good of all people coming here lawfully...
>
> One of the lawyers for the four individual defendants... has made several loud objections to the pronouncement of the word NEGRO by counsel for the plaintiff, honorable members of the Bar of this court, men of education. These objections have been made with no citation of authority to sustain them and have nothing whatsoever to do with the merits of the case.... The objections impress the court as being grandstand plays to the negro spectators in the court room. They are simply appeals to race prejudice.... They

lack good taste. The Court has for two days patiently borne them. Their further repetition will invoke the summary contempt power of the Court.

In an obvious dig at the U.S. Supreme Court, he noted that "it is quite the fashion in high judicial places to work the XIV Amendment over-time." "The XIV Amendment has no standing whatever in this court, it is a pariah and an outcast," Jones declared.

> There is not one word in the XIV Amendment, there is not one suggestion in the history of this amendment, which by the wildest flight of imagination into space, can be constructed to take from a state judge, serving under the construction and laws of his state, his inherent power to control the internal operations of his court....
>
> We will now continue with the trial of this case under the laws of the State of Alabama, and not under the XIV Amendment, and in the belief and knowledge that the white man's justice, a justice born long centuries ago in England, brought over to this country by the Anglo-Saxon Race, and brought today to its full flower here, a justice which has blessed countless generations of whites and blacks will give the parties at the Bar of this Court, regardless of race or color, equal justice under the law.

These remarks were printed in the *Alabama Lawyer*, the organ of the state bar association, which Jones edited, under the title "Judge Jones on Courtroom Segregation."[72] It would become evidence of racial discrimination in the ministers' appeal to the U.S. Supreme Court.

After three days of testimony, the case went to the jury on February 1, 1961. The jurors deliberated for two hours before awarding James $500,000.[73] The total liability against the *Times* and the ministers in the Montgomery cases had now reached one million dollars.

9 A Civil Rights Crisis

The libel cases were being defended on two separate fronts. The lawyers for the *New York Times* pushed papers and made arguments in Alabama courtrooms and behind closed doors in the tony offices of Lord Day & Lord. The SCLC waged its battles humbly in churches and sparsely furnished meeting halls where leaders gave speeches and passed the hat for contributions of twenty-five cents or a dollar. The libel suits silenced the *Times*, but they emboldened the SCLC, which had nothing to lose in publicizing the libel suits and using them to highlight the injustice of the South's racial system.

From the start of the libel suits, civil rights leaders embraced the *Times* as a common victim and ally. The persecution of the *Times* by the Alabama authorities underscored the movement's claims of segregationist brutality. In speeches, editorials, and pamphlets, civil rights leaders publicized the connection between civil rights and freedom of the press.

When the Birmingham commissioners sued the *Times*, Fred Shuttlesworth's Alabama Christian Movement for Human Rights issued resolutions condemning the lawsuits, describing them as "intended to blind the eyes of the local public and cover up ... various violations of law and abuses of citizens' rights." "We see nothing false, slanderous, or calumnious in the articles in question. We submit that there is nothing of substance to be retracted in either; rather, there is more that could be added."[1] The Southern Conference Educational Fund, an interracial civil rights organization based in Birmingham, issued a public statement titled "Is Freedom of the Press to Go Next?" "We view this libel suit as an harassment of these ministers designed to stifle their work for civil rights in the state of Alabama," it stated. "We also see it as a grave threat to freedom of the press, one that if it goes unchecked and unchallenged will make many reporters and newspapers reluctant to print the truth about events in the Deep South."[2]

But civil rights advocates' support of the *New York Times* wouldn't be reciprocated. The *Times* made clear that despite its editorial support of civil rights, it wouldn't be allied with the SCLC in the libel suits, which would jeopardize its precarious defense.

.   .   .   .   .

The sit-ins revitalized the SCLC. Before 1960, the organization had flailed due to King's administrative inexperience and lack of budget and staff. But the impassioned activism of the student protesters inspired the group to pursue a "full-scale assault" on segregation. In the spring of 1960, King appointed Reverend Wyatt Tee Walker executive director of the SCLC and urged him to expand its efforts. By the summer, the SCLC was planning initiatives including supporting the sit-ins, Freedom Rides challenging segregation on interstate transportation, voter registration campaigns, and running the Highlander Folk School that would instruct community leaders in nonviolent techniques to fight segregation.[3]

These efforts took time, commitment, and a great deal of money. The SCLC could not progress if its leaders were saddled with million-dollar libel judgments and defensive litigation battles.[4] The organization was already drowning in legal fees. Defending King in the perjury case had cost $50,000 and required the work of a half-dozen lawyers. On top of this, the SCLC faced a new crop of litigation stemming from the sit-ins.[5]

King was certain that the libel suits threatened the SCLC's very existence. He charged two of his closest advisors, attorneys Stanley Levison and Clarence Jones, with ensuring that the Montgomery verdicts were overturned and that the remaining libel suits were quashed. Jones was the son of poor, black domestic servants from Philadelphia who had pulled himself up by his bootstraps to graduate from Boston University Law School and built a career as a successful entertainment attorney in Los Angeles. King recruited Jones to help represent him in the tax fraud matter, and Jones stayed on as King's legal advisor.[6]

Like King and Levison, Jones saw the defeat of the libel suits as essential to the SCLC's survival. Jones also saw success as a matter of principle. Sullivan's case was petty—"the kind that would either be not filed today or immediately tossed out as frivolous," Jones recalled. "Petty or not, the suit confirmed Martin's belief that the greatest weapon against civil rights was not a fire hose but a lawyer on the wrong side of history." The "political objective of the lawsuit was to bankrupt and decapitate the SCLC and its leadership and intimidate the northern press. Which meant that this suit would not go away by itself. It would have to be won—and decisively—to act as a deterrent against future suits...a lot was riding on this."[7] Jones believed that the success of the civil rights struggle required the robust protection of freedom of speech, and he embarked on a personal crusade to make sure that the libel suits were defeated. If politicians in the South could weaponize libel law, "it would decapitate and bankrupt the civil rights movement," he believed. The "Southwide civil rights movement" could not move forward with "liability hanging over the heads of the [ministers]," Jones explained to King.[8]

The SCLC knew that the *Times* wasn't eager to cooperate with it in the libel defense. King believed nevertheless that Levison and Jones should communicate with the *Times* lawyers "to see what the thinking is." Not long after Patterson filed suit, Loeb, Daly, Levison, and Jones convened around a conference table in the Lord, Day & Lord office.

The lawyers for the newspaper explained how the *Times* had granted Patterson's retractions and insisted that the ministers also issue a retraction to reduce or mitigate the damages. Jones was outraged. The *Times* was backing down, and it was asking the SCLC to share in its cowardice. "No, no. We're not going to issue a retraction," he said indignantly. He turned to Levison. "Stanley, under no circumstances can we consent to a retraction," he said. "We have to stand firm on this, okay?" The ministers never issued a retraction.[9]

Meanwhile, the SCLC was hemorrhaging money in the libel cases. By

October 1960, the SCLC had spent $50,000 on legal expenses, including defending libel cases. In 1961, the New York office of the SCLC spent $27,000 on the defense of the libel cases, nearly one-tenth of its budget. The SCLC also raised $12,000 in an "Emergency Defense Fund," a "Special Fund for the Defense and Restoration of Losses" to assist the ministers.[10] This was essential after the state of Alabama began seizing the ministers' property.

Right after the Sullivan trial, the New York Times lawyers moved for a new trial. The Times managed to have the cases separated, so that the Times and the ministers would pursue separate appeals. The Times lawyers argued that the judgment was invalid because the Times couldn't be sued in Alabama, the ad didn't refer to Sullivan, and the award was excessive based on the evidence before the court. The ministers' lawyers also moved for a new trial, claiming that they didn't consent to the use of their names, that the jury excluded black citizens, and that segregated seating in the courtroom violated the Fourteenth Amendment.

Making a motion for a new trial was a standard, pro forma move. Of course, the Times and the ministers had no expectation of winning—the motions would be heard by none other than Judge Jones—but they had to make the gesture to appeal to a higher court. In addition to requesting a new trial in the Sullivan case, the Times planned to appeal through the state court system. Under Alabama statute, as a condition for taking an appeal from a trial court verdict with a stay of execution during the appeal, a supersedeas bond (a bond required from an appellant who wants to delay the payment of a judgment until an appeal is over) must be posted in an amount double the size of the verdict.

The Times posted a bond for $1,000,500 (twice the amount of judgment plus $500, as required by law). But the ministers couldn't afford to post a bond. The attorneys for the ministers had asked the Times' lawyers if they would permit the clergymen to "piggyback" on the newspaper's bond. The Times attorneys refused, saying that the Times had raised the question of jurisdiction and that they believed that if the case were appealed to the U.S. Supreme Court, the Court would hold that Alabama did not have jurisdiction. But if the ministers were "tagging on" the supersedeas bond, the Alabama court would have jurisdiction over the Times.[11]

The lawyers for the Times and the ministers' lawyers appeared before

Judge Jones on December 16, 1960, asking for an extension of their motions for a new trial, which they received until January 13, 1961. On that day, the *Times* lawyers filed the motion and were granted a postponement of the arguments until March 3. But the ministers didn't make their request for postponement until five days later. Jones ruled that the ministers should have filed a separate request and that their extension had expired the previous Saturday. He refused to hear the ministers' argument or even to allow them to make a statement for the record, saying "you're dead, you're dead" and shooing them from the courtroom.[12]

Because the ministers had no motion pending, and because they hadn't posted a bond, their property could be seized to satisfy the $500,000 judgment. On the instructions of Nachman, who was living up to his reputation for aggressive lawyering, Jones instructed the Montgomery sheriff to confiscate the ministers' possessions. Fred Gray recalled, "Under normal circumstances, the plaintiff wouldn't levy on property, especially when one of the defendants had posted a bond and the case was pending. But these were not normal circumstances." "This was still Alabama and this was still a civil rights case.... The plaintiff did not have the human decency to wait until the appeal was over before levying on the ministers' property."[13]

When Abernathy returned home one day in February, he found that his five-year-old Buick Century had disappeared. Authorities towed it away earlier in the day. The state auctioned it for $400, even though its "book" value was $695.[14] Abernathy told the press that the seizure of his car would not "in any way deter me from fighting for the rights of my people. I shall walk now on the road to freedom."[15] Shortly after, authorities went after Abernathy's other significant possession, his one-twelfth interest in a 307-acre tract of land in the western part of the state, in Marengo County. His father and mother, both dead, worked hard as sharecroppers to buy the land and left it to their twelve children. The land was auctioned on March 20. Abernathy's eleven siblings purchased his share for $4,350.[16] Civil rights supporters from around the country sent donations to help Abernathy reclaim his property.[17] The Victory Baptist Church of Los Angeles bought Abernathy a brand-new Electra Buick.[18]

Seay owned a small tract of land outside Montgomery that he used for farming. This was the only possession in his name. The state attached the land and scheduled it for "quick sale." He pleaded for a loan of $500 from Levison. "I am the pastor of a small church, but my main income is from a farm I operate," he wrote. As a result of the seizure, his credit was "completely nullified here in the community."[19]

Sheriffs J.M. Jones and O.E. Kinney arrived at the Bethel Baptist parsonage in Birmingham to take Fred Shuttlesworth's car, a tan 1957 Plymouth with a cream-colored streak on the side.[20] Before the car was seized, Shuttleworth replaced the good tires with bald ones and let out the air. He laughed as he watched a deputy pump up the tire so that the car could be towed. "I believe in harassing the harassers," he said.[21] Without his car, Shuttlesworth found a taxi service provided by a fellow minister. His followers took up donations to buy him a new car, which they proposed to register "in the name of Jesus" to protect it against further seizures.[22]

The only property the authorities could take from Joseph Lowery in Mobile was his 1958 Chrysler. His parishioners bought the car at auction for nine hundred dollars, then gave it to his wife. Lowery recalled: "I'm the only one who didn't get a new car!" "Those astute Methodists went down and bid for the same car and saved money. But the Baptists let them take the car, and they bought Abernathy and Shuttlesworth and Seay new cars. But I drove my same old car."[23]

In all, Alabama authorities took about $7,500 in property from the ministers as partial payment of the judgment. Their bank accounts at the Tuskegee Federal Savings and Loan were seized and their salaries garnished. This harassment was not a trivial matter. Though all the men were college-trained ministers, none of them had a salary of more than $100 a week. This persecution was driving the SCLC's leadership from Alabama. Shortly after his car was seized, Shuttlesworth left to become a pastor in Cincinnati.[24] Not long after, Lowery left Mobile for Nashville.

The unfortunate episode generated unexpected support for the libel defense and made it easier for the SCLC to fundraise. The dramatic events—the ministers' humble autos being hauled away before crying children, hard-won family property on the auction block—were covered sympathetically in the national press. The events were also reported in black newspapers throughout the country and in the prominent black magazine *Jet*. Donations flowed into the SCLC. Just as the libel suits had mobilized segregationists, they were bringing together an interracial coalition of civil rights advocates in the North. Wyatt Tee Walker noted in

Figure 6. Martin Luther King Jr., Fred Shuttlesworth, and Ralph Abernathy (*left to right*) at a press conference in Birmingham. Alabama Department of Archives and History. Donated by Alabama Media Group. Photo by Tom Self, *Birmingham News*.

his semiannual report that "the intense involvement of these four of our compatriots has been, paradoxically, a means of extending our work and message." "We cannot gainsay how much anxiety and sacrifice has been expended by Abernathy, Lowery, Seay, and Shuttlesworth. But in another of the strange ways that this struggle continues to evolve, SCLC has been helped at their expense and we owe them more than we can ever pay."[25]

The day before the Montgomery sheriffs took Abernathy's property, the four ministers, through attorney Charles Conley, tried to halt the prosecution of the libel suits. This was to be accomplished through a federal civil rights lawsuit against Governor Patterson, the Montgomery commissioners, and four Montgomery sheriffs, brought under the Civil Rights Act of 1871, which prohibits conspiracies by officials to deprive any persons of privileges and immunities guaranteed to them by the Constitution.[26]

In his complaint brought before the U.S. District Court of the Middle District of Alabama, Conley described a plot by state officials to "deprive Negroes of their civil rights" that began with the attack on the student demonstrators in February 1960. He alleged that Patterson and the commissioners "conspired and planned—utilizing their official positions as well as the judicial machinery of the state, to deter and prohibit the plaintiffs and their supporters from utilizing their constitutional rights by instituting fraudulent actions against the plaintiffs without any basis in law or fact." The libel suits had been weaponized as part of the conspiracy—"manufactured and contrived by these persons to enrich themselves by taking advantage of community sentiment against these four plaintiffs."[27] King lauded these "injunctive suits" as "one of the most significant steps taken in behalf of our conference [the SCLC] in 1961."[28]

Arguments were held before Frank M. Johnson Jr. Johnson was lauded by civil rights advocates for his rulings ordering desegregation of public facilities. Yet he refused the request to stop seizure of the ministers' property because they had not yet exhausted their remedies in state court.[29] This ruling was upheld by the U.S. Court of Appeals for the Fifth Circuit.[30] The ministers appealed to the U.S. Supreme Court. The Supreme Court was a champion of civil rights, yet it refused without comment to hear the case.[31] Conley and King were forced to conclude that this avenue of potential relief had been foreclosed.

Sulzberger read about the seizure of the ministers' property one morning during his breakfast-in-bed perusal of the *Times*. Now in his sixties and disabled by a stroke, he was no longer in control of the paper. His son-in-law, Orvil Dryfoos, took over most of the *Times'* day-to-day operations. Sulzberger nonetheless loomed as a powerful figure who made his opinions known through the chronic issuance of "blue notes."[32]

Sulzberger was horrified and conscience-stricken that the ministers should be imperiled on account of the *Times*. He dashed off a "blue note" to Loeb. "Dear Louis, as you know, four Negro ministers are involved with the suit against the *Times* in the Alabama situation," he wrote. "They have suffered severe losses in having their cars attached and now this further story that we have today about their property being sold. While I have every confidence that we will be able to clear ourselves against the absurd verdicts, it remains true that the ministers are presently sustaining real damage. My question is, how and in what way could we legitimately help them?"[33]

Although Loeb was a liberal like Sulzberger and was genuinely disturbed by the ministers' plight, he was certain that helping them would result in dire consequences for the *Times*. "I can assure you that I and my associates down here are just as revolted as you are at the way in which the authorities in Alabama are persecuting these Negro defendants, especially in light of the fact that they have testified in both trials that they never saw the ad before it was published and never consented to the use of their names as signers or endorsers of its contents," he replied. Loeb admitted that the "most effective way that we could help them, but even that is probably too late, would be if we permit the bond which are going to post in behalf of the *Times* to cover them as well."

> We would advise that that be done if their cases and ours were on all fours, but unfortunately they are not because they do not have the question of jurisdiction, which is the main string to our bow for eventually obtaining a reversal. We certainly cannot advise the directors of the *New York Times* to risk over $500,000 for the protection of the Negroes. The attorneys representing the Negroes made a mistake which is the cause of the present situation...
>
> I am afraid that all I can advise is that we cooperate closely with them in the future course of the litigation, which we are doing, that we bend every effort towards the ultimate reversal of these judgments, which I am confident we will succeed in accomplishing, and then lend every conceivable assistance in recovering the meager assets of which they are being deprived in this heartless and vindictive manner.[34]

The ministers were appalled that the *Times* had abandoned them. "I'm a little reluctant to buy the *New York Times* today," Lowery recalled years later. "I usually read somebody else's paper."[35]

• • •

The SCLC convened in March in Atlanta in King's spare, brick-walled Ebenezer Church. The "chief business" of the meeting, King told fifty assembled members, was "the legal, financial, and other involved phases of the Alabama suits against the *New York Times* and the [ministers]."[36]

The attendees peppered Charles Conley with questions. Could the ministers get their property back? How long would the cases take to resolve? Conley said that the cases could take as long as five years to conclude. The discussion then centered on the Montgomery lawyers, Fred Gray and his colleagues. The lawyers were criticized for charging too much and for being "incompetent" for not filing the motion papers on time. King recommended that they be eliminated from the defense; the defense would consist of Conley and various "national attorneys," meaning elite lawyers from the North.[37] Several prestigious white attorneys who had been touched by the civil rights cause volunteered their services to the SCLC.[38] King, Levison, and Jones worked on bringing some of the lawyers to take over the libel defense.

Jones became so devoted to the libel cases that he moved to New York to coordinate them. One of his new neighbors was Theodore "Ted" Kheel. A dapper, erudite labor lawyer, Kheel was a partner in his prestigious law firm, Battler, Fowler, Stokes, and Kheel, as well as president of the venerable interracial civil rights organization known as the National Urban League. Jones told Kheel how discouraged he was by the SCLC's difficulty raising funds for the defense of the libel cases. Kheel assured him that it would be easy for him to enlist "big New York attorneys" as volunteers.[39] Kheel convened a meeting, the inaugural lunch meeting of the "Lawyers Advisory Committee on the Alabama Libel Suits," to be held in the Lotos Club, an elite social club. The invitation went out on the letterhead of Kheel's firm, from the tony address of 477 Madison Avenue:

> Those of us who have reviewed the cases from the legal point of view believe that the institution of these libel actions, their trial before a tribunal which

maintains a segregated courtroom, and the subsequent hasty leveling and execution of the modest property of the defendants, with full knowledge that satisfaction of the maximum verdicts is impossible, constitutes a flagrant abuse of legal and judicial process for purposes other than those for which a legitimate civil action in libel was designed. The record clearly indicates that no lawful basis exists for a civil action in libel.... They have been sued ... for their views and the activities of their supporters in seeking equality of treatment under the law.[40]

King, the keynote speaker at the luncheon, spoke movingly of the threat the libel suits posed to "the political and social interests of our nation." If the judgments weren't reversed, "victims of injustice dare not express opposition to their oppressors.... These cases are a classic example of tyranny over the minds and tongues of men making a nullity of the First Amendment to the Constitution":

Brutality and intimidation can wear many guises. They need not openly be flaunted, as in Mississippi, by setting police dogs trained in viciousness on human beings. Nor need they be expressed only by the howling lynch mob. These have the disadvantages that the sense of decency and justice of the American people can in revulsion turn on the perpetrators. So a more subtle form of attack needed to be designed. In this sense the misuse of legal process is a new and potent weapon in the arsenal of the segregationists. It is a sword with two cutting edges. It not only deprives the victim of his economic security, but it undermines his confidence in law as he finds himself led through all the processes of a juridical system traditionally designed to insure justice, but which for him is perverted to accomplish oppression and injustice....

The effect of accumulating millions of dollars in judgments against leaders of the integration struggle goes far beyond those directly involved. Every Negro senses the threat to his own security and to his own dignity when he witnesses his leaders stripped of their means of transportation, parcels of land, and the garnishment of their salaries. When the line between poverty and subsistence is paper thin, an economic lynching has terrors not fundamentally less destructive than physical lynching.[41]

King's address spurred eighteen high-profile attorneys to volunteer for the committee.[42] The lawyers represented a broad cross-section of the New York bar; "Protestants, Catholics, and Jews, Negroes and whites, Democrats and Republicans," Kheel told the press. One of the volunteers was William Rogers, who ran his own law firm, Rogers & Wells. Rogers had just spent four years as attorney general under President Eisenhower and was involved in federal efforts to enforce integration, including intervening in the Little Rock crisis. Rogers agreed to work on the case *pro bono* and would argue the case before the U.S. Supreme Court. He saw his involvement in the libel suits as the "continuation of a struggle" that he had been involved in for eight years.[43]

At an SCLC meeting in Montgomery in May, King described to a standing-room-only crowd the formation of the "Kheel Committee," as it was known. It was the first time King had been to Montgomery since the perjury charges. The group passed a resolution launching an immediate drive to raise funds for $75,000 for the libel defense. King announced his intention to litigate the cases "all the way to the Supreme Court if necessary," he declared. "We will not let these freedom fighters down."[44]

.   .   .   .   .

On March 3, 1961, the *Times* lawyers returned to Judge Jones's courtroom for the obviously futile exercise of arguing for a new trial in the Sullivan case. The *Times* contended that Jones had erred in ordering it to produce business records from the *Times*, in finding that the paper was "doing business" in Alabama, and in charging the jury that the statements in the advertisement were *libelous per se*. The verdict was "so excessive as to clearly show that it was the result of bias, passion, and prejudice or other improper motive on the part of the jury," the lawyers argued. Moreover, the *Times* was deprived of a fair and impartial trial in that Sullivan's lawyers were allowed to present the case to the jury as a sectional conflict rather than a libel case.[45]

"Half of Montgomery County would have to have been held in contempt of court if evidence of jury pressure had been introduced in the libel suit," Embry told the judge. Jurors who heard the case were "put in the spotlight," and "couldn't fail to realize they were expected to do what the population wanted them to do." The *Advertiser* published pictures of the jury during the trial and part of the trial was broadcast on television. These pressures made a fair and impartial verdict impossible, the lawyers for the *Times* argued.[46]

Nachman "deeply resented" Embry's statements about the jurors' bias,

Figure 7. Shuttlesworth, Abernathy, King, and others during a civil rights demonstration in Birmingham. Alabama Department of Archives and History. Donated by Alabama Media Group. Photo by Ed Jones and Robert Adams, *Birmingham News*.

he told the judge. "No jury has ever been faced with such monstrous action on the part of a newspaper." The *Times* would have "laughed off $50,000 or $100,000 as a mere bagatelle, but they won't laugh off half a million. I don't know of any case of a newspaper being guilty of such monstrous actions, cavalier conduct, or gross misbehavior. The *Times*, considered one of the leading newspapers in the world, could have apologized, it could have said it was sorry. The paper chose to fight it out, bull its way through a suit it could not defend with the truth."[47] "They gambled on the outcome of this trial and they lost," he said. "And now they want a new trial."[48] Jones denied the motion, as well as the motion for a retrial in Mayor James's case.[49] Clyde Sellers, who had been city commissioner when King was arrested in 1958, sued the *Times* and the ministers, bringing the number of libel suits over the "Heed Their Rising Voices" ad to five.[50]

Now desperate, the *Times* lawyers tried to remove the Parks, Patterson, and Sellers cases to the federal district court for the Middle District of Alabama. They were convinced that they could prove that the ministers had been brought into the libel suits for the sole purpose of preventing the cases from being filed in the more liberal federal courts. [51]

This was the first time King had been involved in the proceedings. Judge Frank Johnson had asked for King's testimony to determine whether the SCLC had approved the use of the ministers' names. King testified that there was no relationship between the SCLC and the Committee to Defend Martin Luther King, and that he hadn't authorized Rustin to use his name or those of any on the SCLC. [52]

Johnson upheld the removal of the cases to federal court. After studying the evidence, he concluded that there was "no legal basis whatsoever" for the claim against the ministers. The "theory that the article was authorized ... [by] the individual resident defendants is without any evidentiary basis whatsoever," he wrote. "The joinder in each of these cases therefore was fraudulent as that term is applied in removal cases."[53] Parks and Patterson appealed the ruling to the federal appeals court, which was then hearing ten libel cases involving the *New York Times* in Alabama.[54]

.   .   .   .   .

That spring, the *Times* acknowledged an unpleasant milestone. For the first time in its history, its annual financial report mentioned libel litigation. Footnote 8 of the annual report reported that despite gains in circulation and advertising, earnings had fallen sharply in 1960. Expenses involved in covering the presidential election of 1960 had cut into profits.[55] So had the libel suits. A footnote titled "contingent liabilities" explained, "There are various libel and other legal actions which have arisen in the ordinary course of business and which are now pending against the company."[56]

Sulzberger commented on this in a published statement:

> Many years ago, Mr. Adolph Ochs, former publisher, established a general policy of not settling a libel suit out of court. He was able to boast at one time the *Times* spent more for lead pencils than for libel judgments. As a result, I don't think we have ever before reported on this business risk, which, of course, is always present. Now for the first time that I can recall we have had to comment in the financial footnotes the status of libel litigation. Footnote eight describes certain libel actions now pending against the *Times* in Alabama. These suits raise important questions of constitutional

law and freedom of the press. I am glad to report that our attorneys believe that the final disposition of these cases will not result in any substantial liability, if any, for the *Times*.[57]

Shortly after, Sulzberger retired from the position of publisher on account of his health but remained chairman of the board. Orvil Dryfoos became *Times* publisher. For the second time since Ochs's death, the *Times* passed into the hands of the publisher's son-in-law.[58]

Editors in the South connected Sulzberger's retirement to the paper's libel troubles, though there is little evidence to suggest that this was actually the case. The *Times* "has made what, in the eyes of newspaper men, are terrible bulls, some of which relating to the South have resulted in unprecedented libel suits," according to the *Alabama Journal*. "The changes now being made indicate that the stockholders of the paper see things going wrong since the Sulzberger illness and they proposed to do something about it. The *Times* deserves better direction than it has been receiving." "Well-conducted newspapers do not make the bulls of which the *Times* has recently been guilty," it concluded, "bulls which are costly both in money and prestige."[59]

10 The Iron Curtain

In the spring of 1961, activists launched a new phase in the direct-action movement with the Freedom Rides. Thirteen black and white activists from the Congress for Racial Equality (CORE) left Washington, DC, in two Greyhound buses. They headed South, intending to challenge segregation on interstate buses and in bus terminals. In 1946, the U.S. Supreme Court had ruled that Virginia's state law enforcing segregation on interstate buses was unconstitutional; in December 1960, it ruled in *Boynton v. Virginia* that segregation in bus terminal restaurants violated the non-discrimination provision of the National Motor Carrier Act. CORE came up with the idea of an interracial bus trip, with the intent of eliciting a violent reaction from segregationists that would draw national attention to Southern disobedience of the Court's decisions.[1]

The response to the Freedom Riders in Alabama was near-deadly. In Anniston, one busload of Freedom Riders was firebombed by a mob of Klansmen. Shortly after, another bus reached Birmingham, where the local KKK had worked out a deal with Bull Connor. The Klan would have fifteen minutes to attack the Riders at the Greyhound station before police intervened. KKK members met the Freedom Riders in the bus terminal and pounded them with bicycle chains, lead pipes, baseball bats, and steel knuckles.

Pressured by the Kennedy administration, Governor Patterson consented to have the highway patrol guarantee the safety of the Freedom Riders bus as far as Montgomery. At the city limits, the escort left the bus; Montgomery police were charged with its security. Sullivan's officers delayed arriving at the terminal to allow KKK members to pummel the Freedom Riders for over an hour.[2] Recalled John Doar, a Justice Department attorney who witnessed the arrival of the bus into Montgomery: "Oh! There are fists, punching! A bunch of men led by a guy with a bleeding face are beating them! There are no cops ... There's not a cop in sight."[3]

Rioting engulfed Montgomery. Angry whites overturned cars and tossed Molotov cocktails at black homes. King and Shuttlesworth were attending a service held at Abernathy's First Baptist Church in support of the Freedom Riders when a white mob surrounded the church and vandalized parked cars. King likened the violence to "barbarity comparable to the tragic days of Hitler's Germany."[4] Patterson put the city under martial law and directed National Guardsmen to restore order.[5] Despite the "libel attack" on the press and the risk of being sued, not to mention being subjected to violence, many national news outlets continued to send reporters to the South, and the coverage provided the public with shocking images. Even indifferent Americans had begun to believe that something must be done about the South's racial problems. In the words of historian Michael Klarman, "Alabama politicians had handed the civil rights movement an important victory on a silver platter."[6]

The Civil Rights Commission of the Department of Justice filed a complaint in federal court alleging that the Montgomery Police knowingly failed to protect the Freedom Riders. Sullivan was again thrust into the spotlight. He insisted that his police were caught off-guard and didn't know the Freedom Riders were coming. "There was no request," he said. "We all sincerely regret that this happened here in Montgomery. It could have been avoided had outside agitators left us alone."[7]

Claude Sitton heard about the riot on the radio while sitting on his front porch in Atlanta. Furious that he couldn't go to Montgomery because of the "iron curtain" policy, he called Hal Faber, the *Times'* assistant national editor. "How much longer are we going to let the goddamn lawyers run this newspaper?" he asked.[8]

In less than an hour, the National Desk called him and told him he could go. Sitton caught the next plane out of Atlanta and was on the first bus carrying the Freedom Riders out of Montgomery as it headed toward Jackson, Mississippi. Sitton's article, "Montgomery Tension High after Threats of Bombing," was published three days later.[9]

Sitton wasn't served with process, and he hoped he could return to Alabama. But the *Times* lawyers insisted that he had to stay out. Sitton cussed out Salisbury: "Your damn stories kept me out of Alabama for a year."[10]

Media coverage of the Freedom Riders in Alabama yielded yet another round of "libel attacks."

Five months earlier, Fred Friendly, president of CBS, had called Harding Bancroft of the *Times* to tell him that CBS intended to do a documentary titled "The Case of Birmingham against the New York Times," about the *Times* libel suits. The network felt strongly about the implications of the libel suits for freedom of the press and thought that "all newspapers and news gathering media should take a much more active part in it and see to it that the public knew more about it," Friendly explained to Bancroft.[11]

Producer David Lowe and acclaimed journalist Ed Murrow went to Birmingham to conduct interviews. They found conditions in the city to be even worse than Salisbury reported. People telephoned them from phone booths, put anonymous notes under their hotel doors, and arranged to see them only in parks and on street corners.[12] "There is a conspiracy of fear... People are afraid to talk. The words I have heard more than any others are, 'I'm afraid,'" Lowe observed. Murrow and Lowe decided that the "Birmingham story" was a "bigger story than the freedom of the press and the *Times* story" and decided to focus their report exclusively on racial conditions in the city.[13]

CBS reporter Howard K. Smith, who replaced Murrow on the project in early 1961, was finishing up the program when the Freedom Riders arrived in Birmingham. Smith was a liberal Southerner whose radio broadcasts from Europe during World War II had made him a familiar name in American households. Smith got a phone call telling him to go to the Greyhound station. There, he witnessed brutality that reminded him of Nazi attacks on Jews he'd seen in Europe. He closed the documentary by quoting Edmund Burke: "The only thing necessary for the triumph of evil is for good men to do nothing." When CBS lawyers screened the film— with visions of libel complaints no doubt passing before their eyes—they declared that the quote was "straight editorial" and needed to be cut.[14]

"Who Speaks for Birmingham" was broadcast four days after the Freedom Riders incident in Birmingham. With news footage of beaten activists, bombed cars, and segregationist rallies, it was a damning indictment of the violent and hate-filled city. The documentary opened with scenes from Birmingham, went on to describe the libel suits, and proceeded to air interviews responding to Salisbury's assertion that Birmingham was full of fear and tension.[15] *Birmingham Post-Herald* columnist John Temple Graves spoke as the unofficial voice of the city's establishment. "I am amazed to find that in your mind," he told Smith, "and in the mind of so many, we're the villain of the Southern piece, that this is the worst city in the South for oppression of the races. . . . It isn't so and how can we have the thing denied? Not through one newspaper, not through winning a libel suit against the *New York Times*."[16] Black residents of the city, including Shuttlesworth, described brutality they experienced at the hands of extremists, their narratives more compelling because of the recent Freedom Rides. One black interviewee said, "Life in Birmingham is hell."[17]

"Who Speaks for Birmingham" was described as "explosive." It stirred up the "Salisbury issue" all over again, said the *Birmingham News*. The *News* wondered editorially whether the series had been instigated by the *Times* in retaliation for the libel suits.[18] After the program aired, the local CBS station disaffiliated from the network. CBS fired Smith over the controversy.[19]

Birmingham officials wasted no time in suing CBS for libel. Bull Connor, Mayor James Morgan, and Commissioner James Waggoner asked $500,000 in damages each, alleging that they were falsely accused of abetting and encouraging delay in the arrival of police to the Greyhound station.[20] Shortly after, Samuella Willis and George Penton, members of the city's board of registers, sued CBS for $100,000 each for reporting that they had been working to prevent the registration of black voters.[21]

Figure 8. In 1963, iconic news photographs of a police dog lunging at a high school student in Birmingham changed the course of the civil rights movement. Alabama Department of Archives and History. Donated by Alabama Media Group. Unknown photographer, *Birmingham News.*

CBS's interest in the *New York Times* libel cases had condemned the network to the fate of the *Times*. CBS confronted nearly two million dollars' worth of libel judgments for its coverage of race relations in Alabama.

In June 1961, a milestone took place in the libel cases when the Fifth Circuit Court of Appeals ruled that the *Times* and Salisbury couldn't be sued in Alabama. The basis for the ruling was that under Alabama's own laws, all the action on which a libel suit is based must take place in the state. Chief Justice Elbert Tuttle said that the publication of Salisbury's stories hadn't been completed until they were printed in New York.[22]

The ruling effectively nullified the Birmingham libel cases. The decision "ended" the Birmingham suits, reported the *Times*, the *Washington Post,* and other newspapers.[23] Catledge was in New Orleans when the ruling came down, and he celebrated into the wee hours.[24]

Catledge found dozens of congratulatory letters on his desk when he returned. "All of us are grateful for your warm and encouraging telegram about our victory in the Birmingham suits," he replied to Ralph McGill, anti-segregationist editor of the *Atlanta Constitution*. "That part of our difficulty, I hope, is over. We still have the cases in Montgomery."[25]

He took the opportunity to chastise his colleagues in journalism. "As [one] newspaperm[a]n—and between you and me—I thought our noble profession as a whole acted with singular and eloquent disinterest," he told McGill. "Some of our publisher friends seem to want to avoid looking at the facts for fear they will be frightened. Also, they seem to take the attitude of, 'Let the New York Times go ahead and pay: it has the money.' We are sure as hell going ahead and pay[ing]—and plenty. But we're not all that rich."[26]

.   .   .   .   .

The *Times* lawyers weren't certain that the Fifth Circuit's ruling meant victory. The Birmingham commissioners were planning to appeal the decision. And there were still the Montgomery cases. Loeb feared that letting up too soon on the "iron curtain" could subject the *Times* to even more trouble.

The "iron curtain" policy raised a good deal of conflict at the *Times*. Many angry memoranda were circulated and voices raised over the unpopular policy. Loeb was, in his words, "constantly besieged by the News Department to lift the embargo on the *Times*."[27] The reporters were facing one of the biggest stories of their lifetimes, and they couldn't cover it because of the libel suits. The lawyers were accused of "interfering with a free press."[28]

After the Freedom Rides and the dismissal of the Birmingham cases, Harding Bancroft asked Loeb about lifting the "iron curtain." Loeb said that it couldn't be done unless the story was "of the magnitude of the riots against the Freedom Riders in Montgomery." Loeb was afraid that Sellers, Parks, and Patterson would try to revive their cases in state court by serving process directly on a *Times* reporter.[29]

Loeb continued to deny staff requests to travel to Alabama. Catledge was barred from attending a conference of editors in Birmingham. When an editorial writer named Harry Schwartz wanted to give a talk at an air base outside Montgomery, Lord Day & Lord instructed him that it would be "inadvisable." Loeb explained to Bancroft, "There is a 900-1 chance against the possibility that he will be served with process....However, [we] do question the wisdom of taking even that chance of complicating the litigation until the appeal to the Fifth Circuit Court of Appeals is decided....Once this appeal is out of the way the iron curtain will be lifted."[30]

The *Times* lawyers were also working overtime on libel vetting, "censoring" anything that might be seen as disparaging to the South. In April 1962, the News Department presented the lawyers with an article that was slated to run in the Sunday *New York Times* Magazine titled "The Mob vs. The College in the Deep South," a feature on the racial policies of Southern colleges. Loeb put a stop to it, concluding that it could be libelous. He wrote apologetically to the magazine's editor, Alan Sweetzer:

> It embarrasses me again to have to take a negative attitude about an article which the Magazine wants to run, but this one literally scares me to death. I would remind you that there are still 12 libel suits pending against the *New York Times* in the State of Alabama.
>
> The whole gist of the attitude of the plaintiffs and their lawyers ... is that the *Times* is unfair to the South, doesn't understand it, and goes out of its way to paint it in an unfavorable light on the integration question. For the *Times* now to come out in the magazine with an article of this nature, which rehashes much of the story in Alabama which is the subject matter of five of the lawsuits, and to put a great deal of stress on conditions in Louisiana when we have important appeals pending before the Fifth Circuit Court of Appeals sitting in that state, is really, in my humble opinion, carrying coal to Newcastle.
>
> Now I know that the answer will be that I am attempting to interfere with a free press and the right of the *Times* to tell its readers the story of what goes on in the South in institutions of higher education. But my reply is that the *Times* does not have to go out of its way under the circumstances further to inflame Southern feeling against it. Give us a chance to get rid of these libel suits, rather than invite the institution of new ones.[31]

The tension between the lawyers and news staff came to a head at a meeting in April 1962. Clifton Daniel, a high-level member of the news staff, was attending for Catledge. Daniel argued strenuously for sending reporters into Alabama. He could see that the lawyers were resisting. He reported to Catledge, "Tom Daly said that we would still be running a 'grave risk' if we sent any reporter to Alabama." Daly suggested that the *Times* wait until the libel cases ran their course and a new governor took office. Daly mentioned the governor because he knew that the Patterson administration was helping to finance the lawsuits against the *Times*.[32]

Dryfoos suggested that the *Times* contract with a reporter from another newspaper such as the *Atlanta Constitution* to buy their news from Alabama. Daniel protested taking news from somebody else, "which is contrary to our general practice." But he had no choice. He told the lawyers that they "would be bound by [their] legal advice and that in the meantime we would do what we could to cover news from Alabama in the best possible fashion."[33]

In late 1961, the *New York Times* made its arguments in the *Sullivan* case before the Alabama Supreme Court, state's highest tribunal. This was a lost cause, as all knew well. The court, notorious for its unrepentant white supremacy, was a zealous participant in the state's efforts to enforce segregation. In 1956, Judge Jones had issued a temporary restraining order against the NAACP without giving it a hearing, then held the NAACP in contempt for not producing its membership lists on demand. When the U.S. Supreme Court set the contempt order aside, the Alabama Supreme Court refused to carry out the judgment.[34] The presiding judge, Justice Thomas Seay "Buster" Lawson, a twenty-year veteran of the bench, had risen to fame in 1935 when, as attorney general of Alabama, he participated in the prosecution of the Scottsboro Boys.[35]

Despite the futility of the appeal, the *Times* prepared a lengthy brief with eighteen separate arguments. It alleged that the newspaper couldn't be sued in Alabama, and that the motion for a new trial should have been granted because the prejudice of the jury. The *Times* argued that the state's exercise of jurisdiction over the newspaper limited newsgathering and freedom of expression.[36]

The *Times* further contended that the verdict was so excessive that it was an infringement on freedom of the press. It made a passing First

Amendment argument—that the ad was addressed to "questions of wide public interest and importance" and therefore within the scope of constitutional freedoms.[37] In a separate brief, the ministers asked the court to dismiss the complaints, claiming that there was no evidence that their clients consented to the use of their names and that the trial took place in a segregated courtroom in violation of the Fourteenth Amendment.

Nine months later, on August 30, 1962, the Alabama Supreme Court unanimously affirmed the judgments against the *Times* and the ministers. Associate Justice Robert B. Harwood, a former member of the state legislature and attorney general of Alabama, delivered the opinion. He went through Embry's list of arguments and demolished them each with little discussion.

The court agreed with Judge Jones that when Embry made a "general appearance" in Jones's courtroom, he submitted the newspaper to the jurisdiction of the state court.[38] The activities of the *Times* in Alabama were more than sufficient to meet the minimal standards required for jurisdiction, it said. Moreover, it is "clear under our decisions that when a nonresident prints a libel beyond the boundaries of the state and distributes and prints the libel in Alabama, a cause of action arises in Alabama as well as in the State of the publishing and printing the libel."[39]

Jones had been correct to conclude that the statements were libelous *per se*, the court said. As to the jury finding that the statements were "of and concerning" Sullivan, "we think it common knowledge that the average person knows that municipal agents, such as police and firemen and others, are under the control and direction of the city governing body, and more particularly under the direction and control of a single commissioner. In measuring the performance or deficiencies of such groups, praise or criticism is usually attached to the official in complete control of the body."[40] This was a dangerous proposition: the court was declaring, in effect, that an attack on a government entity could constitute a libel of an individual member of government.

The court also sustained the damage award, concluding that it wasn't excessive. On this point, the court held it critical that the *Times* had in its own files articles which would have demonstrated the falsity of the allegations, that the *Times* retracted the advertisement as to Governor Patterson but ignored Sullivan's demand for retraction, and that in "the trial below none of the defendants questioned the falsity of the allegations in the advertisement."[41] The court emphasized, in particular, the trial testimony of *Times* secretary Harding Bancroft stating that the advertisement was "substantially correct." This, the court said, showed "the bad faith of the *Times* and . . . maliciousness inferable therefrom."[42]

The First Amendment argument was dismissed with the terse statement that "the First Amendment of the U.S. Constitution does not protect libelous publications."[43] The court stated further that the Fourteenth Amendment couldn't be invoked, since it applied only to state action and not to private action. Read the last sentence of the fifty-nine-page opinion: "It is our conclusion that the judgment below is due to be affirmed and it is so ordered. Affirmed."[44] The ministers' claims of racial discrimination were dismissed as mere "quibbling."[45]

That evening, the *Times* announced that it would appeal to the U.S. Supreme Court, although the newspaper executives weren't sure if they were really going to take that step.[46] They did, however, lift the "iron curtain." After eighteen months of exile, reporters and other representatives of the newspaper could go back to Alabama.

"Did our attorneys advise us that it was all right to send our reporter into Alabama? And by that I don't mean that we can assure him that he won't be shot—just arrested," Sulzberger asked Catledge.[47] Catledge replied: "Our attorneys did advise us that it would be all right to send a reporter into Alabama. After the Alabama Supreme Court's ruling, nothing worse could happen to us from now."[48]

11   Make No Law

Not long after the Alabama Supreme Court's decision in the Sullivan case, the libel cases intersected, rather fortuitously, with First Amendment theory.

In 1962, U.S. Supreme Court justice Hugo Black, famed for his "absolutist" position on freedom of speech, gave a public address in which he rejected the long-held maxim that libel was outside the First Amendment's protections. "My view is, without deviation, without exception, without any ifs, buts or whereases, that freedom of speech means that you shall not do something to people either for the views they have or the views they express or the words they speak or write," he said.[1] Because the First Amendment's directive that "Congress shall make no law" was an absolute, even false and defamatory statements were protected, he insisted. Black's controversial statements brought national attention to the libel cases and unwittingly inspired the *New York Times'* argument in its appeal to the U.S. Supreme Court.

·   ·   ·   ·   ·

Hugo Black was one of the most liberal jurists on a liberal court. The Warren Court, so named after Earl Warren, former California governor who was appointed to the Court by President Eisenhower in 1953, had undertaken a program of constitutional reform that transformed the lives of ordinary Americans in a way no previous Court had ever done.[2] Expanding its conventional jurisdiction, the Supreme Court reached out to decide important social issues such as civil rights, privacy, reapportionment, due process, and censorship. For the first time, the Court established itself as a forum for the resolution of social problems, an activist, democratic institution that would boldly implement social change.[3]

The Warren Court struck down the censorship of books and films. It supervised the procedures and mechanisms of criminal law enforcement. It initiated a revolution in race, expanded the guarantees of equal protection of the laws, overturned unequally apportioned legislative districts, afforded criminal defendants expanded constitutional protections, and recognized a constitutional right to privacy. This "judicial activism," as it was deemed, attracted no small criticism.[4] In 1957, a coalition of Southern congressmen introduced legislation that would have curbed the Court's power by reversing all or part of particular decisions, curtailing its general appellate jurisdiction, and changing the qualifications for service on the Court. In 1964, a congressional committee considered no fewer than 147 proposals to undo the school-prayer decisions. Thirteen states approved a proposed constitutional amendment to reverse the voting-reapportionment rulings. The right-wing John Birch Society launched a national campaign to drive out Earl Warren.[5]

The Court's rulings on race were among its most sweeping and controversial. Moved by the sympathetic activism of the civil rights movement and an expansive view of equality and citizenship, the Court transformed deeply rooted patterns of segregation and discrimination. In a series of decisions in the 1950s, it extended *Brown v. Board of Education* to end segregation in public beaches, parks, recreational facilities, housing developments, public buildings, eating facilities, and hospitals.[6] In 1955, it ended racial segregation in University of Alabama admissions.[7] *Browder v. Gayle* (1956) declared unconstitutional intrastate segregation on Montgomery's buses.[8] Segregated parks and playgrounds were invalidated in 1958.[9] In 1960, the Court issued its decision in *Gomillion v. Lightfoot*, striking down, as a violation of the Fifteenth Amendment, the boundaries of Tuskegee, Alabama, which were drawn in a twenty-eight-sided figure to disenfranchise black citizens.[10] During the 1961 and 1962 terms, the Court turned back the efforts of Southern states to frustrate the desegregation movement by jailing peaceful sit-in protesters.[11] The records of the Supreme Court from this time are marked by cases striking back against the South's efforts to enforce segregation and defy the Court's equal protection rulings.

Some of the most consequential free speech decisions of the era emerged from the Court's desire to protect the civil rights movement. The Court expanded the First Amendment's protections in a series of cases involving the South's efforts to undermine the movement by limiting activists' rights of free speech and freedom of association. In *NAACP v. Alabama* (1958), the Court turned back the state's efforts to drive the NAACP from the state by forcing it to disclose its membership rolls. Justice John Harlan's opinion declared that the NAACP's right to protect the identities of its members was protected by the constitutional right of freedom of association.[12] In *Shelton v. Tucker* (1960), the Court invalidated on First Amendment grounds a loyalty oath in Arkansas that was intended to rid public schools of employees who belonged to the NAACP.[13] *NAACP v. Button* (1963) struck down laws in Virginia that prohibited the solicitation of legal clients, enacted to sink the NAACP's litigation efforts. Justice Brennan's opinion in *Button* classified civil rights litigation as a protected form of political expression for the black community.[14] The Court recognized that the implementation of its equal protection goals depended on robust enforcement of the First Amendment.

Yet the Warren Court, overall, was not a reliable guardian of freedom of speech before *New York Times v. Sullivan*. Developments in the Supreme Court's First Amendment jurisprudence in the 1930s and '40s, including the adoption of the Holmes-Brandeis "clear and present danger" approach, were abandoned during the Red Scare of the 1950s. Capitulating to the forces of repression, the Court approved state and federal laws providing that Communist-front organizations register with the government, and for loyalty oaths and legislative investigations of suspected "subversives." In *Dennis v. U.S.* (1951), regarded as one of the Court's most disreputable First Amendment decisions, a 6–2 majority upheld the convictions of eleven leaders of the American Communist Party who had been charged under the Smith Act with being members of an organization whose teachings advocated the violent overthrow of the government. The leading opinion by Chief Justice Vinson, though it purported to use the "clear and present danger" test, in reality used a balancing test. Vinson determined that the government's right to self-preservation outweighed the individual's right to speak.[15]

The Supreme Court did advance free speech in some regards in the 1950s. The Court restricted the use of the Smith Act in *Yates v. United States* (1957) and *Scales v. United States* (1961).[16] In *Roth v. United States* (1957), it distinguished obscenity from pornography, which it declared a protected area of speech, and set in motion a revolution in the dissemination of pornographic materials.[17] In *Speiser v. Randall* (1959), the Court ruled 7–1, in an opinion by Justice Brennan, that a state cannot condition the receipt of a government benefit on the requirement that an individual swear an oath not to advocate overthrow of the government by unlawful means.[18] In *Smith v. California* (1959), the Court held that the First Amendment rights of a Los Angeles bookstore owner had been violated when he was sentenced to thirty days in jail for selling a pulp novel under a law that held that booksellers could be criminally liable without knowledge of a book's contents.[19]

The Court had no systematic approach to adjudicating free speech claims. Its First Amendment jurisprudence was vague, simple, and incomplete.[20] The predominant method used in First Amendment cases was "ad hoc balancing," in which the respective interests in each case were balanced—in most cases, the government's right to self-preservation against the rights of the individual litigant—without granting particular weight to free expression or considering the damage that the repression of speech inflicted to society as a whole.[21]

First Amendment scholars proposed models and theories of free speech, including "absolutism." Alexander Meiklejohn, perhaps the most noted First Amendment theorist of his time, advanced a particular kind of absolutism that he described in his 1948 book *Free Speech and Its Relation to Self-Government*. Freedom of speech was an "absolute" when it came to "public speech," he believed. Meiklejohn defined "public speech" as speech that was essential to democratic self-governance.[22] He argued that the Constitution made the people their own governors, and therefore anything that they said in their capacity for self-government could not be punished.[23] "Private speech" included obscenity, incitement, and libels against private citizens, which had "no relation to the business of governing" and were unprotected by the First Amendment.[24] Hugo Black became an outspoken proponent of an even broader absolutism, in which the government was prohibited from regulating speech of all kinds.

Justice Black hailed from Alabama, of all places. Hugo Black was born in 1886 in rural Clay County to a father who had collected taxes for the Confederate Army. Although the South despised Black for his liberal civil rights and civil liberties rulings, he retained strong emotional ties to the region. "I love Alabama. I love the South ... So far as I know not a single ancestor that I ever had settled north of the Mason & Dixon line," he proclaimed in a 1970 speech.[25]

Black was famous for his obsession with the Constitution. He was so fanatical that he carried a copy of the document in his jacket pocket, imitating the manner in which evangelicals carried copies of the Bible.[26] He read the document literally, like scripture. The guarantees of the Bill of Rights were to be followed to the letter, he believed, and its provisions were unambiguous in meaning.[27] "I like to read the words of the Constitution," he would say in his soft Southern drawl. "I'm a literalist, I admit it. It's a bad word these days. I know, but that's what I am."[28]

To Black, the First Amendment was the cornerstone of liberty, and freedom of speech was the heart of the First Amendment. Black was an "absolutist" who believed that the government could place no limitations whatsoever on freedom of expression. Occasionally, when a litigant disagreed with his position on a case, he would take out his pocket Constitution and ask him to read aloud the First Amendment. When he said the phrase "no law," Black would say "thank you," indicating that an absolutist interpretation was required, then put the Constitution back in his pocket.[29]

In February 1960, Black publicized his absolutist philosophy in a speech on the Bill of Rights at New York University. He announced that "one of the primary purposes of the Constitution with its amendments was to withdraw from the Government all power to act in certain areas— whatever the scope of those areas may be."[30] Two years later, in an unrehearsed interview conducted with Professor Edmond Cahn of New York University at a banquet in Black's honor, he elaborated his position further. Though Black didn't address the *New York Times* cases by name, he was clearly referring to them when he discussed what he believed were the constitutional dimensions of libel and the need for broad protections for the press in libel law.

"I understand that it is rather old fashioned and shows a slight naivete to say that 'no law' means no law ... I have to be honest about it. I confess not only that I think the Amendment means what it says but also that I may be slightly influenced by the fact that I do not think Congress should make any law" with respect to speech, he said. He went as far as to say that he "had no doubt" that liability for libel was unconstitutional.[31] Cahn was astonished.[32]

CAHN: Do you make an exception in freedom of speech and press for the law of defamation? That is, are you willing to allow people to sue for damages when they are subjected to libel or slander?

BLACK: With the First Amendment, the framers intended that there should be no libel or defamation law in the United States under the United States Government, just absolutely none...
As far as public libel is concerned, or seditious libel, I have been very much disturbed sometimes to see that there is present an idea that because we have had the practice of suing individuals for libel, seditious libel still remains for the use of government in this country. Seditious libel, as it has been put into practice throughout the centuries, is nothing in the world except the prosecution of people who are on the wrong side politically; they have said something and their group has lost and they are prosecuted.

Black was referring to the long-defunct crime of seditious libel, under which government may punish its critics as a matter of self-preservation. Black had been musing on seditious libel since the 1952 case of *Beauharnais v. Illinois*, in which he had voted to strike down a state's group libel or hate speech law, likening it to a form of sedition and state censorship, which was "startling and frightening doctrine in a country dedicated to self-government by its people."[33]

BLACK: Those of you who read the newspaper see that this is happening all over the world now, every week somewhere.... I believe with Jefferson that it

> is time enough for government to step in to regulate people when they
> *do* something, not when they *say* something, and I do not believe myself
> that there is *any* halfway ground if you enforce the protections of the
> First Amendment. [34]

Although public opinion generally disapproved of Black's comments
that there should be no libel or defamation law, contemporaneous events
seemed nevertheless to confirm Black's insight about the threat libel
suits posed to the press and to public discourse.[35] By 1964, inspired by
Alabama's cases against the *Times*, officials in three Southern states had
brought seventeen libel actions against Northern media outlets, primarily
over civil rights coverage, seeking damages of more than $288 million.[36]
Although they were brought by different parties against different publications, these copycat lawsuits would play an important role in the *Times*
cases. In their zeal to sue, segregationist authorities were inadvertently
undermining their own cause.

In 1963, arch-segregationist Edwin A. Walker, retired Army general,
who led a segregationist mob that assaulted reporters and federal officers
to protest the admission of James Meredith to the University of Mississippi, sued the Associated Press and ten other media outlets for $33 mil-
lion in damages over accounts claiming, correctly, that he had encouraged
the rioting.[37] The first jury to hear the case, in Fort Worth, awarded him
$800,000, with the judge stating that "the jury has reflected the attitude
of the entire country with respect to false and one-sided reporting of the
news."[38]

Director of the Mississippi Highway Patrol, T.B. Birdsong, then sued
the *Saturday Evening Post* over an article, "What's Next in Mississippi,"
which imputed "official misconduct" to patrolmen during the Ole Miss
riots, alleging that state troopers failed to help federal marshals rein in
the mob, and that patrolmen stood by while a white vigilante posse beat
up a news photographer. Birdsong sought $276 million in damages—$1
million for himself and $1 million for each of the state's 275 highway
patrolmen.[39] Shortly after, the sheriff of Etowah County, Alabama, sued
the publisher of the *Ladies' Home Journal*, Curtis Publishing, for $3 mil-
lion for an article that accused the sheriff and his deputies of brutality in
racial demonstrations.[40] Tom King, a candidate for mayor of Birmingham,

threatened a libel suit against the *Saturday Evening Post* for describing Birmingham as the most "backwards" city in America on race.[41]

Many "publications are now under the shadow of potentially expensive actions," noted the *Columbia Journalism Review*. "The characteristic actions of the 1960s," it observed, "appear to be suits growing out of local or regional retaliation for reporting or comment by a national news organization." "Large awards and wide publicity seem to be encouraging more and more of the offended to sue." This was putting it rather mildly.[42]

· · · · ·

In November 1962, the ministers suffered a huge setback when the Fifth Circuit Court of Appeals held that they could be sued in Alabama in the remaining Montgomery cases. The same court then reversed itself in the Birmingham cases, stating that the *Times* could be sued in the state for the Harrison Salisbury articles. The court based its decision on the ruling of the Alabama Supreme Court in the *Sullivan* case that "when a nonresident prints a libel beyond the boundaries of the state and distributes and publishes the libel in Alabama, a cause of action arises in Alabama as well as in the state of printing and publishing of the libel." The ruling revived all the Birmingham cases.[43]

Panicked, King and Clarence Jones pressured Ted Kheel to revive the Lawyers' Committee on the Alabama Libel Suits, which had disbanded at the end of the previous year. Another group working on the libel defense was the Gandhi Society for Human Rights, founded by Harry Wachtel, a wealthy, liberal New York attorney and King supporter.[44] Wachtel wanted to use the defense of the libel suits to help build coalitions between the SCLC and the labor movement and to solicit donations from labor unions. But the Gandhi Society never obtained significant donations, and it failed to make a significant contribution to the SCLC's battle against the libel cases.[45]

The reinvigorated Lawyers' Committee on the Alabama Libel Suits produced a 2,500-word leaflet titled "Statement of Facts on the Alabama Libel Suits" with an accompanying letter describing the implications of the libel cases for civil rights, freedom of the press, and the democratic process. It

sent the materials to Attorney General Robert Kennedy, the heads of state
and local bar associations, and deans of law schools.[46] The libel laws of
Alabama were being used as "a device to stifle truthful reporting and open
discussion of conditions arising in the South in the wake of Federal court
decisions outlawing racial segregation in schools, transportation, housing
and other phases of our national life," the letter read. This abuse of process
was "fraught with danger for all Americans."

> The continued misuse of judicial process to penalize fair comment and the
> exercise of constitutional rights in the foregoing manner would be tragic
> enough, even if it were limited—as it has been so far—to the attempted pun-
> ishment and intimidation of those who dared to publish facts or to voice
> unpopular opinions on race relationships and tensions in the South.
>
> Yet if libel actions brought under no recognized theory of law can yield
> astronomical verdicts from angry or biased juries, it is at once apparent that
> extremists everywhere, on civil rights or other issues, will have a powerful
> new weapon to suppress the thoughts they cannot tolerate. No person will
> remain immune from legal and economic attack if he utters beliefs contrary
> to those held by his fellow citizens any one of whom has the time, disposi-
> tion and resources to initiate retaliatory legal action. No newspaper will be
> free to print the truth, where the facts about social injustice would inflame,
> without risk of bankruptcy....
>
> We believe the time has come for those of us most directly concerned
> with abuse of judicial process—the members of the Bar—to alert our fellow
> members of the Bar and citizens generally to this latest challenge to free-
> dom in America.... The courts of America must not become instruments to
> destroy the very rights the law is designed to uphold.[47]

Alabamians railed against the further humiliation of the state on the
national stage. The *Alabama Journal* denounced "the surprising and
unusual...outburst of lawyers...made while cases are still pending in
Alabama against the *New York Times*." "Alabama cannot help resenting
suggestions made by these outside lawyers on 'Alabama's angry and biased
juries.' Their statement itself is a libelous outburst about Alabama."[48]

James Simpson, the attorney for the Birmingham commissioners, took
the *Journal*'s lead and proposed suing the committee for libel. Nachman
agreed that the statements were an "unconscionable commentary on the
actions of the lawyers" but advised against suing. "We here feel strongly
that the committee is designed to obtain extra-judicial pressure and to

create federal questions which do not exist in the Sullivan case on the record," he wrote, referring to the issue of racial discrimination. "Accordingly, we feel that any actions which we may take at this time would create just the sort of disturbance and atmosphere which the *Times* would desire." Nachman believed that the committee's actions "indicate a state of near panic on the part of the *Times*."[49]

12 Herbert Wechsler

It was indeed a moment of reckoning at the *New York Times*. The newspaper confronted millions of dollars in liability and the possibility of bankruptcy. Would it appeal to the Supreme Court? Or would it settle, in violation of the Ochs policy?

The top brass began to think that settlement was the only option—if the Alabama officials would in fact settle, which wasn't clear. An appeal to the Supreme Court would be phenomenally expensive, and the law wasn't on their side.

For one of the first times in the history of the newspaper, the hardheaded, fight-to-the-end leaders of the *Times* were ready to call it quits in a libel case. And it was Louis Loeb who stopped them. Loeb had always advocated the cautious, conservative route, but this time he wasn't sure that the *Times* should give in. The Ochs policy had been established for a good reason. If the *Times* caved in, who else would sue the paper for millions? Would segregationists, in the next round or two of libel suits, sue the *New York Times* out of existence? Loeb told the executives that the future of the paper was on the line and that they had to take a chance.

The *Times* leaders weren't convinced, but they gave him the authority to seek the advice of a constitutional law expert. Loeb called Herbert

Wechsler of Columbia Law School, one of the most prominent academic lawyers in the country. The *Times'* decision to use its prestige to employ Wechsler was one of the most important in the history of the *Times* and perhaps even in the history of journalism.[1]

.   .   .   .   .

In 1962, fifty-two-year-old Wechsler stood at the top of three fields: constitutional law, criminal law, and federal courts. Wechsler had argued a dozen cases before the Supreme Court, served in the Department of Justice, written influential law review articles, and authored for the American Law Institute the Model Penal Code, which would be used as a guide by state legislatures to create their criminal codes. Shortly after the *Sullivan* case, Wechsler began a lengthy term as director of the American Law Institute.[2] It was without exaggeration that he was dubbed a "modern-day Blackstone."[3]

Wechsler was short and sturdily built, with thick eyebrows and a stern gaze. His voice was deep and nasal, with a strong, pinched New York accent. His piercing intellect, caustic remarks, and robust sense of self-importance intimidated colleagues and students alike. When one of his students exhibited superficiality in posing a question or answer in one of his classes, he would exclaim: "That remark betrays not the slightest degree of cerebration!"[4] A colleague once described Wechsler's ability to cut the heart out of an argument before the speaker even realized that they had more than a flesh wound.[5]

.   .   .   .   .

Wechsler had been groomed for a life of the mind. Wechsler was born in 1909 in the Bronx to a middle-class Jewish family that prized literacy and learning. His grandfather, an immigrant from Hungary, had been a rabbi and journalist, and his father was a lawyer. His younger brother, James, became a celebrated and controversial editor for the *New York Post*.[6]

Wechsler attended public elementary and high schools in New York and graduated from City College at the age of nineteen. Determined to become a French teacher—an unusual aspiration for a prodigy—he applied to teach

French at City College. The application was rejected because his father convinced the department head that his son should be a lawyer instead of a French teacher. In an interview late in his life, Wechsler avowed that he would have been "a colossal flop" as a French instructor and was grateful that he'd been saved from that "misfortune" by his father.[7]

Wechsler graduated from Columbia Law School during the depths of the Great Depression in 1931. He took a teaching position at Columbia briefly, then headed to Washington to pursue a prestigious clerkship with Supreme Court justice Harlan Fiske Stone. Stone became a role model for Wechsler, who praised his vigorous defense of judicial review and his embrace of a flexible, "living Constitution."[8]

It was during his Supreme Court clerkship that Wechsler first witnessed the intensity of racial animus in the South. Only weeks after he arrived in Washington, the Court heard an appeal from the Communist-affiliated International Labor Defense in the Scottsboro case. Wechsler was so moved by the wrongful conviction of the Scottsboro Boys that he published a piece in the *Yale Law Journal* calling for a federal "reconstruction" of the South, including anti-lynching legislation.[9] Wechsler saw how the suppression of speech could be used to further racial oppression. In 1935, the International Labor Defense invited Wechsler to work on the case of *Herndon v. Lowry*, involving a black Communist Party organizer convicted by the State of Georgia of attempting to incite insurrection. In *Herndon*, a landmark in First Amendment law, the Court used the clear and present danger rule to strike down the Georgia insurrection statute.[10]

By the time he was in his early thirties, Wechsler had accrued a string of accomplishments that most never approached in their lifetimes. He became a professor at Columbia, co-authored the longest article ever written on homicide, and co-wrote a monumental casebook on criminal law. In 1941, Wechsler took a sabbatical and went to work in the Office of the Solicitor General, where he spent the year arguing cases for the government in the Supreme Court. From 1944 to 1946, Wechsler served as assistant attorney general in charge of the War Division. He argued the unpopular case of *Korematsu v. United States* before the Supreme Court, which upheld the internment of Americans of Japanese ancestry, and continued to defend the case long after it was discredited. At the close of the war, Wechsler served as a key advisor to the judicial tribunal at Nuremberg.[11]

Wechsler returned to Columbia and recommenced his brilliant and productive academic career. He co-authored, with Professor Henry M. Hart of Harvard, one of the most influential American legal casebooks, *The Federal Courts and the Federal System*. In 1950, Wechsler drafted the Model Penal Code.[12] Another of Wechsler's achievements was his 1959 article in the *Harvard Law Review*, "Toward Neutral Principles of Constitutional Law," one of the most cited law review articles of all time.[13] The work is referenced as an exemplar of the legal process school of thought, which believes that the evaluation of judicial review should focus not on interests or values served by the decision but rather the method of decision.[14]

Wechsler agreed with the result of *Brown* but contested the reasoning behind the decision. He believed that *Brown* and the Warren Court's other decisions on race were inadequately "principled." *Brown* raised an issue of "competing freedoms: freedom to associate and freedom not to associate," he wrote. Was there "a basis in neutral principles for holding that the Constitution demands that the claims for association should prevail"?[15] He believed that his conclusion was helping, rather than hurting, the cause of civil rights. If guided by neutral principles, constitutional adjudication was likely to be consistent, and as a result, to command greater respect, than if guided by considerations of policy. Wechsler was an ardent defender of racial equality, although the article gave the impression that Wechsler opposed civil rights, and it contributed along with *Korematsu* to Wechsler's mixed legacy among liberals.

Wechsler was immediately intrigued by Loeb's proposal to help the *New York Times* appeal the Sullivan case. Wechsler was intellectually engaged by the issues; he also, frankly, needed the money. Wechsler was supporting two sick parents and an ex-wife at the time. (The *Times* would pay Wechsler $40,000 for his work on the case, underscoring how a newspaper of lesser standing and means could never have afforded such legal talent.)[16] Wechsler had recently started a consulting law practice for extra income. He served as a consultant to Lord Day & Lord in connection with various libel suits and had advised CBS on libel cases.[17]

Through this work for media outlets, Wechsler had begun contemplating the maxim that libel was "outside" the First Amendment. He knew there had been important Supreme Court decisions that brought formerly excluded areas of speech under the First Amendment's protections.

Bridges v. California (1941) held that the First Amendment protected critical statements about judges that had once been punishable as contempt. Pornography had once been totally excluded from the First Amendment until *Roth v. U.S.* (1957). Wechsler believed that the time had come to bring libel law in line with these developments. "The Supreme Court could not on one hand be sensitive to First Amendment claims in practically every area of speech and expression... and still take the view that defamation was not an area to be treated in the same way," he believed.[18]

It was with these thoughts in mind that Wechsler met Loeb to discuss the *Sullivan* case. Loeb explained that there was "great resistance" in *Times* headquarters to appealing the case on First Amendment grounds. The *Times* had never lost a libel case that hadn't been reversed or otherwise ended up in a favorable way for the *Times*, and they were reluctant against that background to risk their prestige, Loeb said.[19]

At the end of the meeting, Loeb told Wechsler that the decision to appeal had to be made by the leaders of the *Times*. He asked Wechsler to come to a gathering in the Publisher's Dining Room to discuss the issue. It was, Wechsler recalled, "one of the most important meetings I ever attended."[20]

The Publisher's Dining Room on the eleventh floor was the prestigious inner sanctum of the *Times*. The managerial staff lunched there on shrimp and steak, served on gold-rimmed china plates. Presidents, foreign leaders, industrialists, and other dignitaries attended these luncheons. The walls were embossed with an eagle, the *New York Times'* emblem. Distinguished guests were assured by Sulzberger, who never tired of puns, that anything they said was *sub rosa* (the ceiling was decorated with roses).[21]

When Wechsler walked in at noon on Tuesday, November 6, 1962, he saw all the top brass at the table—John Oakes, editor of the editorial page, Orvil Dryfoos, Clifton Daniel, Harrison Salisbury, Turner Catledge, Harding Bancroft, Lester Markel, the Sunday editor, and Arthur Krock. Arthur Hays Sulzberger was seated on the side, in a wheelchair. Wechsler described it as a "council of war."[22]

Wechsler explained the history of the Alabama cases and the legal issues involved. The facts of the case could be very "sympathetic" to the Supreme Court, he said. Wechsler then proceeded to embark on a kind of "law school lecture," as he put it, to tell the newspaper officials "what had happened regarding the judicial interpretation of the First Amendment over the preceding thirty years." He explained how the Court had taken previously unprotected areas of speech like pornography and contempt and subjected them to judicial scrutiny and constitutional standards. The time was now ripe to bring libel under the First Amendment, he argued. Wechsler told the executives that the *Times* owed it to itself and to the newspaper profession not to pass up the opportunity to pursue the First Amendment claim. He asked, "If the *Times* didn't take this [argument] up in what was overall a very significant case who could be expected to make it?"[23]

Several of the men aggressively questioned Wechsler. Wouldn't it be better to settle the case out of court? What was the likelihood of reversal? A few, including Harrison Salisbury, seemed receptive to Wechsler's arguments. They finished their lunches, and Wechsler left. He could see that he hadn't convinced most of them. But he felt confident that he did win over the most important man in the room, publisher Orvil Dryfoos. Shortly after, Dryfoos met with Loeb, and Loeb called Wechsler and told him to seek Supreme Court review.[24]

The *Times* was betting it all on Wechsler, who thereafter became the lead attorney on the case. Of course, this was a good bet. Yet what lay ahead, even for a scholar and advocate of Wechsler's stature, was daunting. Even Wechsler wasn't sure he could win. He was confident of his intellectual powers and his knowledge of law, but he was uncertain that he could convince the Court to make a sweeping change in its position on libel and the First Amendment. For the Court to conclude that the traditional, well-established doctrines of libel law violated constitutional guarantees of free speech would be a remarkable leap.

•   •   •   •   •

The Supreme Court hears questions of federal law. In appealing from a lower court decision, the petitioner, the appealing party, must show that there are important issues of federal law involved and that the lower court either failed to take them into account or got them wrong. There were two possible federal questions in the *Sullivan* case. One was the constitutional validity of the "long-arm" statute involving Alabama's jurisdiction over the *Times*. The other was whether Alabama's libel law violated the First Amendment. If the jurisdictional question was to be the basis of review, the approach would be by appeal, since the argument would be that the application of the Alabama statutes was unconstitutional. Review would be obligatory, meaning that the Court was required to hear the case. But if the issue was the constitutionality of Alabama's libel law, the petitioners would have to file a petition for *certiorari* to get the Court to hear the case. This is a request that the Court order a lower court to send up the record of the case for review. The Court received thousands of such petitions each year and granted just a handful.[25]

Wechsler called on his junior colleague Marvin Frankel, one of his former students, to help him with the petition. Frankel, forty-two, had just been hired as a professor at Columbia. Frankel was a man of great smarts and determination. As an undergraduate at Queens College, he had driven ice cream trucks and pushed clothes racks in the garment district of Manhattan to pay for his studies. After Army service, Frankel attended law school, then worked for the solicitor general's office in Washington, helping to write briefs and argue cases before the Supreme Court. He was a partner in the New York law firm Proskauer Rose for six years before going to teach at Columbia.[26] Frankel idolized Wechsler. The younger man would come up with the most important ideas of the appeal, but he ceded the credit to his mentor.

Before they could write, Wechsler and Frankel had to decide an important matter. They debated whether they should emphasize the First Amendment argument or the subjection of the *Times* to the jurisdiction of Alabama. Wechsler concluded that the jurisdictional argument would not be a winning one and that the First Amendment point had "greater sex appeal." The jurisdictional argument was flawed, he believed, because Judge Jones had held early on that Eric Embry made a general appearance and that the *Times* forfeited any right to claim that Alabama lacked personal jurisdiction over the *Times*. Wechsler recommended that the *Times* file a writ of *certiorari*, leading with the libel claim and making the jurisdictional claim secondary.[27]

Wechsler told Loeb why they should emphasize the First Amendment point: the massive libel judgment inflicted on the *Times* for criticizing a public official—without direct reference to that official, and arguably without inflicting any damage to his reputation—was an infringement of freedom of speech and press. He told Loeb that "if we couldn't interest the Court in a petition for a writ of certiorari on this issue, we really had to withdraw from the South in the distribution of the *Times*, because so long as the civil rights struggle lasted, we were going to be sitting ducks for libel actions everywhere." But he was pessimistic about how the point could be made as a technical matter.[28]

Wechsler could argue that the clear and present danger test should apply to defamation. Yet he found it hard to see how the formula would work, as the danger of injury to reputation would almost always be clear and present. Moreover, the doctrine was in disrepute after the way it had been used in *Dennis v. U.S.* to justify repression of the Communist Party leaders. The other main First Amendment test was the balancing test. But balancing was already used in libel cases under state law, and Wechsler wasn't sure that it would be useful to try to convince the Court to rebalance the interests between free speech and reputation.[29]

It was Frankel who came up with a brilliant way to turn the common law of libel into a constitutional issue. "Let's pursue a Sedition Act strategy," he told Wechsler. Frankel wanted to shift the issue in the case from the right to protect reputation to the right to criticize the government. He believed that the *Sullivan* case could be recast so that it resembled not so much an ordinary libel suit as it did cases like *Abrams v. United States* and *Whitney v. California* in which the government had prosecuted speech that was critical of official policy. The seditious libel analogy had likely been inspired by Hugo Black's comments a few months earlier. Frankel prepared a memorandum for Wechsler on how the case could be "played up with the seditious libel angle."[30]

Wechsler would argue that a massive damage award levied for criticizing an officer of government for his official conduct was akin to the crime of seditious libel, long assumed to be unconstitutional. As a technical matter, an action for civil libel and the crime of seditious libel are different: civil libel involves money damages for injury to individual reputation, while seditious libel involved criminal punishment for an attack on the government or its officials. Wechsler would claim, nevertheless, that permitting Sullivan to recover on the theory that he was defamed by criticism of the "police" in Montgomery constituted liability for criticizing government. Wechsler would attempt to convince the Court that in hearing the case and granting protection for libelous statements about public officials, they were following existing constitutional tradition and not doing anything revolutionary at all.

· · · · · ·

For their petition, Wechsler and Frankel did something that is now common, but that was not yet typical in Supreme Court briefs. They went back in time, to show that "history and tradition" supported their position that Sullivan could not win damages for criticism of his official conduct.

The petition for *certiorari* started in medieval England, with *De Scandalis Magnatum*, an edict from 1274 that outlawed seditious criticism. Under the law, statements that threatened to diminish respect for the government or public officials were punishable by death as treason. Seditious libel eventually became a misdemeanor, punishable by fines, imprisonment, and the pillory.[31] The law allowed no defense of truth, as truthful criticism was regarded an even greater threat to preserving respect for government than falsehood. Judges had the power to determine whether the intent of the speaker was seditious; the jury was only allowed to decide whether the speaker had uttered the words charged.[32]

Seditious libel was transplanted to colonial America and was used against critics of local representatives of the crown. It was highly unpopular, and many complained that the doctrine punished legitimate criticism of government. The issue came to a head in the famous 1735 trial of John Peter Zenger, a printer who had criticized the royal governor in New York. Zenger's lawyer argued that he should be permitted to defend Zenger by proving the truth of the publication, and that the jury should decide whether the words were libelous. The judge rejected these arguments, but the jury nevertheless acquitted Zenger. There were subsequently few successful common law prosecutions in the colonies. The intended effect of the First Amendment, ratified in 1791, on the crime of seditious libel was unclear.[33]

The reigning Federalist party feared that it would lose the election of 1800. The Federalists believed that one way they could secure their advantage was to silence their critics in the Republican press. They made "seditious" writing about either house of Congress or the president of the United States a crime. The Sedition Act of 1798 essentially codified seditious libel, but its provisions were less strict than the common law. The act punished political criticism only if it was false, scandalous, and malicious, and only if the author intended to defame. But the federal courts interpreted the requirement of falsity to make the defendant bear the burden of proving the truth; a critical statement was presumed to be false unless the defendant could prove it true in all respects. Intent to defame was inferred from publication of words that had a "bad tendency." Between 1798 and 1801, Federalist prosecutors indicted fourteen Republicans, ten of whom were brought to trial in federal court. The judges charged the jury in so biased a manner that the cases resulted in jury verdicts, despite the triviality of the comments alleged to be seditious.[34]

It was in the debate over the Sedition Act that Congress first began exploring the meaning of the First Amendment. James Madison and Thomas Jefferson argued that the Sedition Act was unconstitutional and tried to raise opposition to it in the state legislatures. Madison drafted, and the Virginia legislature approved, resolutions arguing that freedom of speech and of the press were essential to safeguard a republican political system. The Virginia Resolution argued that the Sedition Act violated the First Amendment because it was leveled against that right of "freely examining public characters and measures" that is the "only effectual guardian of every other right." The Constitution created a form of government under which "the people, not the government, possess the absolute sovereignty," Madison had written. The government dispersed power in reflection of the public's distrust of concentrations of power. This form of government was "altogether different" from the British form of government, under which "the Crown was sovereign and the people were subjects." "Is it not natural and necessary, under such different circumstances," he asked, "that a different degree of freedom in the use of the press should be contemplated?"[35] As president, Jefferson pardoned editors who had been convicted under the Sedition Act and remitted their fines, stating: "I discharged every person under punishment or prosecution under the sedition law, because I considered, and now consider, that law to be a nullity, as absolute and as palpable as if Congress had ordered us to fall down and worship a golden image." The Sedition Act expired on its own terms in 1801 before the Supreme Court could hear any cases brought under it, and the crime of seditious libel fell into oblivion.[36]

The Supreme Court never held that the First Amendment forbids punishment of seditious libel, although a handful of dissenting opinions had expressed the view that the crime of seditious libel was unconstitutional. Justice Holmes, dissenting in *Abrams v. U.S.*, brought under the Sedition Act of 1918, stated that he "wholly disagree[d] with the argument of the Government that the First Amendment left the common law as to seditious libel in force. History seems to me against the notion. I had conceived that the United States had through many years had shown its repentance for the Sedition Act of 1798 by repaying fines that it imposed."[37] In his dissenting opinion in *Beauharnais v. Illinois* (1952), involving a group libel law that had criminalized statements of race hatred, Justice Robert Jackson noted, "I think today's better opinion regards the enactment [of the Sedition Act] as a breach of the First Amendment and certainly Mr. Holmes and Mr. Justice Brandeis thought so."[38] Justice Black had observed in *Beauharnais*, "the First Amendment repudiated seditious libel for this country."[39] Justice Black's off-bench commentary in 1962 was the last time any member of the Court had discussed the relationship between seditious libel and the First Amendment. The doctrine of seditious libel was widely regarded to be odious, and Wechsler was not wrong to think that the Supreme Court would be inclined to condemn it formally.

Wechsler's thirty-page petition for *certiorari* began by stating the facts in the case, the legal issues presented, and "reasons for granting the writ." The first issue was "whether, consistently with the guarantee of freedom of the press ... a state may hold libelous *per se* and actionable by an elected City Commissioner, without proof of special damage, statements critical of the conduct of a department of the city government under his jurisdiction which are inaccurate in some particulars." The second was whether there was sufficient evidence to justify, "consistently with the guarantees

of freedom of the press," the Alabama court's determination that statements "naming no individual" but critical of the police department generally were "defamatory as to [Sullivan] and punishable as libel per se."
There was also the question of whether the $500,000 award was so exces-
sive as to violate freedom of the press. The last issue was whether Alabama's assumption of jurisdiction over the *Times* infringed upon freedom
of the press.[40]

Wechsler stated why it was imperative that the Court hear the case:

> The decision of the Supreme Court of Alabama gives a scope and applica-
> tion to the law of libel so restrictive of the right to protest and to criticize
> official conduct that it abridges the freedom of the press, as that freedom
> has been defined by the decisions of the Court. It transforms the action for
> defamation from a method of protecting private reputation to a device for
> insulating government against attack. If the judgment stands, its impact
> will be grave—not only upon the press but also upon those whose welfare
> may depend on the ability and willingness of publications to give voice to
> grievances against the agencies of governmental power.[41]

"This principle of liability," Wechsler continued—referring to Alabama's
libel law that permitted a public official to recover presumed and punitive damages "for a publication critical of official conduct of a government
agency under his general supervision ... unless a jury is persuaded that the
statement is entirely true"—is "indistinguishable in its function and effect
from the proscription of seditious libel, which the verdict of history has long
deemed inconsistent with the First Amendment." There were some respects
in which a private action for libel brought by a public official over criticism
of his official conduct was more repressive than a criminal prosecution
for seditious libel, he argued. "There is no requirement of an indictment
and the case need not be proved beyond a reasonable doubt. It need not
be shown, as the Sedition Act required, that the defendant's purpose was
to bring the official into 'contempt or disrepute.'...a statement adjudged
libelous *per se* is *presumed* to be false and malicious ... nor is it necessary...
that there be proof of injury in fact to the official's reputation."[42]

"We submit that such a rule of liability cannot be reconciled with this
Court's rulings on the scope of freedom of the press safeguarded by the
Constitution. Those rulings start with the assumption that one of the
prime objectives of the First Amendment is to protect the right to criticize

'all public institutions.'... We do not see how... criticism of an elected, public official may consistently be punished as a libel on the ground that it diminishes his reputation."[43] "Like sedition, insurrection, contempt, advocacy of unlawful acts, breach of the peace, disorderly conduct, obscenity or barratry, to name but prime examples," libel "must be defined and judged by standards which are not repugnant to the Constitution." Alabama's libel law did "not survive that test because it stifles criticism of official conduct no less potently than did seditious libel."[44]

Wechsler conceded that even if liability were justified for criticism of an official in some circumstances, Sullivan's judgment against the *Times* was patently unconstitutional. The advertisement did not name Sullivan and "plainly was not meant as an attack on him or any other individual." There was no real injury to his reputation: "The exaggeration or inaccuracies in these statements cannot be rationally regarded as tending to injure the respondent's reputation." Moreover, the damage award was excessive: "There was no rational relationship between the gravity of the offense and the size of the penalty imposed in his behalf.... any judgment of this magnitude, imposed routinely on these facts and sustained no less routinely on appeal, will necessarily have a repressive influence which extends far beyond preventing such inaccuracies of assertion as have been established here."[45]

Although it is not customary in Supreme Court petitions to refer to other pending cases, Wechsler mentioned, in a footnote, the other Montgomery libel suits, the libel suits in Birmingham, and the cases against CBS. No doubt the justices already knew this, but Wechsler wanted to make clear that libel was being deployed as a weapon in a political and sectional battle. The petition alluded briefly and discreetly yet forcefully to the case's civil rights context: "This is not a time when it would serve the values enshrined in the Constitution to force the press to curtail its attention to the racial tensions of the country or to forego dissemination of its publications in the areas where tension is extreme. Here, too, the law of libel must confront and be subordinated to the Constitution. The occasion for that confrontation is at hand."[46]

Wechsler filed the petition on December 15, 1962. Shortly after, the ministers, now represented by a team led by William Rogers and several members of a law firm run by Harry Wachtel, filed their petition with the Court. Clarence Jones informed King of the filing of the petition, noting that the "libel cases have come a long way" and that he was certain that because of the "gravity and importance" of the constitutional questions, *certiorari* would be granted.[47] The ministers' petition described in strong terms the racial animus that had given rise to the case, which they characterized as violations of due process and equal protection of the law. "Patently, the institution of each and all of these libel prosecutions," they wrote, "was designed to intimidate and penalize petitioners and others giving leadership and religious and spiritual guidance and support to the civil rights movement, and unconstitutionally to stifle all criticism by news media of Alabama public officials in connection therewith, as well as to punish and silence the *Times*."[48]

The libel suits were "further evidence of Alabama's pattern of massive racial segregation and discrimination and its attempt to prevent its Negro citizens from achieving full civil rights under our Constitution. We have already noted ... Alabama's failure to integrate its public schools and its racial discrimination statutes and law maintaining segregation; in addition, it has systematically and intentionally excluded Negroes from voting, from juries, and other related public and civic activities." "Alabama now embarks on more 'refined and sophisticated' policies of repression. It now strikes at the rights of free speech and press—roots of our democracy ...

> If this case stands unreviewed and unreversed, not only will the struggles of Southern Negroes towards civil rights be impeded, but Alabama will have been given permission to place a curtain of silence over its wrongful activities. This curtain of silence will soon spread to other Southern states in their similar attempts to resist civil rights and desegregation. For fear of libel and defamation actions in these states, people will fear to speak out against oppression; ministers will fear to assist the civil rights struggle ... national newspapers will no longer report the activities in the South.
>
> This case, moreover, has impact and meaning throughout our country. What minority can call itself safe now? Who will speak out for an oppressed minority? Today it is the Southern Negro being persecuted. Yesterday it was the Japanese-Americans. Who shall it be tomorrow?
>
> Racists and segregationists will now have a new weapon in their arsenal of oppression. This form of racial oppression and terrorism, with its ominous parallels in the recent history of Nazi Germany, will take on a new and more terrible form through the façade of libel prosecutions.[49]

Nachman's briefs opposing the *Times* and the ministers' petitions for *certiorari* were as bombastic and righteous as one of Grover Hall's *Montgomery Advertiser* editorials. "This lawsuit arose because of a willful, deliberate and reckless attempt to portray in a full-page newspaper advertisement, for which the *Times* charged and was paid almost $5,000, rampant, vicious, terroristic and criminal police action in Montgomery, Alabama, to a nationwide public of 650,000. The goal was money-raising. Truth, accuracy and long-accepted standards of journalism were not criteria for the writing or publication of this advertisement," he ranted. "*The New York Times*, perhaps the nation's most influential newspaper, stooped to circulate a paid advertisement to 650,000 readers—an advertisement which libeled respondent with violent, inflammatory, and devasting language. The *Times* knew that the charges were uninvestigated and reckless in the extreme."[50]

Nachman hammered on the fact that the *Times* had been unable to plead the traditional libel defenses of truth, fair comment, or privilege. There was no federal question for the Court to decide, since "libelous utterances have never been protected by the Federal Constitution." "Moreover, commercial advertisements are not constitutionally protected as speech." This argument relied on the 1942 case *Valentine v. Chrestensen*, which held that a city ordinance forbidding street distribution of commercial and business advertising matter did not abridge First Amendment freedoms, even as applied to a handbill having a commercial message on one side but a protest of official action on the other.[51]

Nachman went on to argue that the *Times* had no basis in the Constitution or in prior Supreme Court decisions to challenge the jury's verdict, and that the Court was bound to follow precedent when dealing with a matter of federalism. The suit had been decided by a state judge and a local jury and was confirmed by the state's highest court. Nachman denied that the civil rights context had any bearing on the case: "The *Times* seems to hint to this Court that because the publication contained statements regarding racial tensions, the law of libel should perforce 'confront and be subordinated to' a constitutional privilege to defame. Surely in a field so tense, truthful statements by huge and influential newspapers are imperative."[52]

Reversal of the verdict became even more urgent for the *Times*. Shortly after Wechsler filed his petition, the *Times'* printers, represented by the International Typographical Union, led a massive strike against seven New York City publications, protesting low wages and automation. The strike, the longest in newspaper history, dragged on for 114 days. The *Times'* working personnel went from 5,000 to 900, and the price of the newspaper went up for the first time since 1946. In April 1963, it reported a loss of $4 million during the first quarter. After the strike, revenues were down by $16 million, and daily circulation had dropped by 80,000, making it the costliest strike in New York's history.[53]

Orvil Dryfoos felt personal responsibility for the financial crisis caused by the strike on top of the libel suits, and the stress took its toll. In May 1963, he died of heart failure at the age of fifty.[54]

13 Before the Court

As the justices read the petitions of the *Times* and the ministers, children in Birmingham were being attacked by police dogs. In April 1963, determined to force the civil rights issue onto the national stage, King and the SCLC joined with Shuttlesworth's Alabama Christian Movement for Human Rights in a series of boycotts and sit-ins in what remained the South's most violent and segregated city. The goals of "Project C for Confrontation" were to desegregate downtown businesses and to win promises to hire black clerks. It marked the culmination of the direct-action movement. If the plan worked, Bull Connor's violent response would attract national media coverage and force President Kennedy to act by proposing civil rights legislation.[1]

When the city government obtained a court injunction against the marches and sit-ins, civil rights leaders decided to use children as protesters. More than a thousand children, some as young as five, marched into downtown Birmingham. They were arrested and hauled off in paddy wagons. Chanting, smiling, and singing, they clogged local jails. Images of children being blasted by high-pressure fire hoses, clubbed by police officers, and attacked by police dogs flashed on television and appeared on front pages throughout the country. Newspapers published an Associated Press image, soon to be iconic, of a police dog lunging at the stomach of high school student Walter Gadsden. King was arrested and kept in solitary confinement, where he penned his "Letter from Birmingham Jail."[2]

Birmingham marked a turning point. After Birmingham, the SCLC turned to more aggressive forms of direct action, provoking continued retaliation and backlash. By the spring of 1963, most of the country had concluded that the number one issue facing the nation was dismantling segregation. The events in Birmingham and their media coverage inspired the passage of the Civil Rights Act of 1964, which effectively ended segregation in public accommodations. On the day Kennedy introduced the bill, meeting with King and Shuttlesworth, he remarked, "But for Birmingham, we would not be here today."[3]

Stanley Levison prepared a fundraising ad for the SCLC describing the situation in Birmingham and sent it to the *New York Times*. He was informed, in his words, that the "bastards at the *Times* wouldn't print [it]." Clarence Jones, after talking with *Times* lawyers, reported that "they want to take out references to brutality and all strong references to segregation and discrimination in Birmingham," even though the ad included text that had appeared in the *Times'* own news stories. Levison understood that the paper was worried about being sued again over a King ad. He arrived at a compromise, with the ad appealing to the "conscience of America" and referring to Birmingham as "one of the largest segregated cities in the Western Hemisphere." It was the SCLC's first newspaper fundraising effort since the "Heed Their Rising Voices" ad.[4]

.   .   .   .   .   .

Three months earlier, the Supreme Court had reviewed the petitions for *certiorari* from the *Times* and the ministers. The review took place at the "justices' conference," a weekly meeting held in the holiest sanctuary of the Supreme Court building, the conference room on the first floor, just behind the courtroom. The oak-paneled room was simple and functional, with a long, rectangular table, covered in green felt like a pool table. The justices shook hands to signify the collegiality of the event, then sat down at the table and presented their views on the petitions in order of seniority. An application for review was accepted whenever at least four justices voted to consider it. If four did not, the decision of the lower court was left standing.[5]

Chief Justice Earl Warren sat at the head of the table. A heavy-set man with tremendous charm and a seemingly perpetual smile, Warren was a seasoned politician who had served as California's popular progressive Republican governor. Warren had no judicial experience when President Eisenhower appointed him to the Court in 1953. Despite the stain on his record caused by his urging of the removal of Japanese Americans from the West Coast during the war, his tenure on the Court was marked by reverence for civil rights and civil liberties. Warren was known for his uncanny talent for putting together majorities, including the unanimous Court that handed down *Brown v. Board of Education*.[6]

Hugo Black, the most senior justice, with the most years of service on the Court, sat at the other end of the table from Chief Justice Warren. The next in seniority was William Douglas, appointed by Roosevelt in 1939. Douglas was a restless, eccentric man who grew up in rural poverty in Washington State and went on to serve as former chairman of the Securities and Exchange Commission and a Yale Law School professor. Douglas became, with Black, the Court's leading civil libertarian. Douglas was willing to constitutionalize rights not explicitly articulated in the Constitution, so long as he considered them essential to individual liberty.[7]

To the right of Douglas was Tom Clark, a Texan and former attorney general appointed by Truman in 1949. Clark was a conservative known for his quiet demeanor and trademark bowties.[8] Next to him was John Marshall Harlan II, grandson of Justice John Harlan, who was known as the "great dissenter" for his prophetic 1896 dissent in *Plessy v. Ferguson*, which had put forth the separate but equal doctrine. The tall, quiet, methodical Harlan, appointed by Eisenhower in 1954, was considered a moderate who espoused respect for precedent and a limited role for the Court.[9]

William J. Brennan Jr., a former justice on the New Jersey Supreme Court, was next in seniority. A moderate Democrat appointed by Eisenhower in 1956, Brennan quickly distinguished himself as a crusader for civil rights and civil liberties and became part of the liberal bloc with Black, Douglas, and Warren.[10] In the opinion of many Supreme Court historians, Brennan, who would play a decisive role in the *Times* case, was not only one of the most important intellectual influences on the Warren Court but one of history's most influential justices, with more impact on public policy than any policymaker in the twentieth century.[11]

Others in the room included Potter Stewart, a former federal appellate judge from Ohio, also an Eisenhower appointee. Described as both "conservative" and "liberal," Stewart was a detached, mercurial figure who aligned himself with none of his colleagues on a regular basis. Byron Raymond ("Whizzer") White, former NFL star and deputy attorney general under Robert Kennedy, was also viewed as a swing vote who was impossible to pin down ideologically.[12] The most recent appointee, Arthur J. Goldberg, former secretary of labor, joined Warren, Black, Douglas, and Brennan as one of the Court's liberals.[13]

There are no records of the Court's deliberations on the petitions, although memoranda of the justices' law clerks have been preserved in the justices' papers at the Library of Congress. Jared Carter, a clerk for Douglas, noted in a memo to the justice that that the verdict and award were outrageous, and that "new rules are going to have to be laid down." "Somehow or other this judgment has to be reversed because the threat of suits such as this will undoubtedly discourage any criticism of Southern leaders.... The limits of rules governing libel actions by public officials which are drawn by the First and Fourteenth Amendments seem to be a very important issue." Harlan's clerk agreed that there were significant free speech issues involved. The judgment, if allowed to stand, could put newspapers "under huge financial pressure" to reject political ads and to stifle reporting.[14]

Six justices—Warren, Black, Douglas, Clark, Harlan, and Brennan—voted to hear the cases of the *Times* and the ministers. White, Stewart, and Goldberg did not and were willing to let the judgments stand—puzzling, considering their later positions in favor of the *Times*. The justices do not issue written opinions in this context, nor have notes of this session been preserved, so we will never know why White, Stewart, and Goldberg voted as they did.

It isn't difficult to figure out why the six justices agreed to hear the cases of the *Times* and the ministers. The "Heed Their Rising Voices" ad barely referred to Sullivan, the misstatements in the ad were relatively minor, there was no ostensible harm to Sullivan's reputation, and the damage award was extravagant. Moreover, the results had been achieved not through any perversion of the law, but through the application of three well-established rules of libel existing in all the states: strict liability, presumed damages, and the presumption of falsity, with the burden on the defendant to prove the truth.

The prosecution of the libel suits was glaringly racist. The litigation represented another example of Southern resistance and intransigence that called out for remediation. The other libel suits by Alabama officials threatened to undermine the critical work of the media in furthering the civil rights movement. If Sullivan's award against the *Times* were sustained, then media outlets might be forever restrained in their reporting on segregation and civil rights.

Concern for the civil rights movement was the primary reason behind the Court's decision to hear the cases, yet the justices were also interested in the free speech issues in their own right. The relationship between libel law and freedom of speech had for decades been an open question, one that the Court had avoided, even as it expanded the First Amendment's reach and scope. Moreover, the way Wechsler had framed it, the judgment appeared to be the criminalization of political speech, which set off First Amendment alarms. The $500,000 damage award, rendered without evidence of any harm to Sullivan's reputation, was effectively a criminal fine leveled by Southern officials to suppress criticism. It took the spectacular circumstances of the Alabama libel cases to get the Court to address the issue of libel law's relationship to the First Amendment, and it was in this way that it made its first, historic foray into libel law.

The following Monday morning, a clerk of the Court posted a list of petitions granted. A *Times* reporter saw the list and reported the news to Loeb. "A very hefty sigh of relief emanated from everybody" when the petition was granted and the case was placed on the calendar, Loeb recalled.[15] The Court's calendar for the spring was full, so the date for oral argument was set for October.[16] Ultimately, the oral argument wouldn't be heard until January of the following year.

King, Jones, and Levison geared up to generate publicity and financial support for the appeal. King flew to New York to address the American Jewish Congress, which through Levison, a member of the group, had become a leading financial backer of the case. Ted Kheel informed the members of the Lawyers' Committee of the Court's decision. He wrote to them individually, as he was afraid that the newspaper strike prevented them from getting the news. This prompted one member to reply: "The news that the Supreme Court has agreed to review the Sullivan case is good news indeed. I can think of nothing that our committee should do in the interim, except to pray."[17]

.   .   .   .   .

Wechsler's next task was to write the main brief in the case, the brief on the merits. The purpose of a Supreme Court brief is to offer the main arguments for one's side. Wechsler also believed that a brief should be a document "that a justice can use when writing an opinion favorable to the briefers."[18] Wechsler was on sabbatical from Columbia that semester, so he was able to work on the brief full-time, which for him meant no less than fifteen hours a day.

Wechsler was a quick thinker but a slow writer. He had to read every-thing on a topic—every book, treatise, article, and case—before putting pencil to paper. Wechsler read copiously in preparation for writing the *Sullivan* brief, which he scrawled longhand on yellow legal pads, as most lawyers did at the time. He studied not only "libraries on the First Amend-ment," in Frankel's words, but ten years' worth of Judge Jones's publication *Alabama Lawyer* and the state court proceedings in the case, which filled five volumes thicker than phone books. It took two months before he felt ready to write. Frankel continued to assist him, and Wechsler's wife, Doris, also worked on the brief. That summer, in Frankel's words, he "drafted discarded reams," "fought, struggled, agonized, and learned."[19]

Wechsler and Frankel's work on the brief took place during an intense period of racial turmoil and violence, dubbed the "long hot summer." In June, Governor George Wallace, who had replaced Patterson and whose campaign speeches promised "segregation now . . . segregation forever," tried to block the integration of the University of Alabama by standing in a doorway in protest. That evening, President Kennedy addressed the nation with a historic speech in which he called on Congress to pass new civil rights legislation and urged the country to embrace civil rights as a moral issue "in our daily lives."[20] Wechsler and Frankel finished the brief just after the March on Washington. On August 28, 250,000 marchers on the National Mall heard King make his "I Have a Dream" speech.

"That's it, all we need now is the cite checking," Wechsler said on the last day of the month. Frankel replied, "Let's call Ron Diana," an associate from Lord Day & Lord who was helping them with the brief. "I'm not going to trust that to anyone else," Wechsler declared.[21] The great legal scholar methodically checked the citations, a task routinely assigned to law clerks and first-year law firm associates.

Wechsler had taken a libel case and turned it into an opportunity for grand First Amendment theorizing. Through his artful framing of the issues, the case had become one about the core functioning of the democratic process rather than mere compensation for personal injury.

Wechsler's analytical, detailed, and theoretical ninety-five-page brief elaborated on the points he had made in the petition for *certiorari*. The document compiled the major writings on the civil libertarian theory of free speech—passages from James Madison, from Holmes and Brandeis, and statements from Supreme Court cases in the 1930s and '40s declaring broad protections for political speech—into a sort of "greatest hits" of the First Amendment. This was to support the principle that the First Amendment protected the right to criticize public officials and institutions, even if the criticism contained false statements that defamed the official.

Wechsler pushed for a radical decision that would not only win the case for the *Times* but that would revolutionize libel law. He did this in a smooth, matter-of-fact way that made the conclusion seem obvious, even foreordained, and in line with history and constitutional tradition. There were no arguments about race or equal protection in the brief, as the *Times* was not a victim of racial discrimination. Such arguments would not have secured the case for the *Times* and, Wechsler felt, would have distracted from the broad First Amendment ruling he hoped to achieve.[22]

After describing the events in Montgomery, the "Heed Their Rising Voices" ad, and the proceedings in Judge Jones's courtroom, Wechsler's brief launched into its main argument:

Under the law of libel as declared below, a public official is entitled to recover "presumed" and punitive damages for a publication found to be critical of the official conduct of a governmental agency under his general supervision if a jury thinks the publication "tends" to "injure" him "in his reputation" or to "bring" him "into public contempt" as an official. The place of the official in the governmental hierarchy is, moreover, evidence sufficient to establish that his reputation has been jeopardized by statements that reflect upon the agency of which he is in charge. The publisher has no defense unless... he can persuade the jury that the publication is entirely true in all its factual, material particulars.... We submit that such a rule of liability works an abridgment of the freedom of the press, as that freedom has been defined by the decisions of this Court.[23]

Wechsler conceded that the Court had long declared libelous statements to be outside the First Amendment's protections. However, he said that this was the case only because prior decisions did not involve criticism of public officials. "Throughout the years this Court has measured by the standards of the First Amendment every formula for the repression of expression challenged at its bar. In that process judgment has been guided by the meaning and the purpose of the Constitution... not by the vagaries or 'mere labels' of state law... Hence like sedition, insurrection, contempt, advocacy of unlawful acts, breach of the peace, disorderly conduct, obscenity or barratry, to name but prime examples," libel "must be defined and judged in terms that satisfy the First Amendment," he wrote. "The law of libel has no more immunity than other law from the supremacy of its command."[24]

The heart of the brief was the Sedition Act argument, which appeared under the heading "Seditious Libel and the Constitution":

If libel does not enjoy a talismanic insulation from the limitations of the First and Fourteenth Amendments, the principle of liability applied below, resting as it does on a "common law concept of the most general and undefined nature," infringes these basic constitutional rights in their most pristine and classic form....

Whatever other ends are also served by freedom of the press, its safeguard, as this Court has said, "was fashioned to assure unfettered interchange of ideas for the bringing about of political and social changes desired by the people."...

Its object comprehends the protection of that "right of freely examining public characters and measures, and of free communication among the people thereon," which, in the words of the Virginia Resolution, "has ever been justly deemed the only effectual guardian of every other right."

The "prized American privilege to speak one's mind, although not always with perfect good taste," applies at least to such speech "on all public institutions." "That national commitment has been affirmed repeatedly by the decisions of this Court, which have recognized that the Amendment 'must be taken as a command of the broadest scope that explicit language, read in the context of a liberty-loving society, will allow' and that its freedoms 'need breathing space to survive,'" the phrase "breathing room" having come from Justice Brennan's opinion in *NAACP v. Button* (1963).[25]

Even false statements pertaining to public issues were protected, Wechsler asserted. "It is clear that the political expression thus protected by the fundamental law is not delimited by any test of truth, to be administered by juries, courts, or by executive officials, not to speak of a test which puts the burden of establishing the truth upon the writer. Within this sphere of speech or publication, the constitutional protection does not turn upon 'the truth, popularity, or social utility of the ideas and beliefs which are offered,'" he wrote, again quoting Brennan's opinions in *NAACP v. Button* and *Speiser v. Randall*.[26]

Wechsler claimed that government officials could not be libeled, referencing cases in which the Court had limited the power of the state to punish speakers for contempt. "It is settled law that concern for the dignity, and reputation of the bench does not support the punishment of criticism of the judge or his decision ... though the utterance contains 'half-truths' and 'misinformation.' Any such repression must be justified, if it is justified at all, by danger of obstruction of the course of justice; and such danger must be clear and present. We do not see how comparable criticism of an elected, political official may consistently be punished as a libel on the ground that it diminishes his reputation."[27] Of course, as a matter of fact, political officials recovered for damage to their reputations under libel laws in all the states.

"If criticism of official conduct may not be repressed upon the ground that it is false or that it tends to harm official reputation, the inadequacy of these separate grounds is not surmounted by their combination." This was, according to Wechsler, the "basic lesson of the great assault on the short-lived Sedition Act of 1798," "which first crystallized a national awareness of the central meaning of the First Amendment."[28]

Wechsler asked the Court to declare the Sedition Act unconstitutional: "The verdict of history surely sustains the view that it was inconsistent with the First Amendment."[29] Further, he pointed out that Alabama's libel laws were even more repressive than the Sedition Act. There was no requirement of an indictment and a libel case need not be proven beyond a reasonable doubt. The libel plaintiff did not have to show, as the Sedition Act required, that the defendant's purpose was to bring the official "into contempt or disrepute." A statement judged to be libelous *per se* was presumed to be "false and malicious." There was no limitation to one punishment for one offensive statement, as would be required in a criminal proceeding. Damages in a libel case were fettered by "no legal measure" of amount. Wechsler opined, "Such a civil sanction is a more repressive measure than the type of sentence the Sedition Act permitted for the crime that it purported to define."[30]

.   .   .   .   .

Wechsler insisted that the First Amendment protected criticism of public officials absolutely and there was no balance to be struck between the protection of official reputation and freedom of the press. He bolstered this point with reference to the immunity given to public officials from libel suits from what they said in the course of their duties. In *Barr v. Matteo* (1959), the Court had ruled that an "utterance of a federal official was absolutely privileged if made 'within the outer perimeter' of the official's duties." The ground of the official privilege was said to be that the threat of damage suits would "inhibit the fearless, vigorous, and effective administration of policies of government." The threat of civil libel lawsuits, Wechsler explained, surely is "no less of a deterrent to the private individual who wants to speak out on public matters than it is to the official." "It would invert the scale of values vital to a free society if citizens discharging the 'political duty' of 'public discussion' did not enjoy a fair equivalent of the immunity granted to officials as a necessary incident of the performance of official duties."[31]

Wechsler knew that an argument in favor of absolute freedom to criticize government officials was not likely to win a majority of the Court. Only Black and Douglas were likely to support it. He knew that if he pressed on this point alone, there was a chance he would lose. So he presented "accommodations," as he described them, narrower grounds for reversal that would protect speech broadly yet offer some protections for reputation.

One "accommodation" was to say that officials would have to prove specific economic losses caused by the libel. Another was to require that the official prove the critic's malice—their intent to defame, inferred from their knowledge that the accusation was unfounded. This was Wechsler's way of characterizing the requirements of the good faith privilege or honest mistake privilege, the "minority" rule of privilege, which had been adopted in less than half of the states by 1963. A footnote inserted in the brief by Frankel listed eleven state cases on the privilege, citing as the lead case the 1908 Kansas Supreme Court case of *Coleman v. MacLennan*. Notably, Wechsler did not propose the definition of actual malice that the Court ultimately adopted: knowledge of falsity or "reckless disregard" of the truth or falsity of a statement. What ultimately became the rule of the *Sullivan* case was never once mentioned in the *Times'* brief. [32]

A third part of the brief presented another take on the First Amendment argument. Even if the libel law of Alabama was constitutional, the law had been applied unconstitutionally to the facts in this case. Wechsler asserted that the Supreme Court may appraise the facts when a state court has found the facts in a manner that threatened constitutional values. This was a provocative claim, as the principles of federalism require respect for findings of fact by a state court. But the Court in past decisions—Wechsler relied on the 1927 case of *Fiske v. Kansas*—made clear that it would review the facts when the Court's findings were intertwined with a claimed federal right. There was nothing in the record to say that Sullivan's reputation had been harmed, or that the ad referred to Sullivan, according to Wechsler. "So read, this publication was a totally impersonal attack upon conditions, groups and institutions, not a personal assault of any kind." "It is, in sum, impossible in our view to see in this mélange of statements, notwithstanding the inaccuracies noted, any falsehood that related to respondent and portended injury to his official reputation.... That such a statement could have jeopardized respondent's reputation anywhere he was known as an official must be regarded as a sheer illusion, not a finding that has any tangible support."[33]

Another section called *The Magnitude of the Verdict* argued that the award should be void because it was so "shockingly excessive that it violates the Constitution." "It is no hyperbole to say that if a judgment of this size can be sustained upon such facts as these, its repressive influence will extend far beyond deterring such inaccuracies of assertion as have been established here." Referring to the civil rights context, he wrote, "this is not a time—there never is a time—when it would serve the values enshrined in the Constitution to force the press to curtail its attention to the tensest issues that confront the country or to forego the dissemination of its publications in the areas where tension is extreme."[34]

In conclusion, the brief asked the court to reverse the judgment of the Alabama Supreme Court with directions to dismiss the case. This was another bold move. Typically, when the Court reverses a state court judgment, the opinion ends by remanding the case for the court to conduct "proceedings not inconsistent with this opinion." But Wechsler was suggesting that given how hostile the Alabama courts were toward the *Times*, the Supreme Court end the case without any further proceedings. Denying the state courts an opportunity to retry the case under the appropriate rule was a major intrusion into reserved powers of the state.

The ministers' lawyers framed their appeal in terms of violations of guarantees of equal protection of the law. The trial was a "race trial," in which the ministers were "placed in a patently inferior position because of the color of their skins," they argued. Read the brief:

> Clearly, when four Negro ministers are sued by a white city commissioner for an ad seeking support of Dr. Martin Luther King and the case is tried in a segregated courtroom in Montgomery, Alabama during a Civil War Centennial, before an all-white jury, and a trial judge elected at polls from which Negroes were excluded, and when that very judge states that "white man's justice" governs in his court and permits respondents counsel to say...Nigra...to the jury, then the Fourteenth Amendment does indeed become the pariah that the trial judge below called it.

The actions were part of a "concerted, calculated program to carry out a policy of punishing, intimidating, and silencing all who criticize and seek to change Alabama's notorious political system of enforced segregation."[35]

Nachman's brief attacked the *Times* for "dressing up" the advertisement as constitutionally protected speech:

> In a vain attempt to transfer these devastating statements from the constitutionally unprotected area of socially useless libel, where they belong, to the arena of constitutionally protected speech, where they obviously have no place, the *Times* and its friends employ various soothing phrases to describe the advertisement. It is called "political expression" and "political criticism" of "public men"; "the daily dialogue of politics"... a "recital of grievances and protests against claimed abuse dealing squarely with the major issue of our time."... But the ordinary, unsophisticated reader of this ad was bound to draw the plain meaning that such shocking conditions were the responsibility of those charged with the administration of the Montgomery Police Department—respondent and the other two city commissioners. Any other conclusion is impossible.... A description of such conduct, at war with basic concepts of decency and lawful government, inevitably evokes contempt, indignation, and ridicule for the person charged with the administration of police activities in Montgomery.[36]

Nachman continued:

> The *Times* and its powerful corporate newspaper friends obviously realize that history and precedent support the holding below that this libelous advertisement is not constitutionally protected. They assert, therefore, at least for themselves and others who conduct the business of mass communication, an absolute privilege to defame all public officials—even in paid advertisements; even when the defamation renders the classic defenses of truth, fair comment and privilege unavailable; even when there is no retraction to show good faith. They urge this Court to write such a fancied immunity into the Constitution.[37]

Nachman's invocation of "powerful corporate newspaper friends" was a reference to the *Chicago Tribune* and the *Washington Post*, which had filed *amicus curiae* briefs on behalf of the *Times*. The *Washington Post* got involved because William Rogers, the *Post*'s attorney, was representing the ministers. The *Post*'s brief put the central issue of the case in dramatic terms: "This case presents the fundamental question whether the State of Alabama may constitutionally so apply its libel laws as to suppress and punish expressions of support for the cause of racial equality and, in so doing, attempt to deny to those actively engaged in that cause access to media of mass communication."[38] The ACLU, now assured of the propriety of inserting itself into what was indisputably a constitutional case, also filed an amicus brief.[39]

After nearly three years, the expenditure of tens of thousands of dollars on the litigation by the *New York Times* and by the Southern Christian Leadership Conference, and thousands of hours invested by attorneys, the case would finally be heard by the Supreme Court. The case was remarkable in many respects. Not only was it the first time the Court would consider the relationship between libel and the First Amendment, but unusual in that the petitioner in the case, in contrast to most free speech cases that went to the Supreme Court, was not an isolated and marginal member of American society, but rather a pillar of the establishment, the serious and respectable *New York Times*.

Shortly after New Years' Day 1964, Nachman boarded a plane for Washington. The oral arguments in the *Sullivan* case were scheduled for January 6. Before Nachman left Montgomery, Sullivan asked him if the Supreme Court might take away his jury verdict. "L.B., for that to happen, they would have to reverse 200 years of settled law," Nachman reassured him.[40]

Nachman was confident that he would have a "bomb-proof" victory, he told Sullivan. "Either I will win the cases or they will change the law of the land."[41] The Supreme Court had said, time and time again, that libel was outside the First Amendment. How could he possibly lose?

14 **Arguments**

It was a momentous term in the Supreme Court's history—one of "extraordinary importance for Court and country," in the words of Anthony Lewis of the *New York Times*.[1] The October 1963 term (which lasted from October 1963 to October 1964) would be known as the "Second American Constitutional Convention" for its decisions radically innovating constitutional doctrine. The Warren Court was at the peak of its powers. Cases involving desegregation, reapportionment, school prayer, and obscenity, as well as five sit-in cases, were being argued at practically the same time as *New York Times v. Sullivan*.[2]

For four hours a day, four days a week, about two weeks out of four during the term, the justices sat in the courtroom and listened to oral argument. The oral argument provided an opportunity to find out what a case is about, in more human terms, than the printed record disclosed.[3] A distinguished group of spectators came to the courtroom to hear the arguments in the *Sullivan* case. They included three former U.S. attorneys general—Francis Biddle, Herbert Brownell, of Lord Day & Lord, and William Rogers, who was arguing the case for the ministers. Lawyers for CBS and the *Washington Post*, which had an obvious interest in the case, were also present. King entered the courtroom shortly after noon and took a reserved seat. His presence was noted by everyone in the courtroom and heightened the importance of the proceedings.[4] Shuttlesworth and Abernathy were also in the room. Harry Wachtel had asked Abernathy and King to attend: "Aside from it being important, I'm sure you will enjoy the spectacle of Mr. Sullivan's counsel attempting to support the oppressive—and in our opinion, illegal—libel judgment," he had written.[5] From the bench, Arthur Goldberg, dispensing with any illusion of impartiality, sent down his copy of *Stride Toward Freedom* with a note asking for King's autograph.[6]

The austere and orderly setting of the U.S. Supreme Court was a far cry from the violence-laden streets of Birmingham and the unfurling flags in Montgomery's "Confederate Square." None of the sectional conflict and racial animus that had brought forth the case was present when the nine justices proceeded through the red velvet curtains into the ornate, marble-walled, Ionic-columned courtroom and sat down in their high-backed, black leather swivel chairs behind the mahogany bench. Nachman and members of his firm were there for Sullivan, and Wechsler, Daly, and Loeb appeared for the *Times*.

Loeb was wearing no socks. There was a reason for this. Loeb and his wife had been in the Caribbean over the holidays. Loeb, an albino, was extremely susceptible to the sun and sustained third-degree burns on his feet. "The distinction I had was that I was the first attorney that ever appeared at the bar of the Supreme Court of the United States without socks," Loeb recalled. He was terrified that he would be thrown out: "if you know how meticulous the Supreme Court is, the way people are dressed." Eric Embry, who was sitting next to him, had unbuttoned his coat, and the bailiff came up to him and asked him to button his coat. "I kept thinking, Eric Embry was going to say, 'what about him?' Here I was without any socks."[7]

Wechsler, as counsel for the petitioner, was first in the argument. By this time, the justices had read all the briefs in the case as well as the record of the lower court proceedings. After Chief Justice Warren acknowledged him, Wechsler stepped to the podium and began his oration.[8]

WECHSLER: Mr. Chief Justice, May it please the Court. This case is here
            together with No. 40 on writ of certiorari granted a year ago in the
            Supreme Court of Alabama. It summons for review a judgment of
            that court which poses in our submission hazards to the freedom of
            the press, of a dimension not confronted since the early days of the
            Republic....

Each of the justices had a copy of Wechsler's brief on the bench before
them. Wechsler had attached the "Heed Their Rising Voices" ad to the brief,
for dramatic effect. Wechsler invited the justices to read the text of the ad,
since "the case not only begins with the publication but ends there as well."
"I suggest that the text was thus a statement of protest, an encomium inter-
woven with a recitation of events. But it names no names but Dr. King's,
and plainly makes no personal attack on any individual," he said.

Wechsler admitted that there were errors in the ad, including the fact
that the dining hall at Alabama State wasn't padlocked. But none of those
mistakes reflected on Sullivan, he insisted. "I submit that the grievance
has nothing to do with the respondent. If anybody has a grievance about
it, it is the state authorities that are referred to in those words, and not the
commissioner of the city of Montgomery, or any other authority."

Several of the justices, especially Brennan and Goldberg, took great
interest in the facts. They asked so many questions about the events in
Montgomery and the circumstances surrounding the ad's publication that
Wechsler ran out of time before he could present his full argument.

After half an hour discussing the facts, Wechsler moved on to his legal
arguments. "Our first proposition," he explained, "is that this action was
judged in Alabama by...a rule of law offensive to the First Amendment,
and offensive on its face to the First Amendment." Though he avoided the
term "absolute" and instead used "seditious libel," Wechsler explained why
he believed that the First Amendment granted, in effect, an absolute privilege to criticize public officials. "We are actually making here, in relation
to this rule of law, the same argument that James Madison made and that
Thomas Jefferson made with respect to the Sedition Act of 1798."

BRENNAN: How far does this go, Mr. Wechsler? As long as the criticism is
           addressed to official conduct?...Are there any limits whatever
           which take it outside the protection of the First Amendment?

WECHSLER: If I take my instruction from James Madison, I would have to say that within any references that Madison made, I can see no toying with limits or with exclusions.

BRENNAN: The First Amendment gives . . . in effect, an absolute prudence to criticize?

WECHSLER: The First Amendment was precisely designed to do away with seditious libel, the punishment for the criticism of the government and criticism of officials. . . .

GOLDBERG: You are not arguing here for a special rule that applies to newspapers?

WECHSLER: Certainly not. We are talking about the full ambit of the First Amendment. I realize the weight of this argument at this time. The Sedition Act was never passed on. But on the other hand, as I see our case, we are in the same position that the contempt cases were in 1940, when the scope of the contempt power had never been considered by this Court. When obscenity was here, that issue had never been considered. In short, this is a field of constitution interpretation that is 35 years old. That is a fact of life. And this is the first time . . . that the opportunity has arisen to make this submission in this Court. But I believe that if James Madison were alive today . . . the submission that I am making is the submission he would make.

GOLDBERG: Mr. Wechsler, your basic position . . . is that under the First and Fourteenth Amendments no public official can sue for libel constitutionally and get a verdict with respect to any type of false or malicious statement made concerning his official conduct?

WECHSLER: That is the broadest statement that I make, but I wish in my remaining time to indicate what the—what the—lesser submissions are, because there are many that I think must produce a reversal in this case. . . .

GOLDBERG: So to follow this through, it is a logical conclusion that a citizen would have the right under that broad proposition to state falsely, knowingly, and maliciously that his Mayor, his Governor, had accepted a bribe of one million dollars to commit an official act. And . . . the Mayor could not sue for libel.

WECHSLER: That is right. What he would have to do is to make a speech, using his official privilege as Mayor, to make a speech answering this charge. And that of course is what most Mayors do, and what the political history of the country has produced.

Wechsler went on to summarize his "lesser submissions" or "accommodations" that would balance the interest in reputation with freedom of speech:

WECHSLER: My further points are these. First, that even if—even if I'm wrong, you have then a situation here where law should surely attempt an accommodation of conflicting interests, the interest in protecting official reputation and the interests of freedom of discussion, but there is no accommodation here. The qualified privilege rule . . . is one way to work out an accommodation . . . And thirdly on this point, we have of course the submission . . . that there was in this record no evidence sufficient to support a finding that these particular statements in this particular advertisement threatened the respondent's reputation in any tangible way. And since that is the finding which justifies on this assumption, the suppression of a constitutionally protected freedom, we submit that the normal scope of Supreme Court review as to the facts on this obtains. [Here he mentioned *Fiske v. Kansas*] . . .

HARLAN: Are we entitled to review the evidence here?

WECHSLER: Yes, I think very definitely, Mr. Justice.

· · · · ·

Nachman was competent and articulate, as he had been before. But this time he was clearly on the defensive, with his unsympathetic client and dramatic upstaging by the brash and erudite Wechsler. Nachman's formal and genteel Southern manner, his oration peppered with "pleases" and "yes, sirs," contrasted starkly with Wechsler's direct and forceful style.

Repeating his arguments in his brief, Nachman presented the case not as a gross conspiracy to silence the press, but rather an ordinary personal injury case that had been tried under well-established rules of libel, with a jury verdict that had been reviewed by the state's highest court and was protected by the Seventh Amendment.[9]

NACHMAN: May it please the Court. I would like to address myself . . . to what I consider to be a short difference between Mr. Wechsler's analysis of the facts and facts as I see them. . . . this case is here obviously after a jury verdict, after the case has been before a trial court on a motion for new trial, after it's been before the highest state appellate court. And we do not rely on there being something in the record to support it. We say there was ample and indeed overwhelming evidence to support the jury verdict.

BRENNAN: May we reexamine (the facts)?

NACHMAN: We—we say, no sir, ...we say that the Seventh Amendment protects this verdict unless this Court finds that there's no reasonable basis, whatever for it. . . . There's no evidence at all to support it. . . .

WHITE: I suppose it is your assertion . . . that libel falls outside the protection of the First Amendment, that someone finally has to decide what libel is that falls outside the protection of the First Amendment? . . .

BRENNAN: The jury isn't the final answer on that I don't suppose.

NACHMAN: Up to now, as we read the cases, "The Court has left the characterization of publications as libelous or not libelous to the States." Now, if we would certainly concede that if a statement was made that somebody had blonde hair and a state court held that this statement was libelous per se, well of course this—this Court should—could review it. But adverting to some of Mr. Justice Black's observations in his questions, we say that when this kind of conduct is charged, this is within the normal usual rubric and framework of libel. . . . It charges them with criminal offenses of the charges which certainly hold them up to contempt . . . ridicule and disapproval and . . . we think, we are well within the classic definition of libel. . . . .We submit that Mr. Wechsler should fail before a jury and certainly before this tribunal on the question of whether or not there was ample evidence to sustain a jury verdict of falsity. We— think that the defendant in order to succeed must convince this Court that a newspaper corporation has an absolute immunity from anything it publishes. . . . And we think that's something brand new in our jurisprudence. . . .

The absolute rule proposed by the *Times* would have a "devastating effect on this nation," he warned.

. . . . .

The arguments concluded at 2:33, three minutes over the planned adjournment time of 2:30. The ministers' case, the so-called "Negro half" of the case, was held over for arguments until the following morning.[10]

That evening, King met with his lawyers at William Rogers's Washington office. The team recapped the day's events and confirmed the strategy for the following day. Harry Wachtel criticized Wechsler's performance, opining that his "accommodations" had been too timid. Rogers disagreed, saying he thought Wechsler's absolute argument had been too bold. King stood up. "I agree with you," he exclaimed, startling the lawyers who assumed he would sympathize with the extreme position. "Just because I'm out there in public, I don't want people to say and print anything they want about me and be protected."[11] King's advisers hailed Wechsler's race-neutral approach, however, suggesting that it would help foster coalitions with groups that were needed for the civil rights movement, such as labor unions and religious groups that could imagine being victimized by Southern juries.[12]

King left the meeting to spend the night at the elegant Willard Hotel. There, he hosted a party in his hotel suite. The FBI bugged his room. The FBI used King's relationship with Stanley Levison, whom they believed to be a Communist sympathizer, to justify surveillance of King, to expose what they believed to be King's moral shortcomings. This produced evidence of what the FBI described as a wild, drunken "orgy" involving several SCLC colleagues and two women from Philadelphia. FBI director J. Edgar Hoover would use the tapes in an unsuccessful attempt to blackmail King.[13]

None of this was known when King returned to the courtroom the following morning to hear arguments on behalf of the ministers by Rogers and Samuel R. Pierce, a young partner at Ted Kheel's law firm. "What did these petitioners do to deserve this punishment?" Rogers asked. "A precise recital of the evidence brings into sharp focus that the petitioners' constitutional rights have been violated.... The petitioners are not in truth being punished for what they did or failed to do in this case... the central fact of this case is that they are being drastically punished because they were Negroes residing in Alabama, who had the courage to speak out in the struggle to achieve the rights guaranteed by the Constitution for all citizens regardless of race or color."[14]

Nachman had little to stand on in his case against the ministers, and the justices made sure he knew it. Nachman insisted that there was evidence connecting the ministers to the ad. The justices pressed him to say what this was. He declared that their names were printed in the ad, and that they failed to reply to letters demanding a retraction, which under Alabama law was an admission of liability.[15]

Goldberg retorted: "If you get a letter from one person you've never heard of accusing you of something you didn't do, surely your failure to answer can't be proof of guilt. I get letters every day that I don't answer." Warren chimed in, alluding to crank letters he received by the thousands. "It is not unknown to at least one member of this Court," he said, "that he gets letters from various parts of the country accusing him of making statements libeling various groups and demanding retractions. Is he under an obligation to answer such letters or risk a half-million-dollar judgment?" Nachman said he wasn't familiar with those letters. "They are far worse than this one, I assure you," said Warren.

Shortly after the arguments concluded at noon, King and his lawyers celebrated at a reception at the Washington Hotel. King thanked Rogers, saying that he never thought he'd see the day when a former attorney general would represent him in the Supreme Court.[16] The lawyers cheered, and one of them offered a toast to Rosa Parks, whose refusal to give up her seat on the bus had sparked the civil rights movement.[17]

.   .   .   .   .

That Friday afternoon, the justices were back in the conference room with the green felt-topped table. After an hour of discussion, they unanimously agreed to reverse the judgment against the ministers and agreed generally to reverse the judgment against the *Times*.

In the *Times'* case, the justices divided substantially on the scope of the First Amendment. Justice Black, not surprisingly, felt that the Court should follow Wechsler's broadest argument, that liability for criticism of a public official in his official capacity could never be imposed consistently with the First Amendment.

BLACK: The purpose of the First Amendment is to keep public affairs open to discussion and not to outlaw public discussions, even where there is falsity. . . . If there is anything clear to me, it is that in public affairs it was intended to foreclose any kind of proceedings which would deter free and open discussion. At least in the field of public affairs, a state cannot keep a person from talking.

Douglas and Goldberg felt the same way. Yet the other justices weren't prepared to go that far. They were sure that the judgments should be reversed, yet they didn't want to go down the absolutist route. Brennan, Clark, Stewart, Harlan, Warren, and White proposed retaining the existing rules of libel as they applied to private persons but imposing stricter standards of proof for libel involving the official conduct of public officials.

BRENNAN: I reverse. The First Amendment does not outlaw all libel laws . . . but the press is entitled to broad freedom in criticizing public officials. I am not far from John [Harlan] in saying that there must be federal standards and actual malice. I would embrace "clear, convincing, and unequivocal" evidence from our expatriation cases. It applies to each element.[18]

The conclusion of the majority was that the judgment should be reversed on the narrow ground that Sullivan was not named in the ad, and that when a public official sued a critic of his official conduct, the First Amendment required clear proof, "clear and convincing evidence," of every element. This would not have shifted any of the traditional elements of libel; it would only require stronger evidence of what the plaintiff had to prove. This was far less radical than the doctrine that eventually emerged as the main rule of the case.

In the discussion of the ministers' case, *Abernathy v. Sullivan*, all the justices agreed to reverse. The reasoning was not that the prosecution of the libel cases and the trial proceedings were so tainted with racial bias as to violate the Fourteenth Amendment, but that there was no evidence against the ministers, and that therefore the judgment against them violated the due process clause of the Fourteenth Amendment. This basis for the decision for the ministers would ultimately disappear in the final version of the opinion.

Traditionally, the chief justice, if he is in the majority, assigns the writing of the opinion to another justice in the majority. The day after the conference, Warren sent a note to Brennan asking him to write the opinion. The fate of the *New York Times* and the ministers was now in the hands of Justice Brennan.

·   ·   ·   ·

Fifty-six-year-old William Brennan was a "chunky, hearty, informal jurist...[who] cusses moderately, dresses neatly, wears button-down shirts, [and] smokes both pipe and filter-tip," as *Look* magazine recently described him.[19] Brennan was one of the most respected justices on the Court in his own right, but he was also Chief Justice Warren's right-hand man, his unofficial strategist and advisor. Warren had a habit of turning to Brennan to draft opinions in high-profile cases in which the justices were unanimous in the result they wanted to achieve but didn't agree on how to get there.

Warren relied on Brennan for this important task because he knew that Brennan shared his commitment to civil liberties and civil rights, and the "living Constitution." Warren also knew that Brennan had the intellect and technical skills to be able to assert a principle and attend to details in a way that would strengthen the Court's image in the eyes of the public. Brennan was a remarkable unifier on the Court, with an ability to draft opinions that would secure the five votes needed for a majority. Though Brennan's opinions usually reached liberal results, he tended to avoid absolutes in favor of balancing competing interests. Through this measured and pragmatic approach, he was able to forge a majority consensus in a way that his more doctrinaire colleagues on the left, Black and Douglas, could not.

Brennan's gregarious personality served him well in this endeavor. Perhaps from his experience as a labor lawyer, Brennan was a remarkable negotiator who treated his opponents with respect and who never forgot that adversaries could be allies in the next battle. Brennan had a mischievous Irish grin and a springy step reminiscent of actor Jimmy Cagney.[20] In the justices' conferences, he was known for "having more than one vote," as he genially grabbed his colleagues by their elbow, or put his arm around their shoulder, and started his comments with, "Look, pal..."[21]

Brennan's perspectives on civil rights and liberties reflected his innate sympathies with outsiders and underdogs. Brennan was born in Newark in 1906, the eighth child of Irish immigrant laborers. After graduating from Harvard Law School in 1931 and working at a Newark law firm for over a decade, he accepted an appointment to the state superior court, and in 1952 was appointed to the New Jersey Supreme Court. Eisenhower, a Republican, selected Brennan to fill the vacancy on the U.S. Supreme

Court in 1956. Eisenhower wanted a Catholic and Democrat to appeal to independent and Democratic voters in the Northeast.

Brennan had been considered a moderate at the time he was appointed, but it was not long into his tenure on the Court that he embraced the liberal worldview that would define his legacy as a justice. Brennan's rulings expressed strong tendencies toward personal rights and freedoms, and a tenacious commitment to advancing the Constitution's promise of fairness and equality. He believed that law should be a moral force, and he read the Constitution expansively to find new rights and to broaden existing ones.[22]

Brennan was arguably the most important justice on the Warren Court in the advancement of civil rights. He had authored the opinions in *Cooper v Aaron*, the 1958 decision enforcing *Brown v. Board of Education*, and in *NAACP v. Button* (1963), protecting the right of the NAACP to litigate in Virginia. Though he was considerably more conservative than Justice Black on the First Amendment, Brennan was one of the Court's most influential justices on freedom of speech. By 1963, he had written seven majority opinions in free expression cases, including the landmark 1957 obscenity decision in *Roth v. United States*, involving the distribution of an erotic magazine, an opinion that Brennan would come to regret.

Brennan's approach in *Roth* had been highly formalistic, reflecting the dominant free speech jurisprudence of the time. Brennan concluded that because obscenity was one of the well-defined "low-value" areas of speech, it could be restricted. Yet in later free-expression cases, Brennan developed new methods of analysis and a more expansive view of free speech. This was based, in part, on his observations during the McCarthy era of the ways that the government restricted dissent.[23]

Brennan's next First Amendment opinion, *Speiser v. Randall* (1958), offered a more strategic approach to First Amendment decision-making. The case involved a California law that established a special property tax exemption for veterans, but it denied the exemption unless the individual swore an oath not to advocate overthrow of the government by unlawful means. Brennan rejected the state's argument that the disqualification was lawful because it merely withheld a "privilege." "To deny an exemption to claimants who engage in certain forms of speech is in effect to penalize them for their speech," because the "deterrent effect is the same as if the

State were to fine them for this speech," he wrote. The idea came to be known as "unconstitutional conditions." Brennan also concluded that the statute violated the First Amendment because it required the applicant to prove that he had not advocated the violent overthrow of government. Such an allocation of the burden of proof could have a "chilling effect," inhibiting free expression since "[t]he man who knows that he must bring forth proof and persuade another of the lawfulness of his conduct necessarily must steer far wider of the unlawful zone than if the State must bear these burdens."[24] Under the chilling effects doctrine, the First Amendment could be violated not only by direct sanctions, but also by a wide range of measures that were likely to inhibit constitutionally protected speech, even if they were indirect or incidental.[25]

In *Smith v. California* (1958), Brennan elaborated on his concept of "chilling effects." In *Smith*, the Court held that the First Amendment rights of a Los Angeles bookstore owner had been violated when he was sentenced to thirty days in jail for selling a pulp novel under a law holding that booksellers could be criminally liable for selling an obscene book even without knowledge of the book's contents. Brennan concluded that booksellers would tend to restrict the books they sold to those they had inspected, and thus the state would have imposed a restriction upon the distribution of constitutionally protected as well as obscene literature.[26] *Smith* and *Speiser* suggested a new category of invalid regulations: laws that tend to inhibit freedom of speech by generating a kind of "self-censorship." Brennan's opinion in *NAACP v. Button* (1963) invalidated a statute because it was written so broadly that it punished protected speech along with activity government has the right to proscribe. "Because First Amendment freedoms need breathing space to survive, government may regulate in the area only with narrow specificity," Brennan had written.[27]

With his strategic and technical vision of the operation of free speech—his concepts of "chilling effects" and "breathing space"—Brennan was well qualified to deal with the issues presented by the Alabama libel cases. No one on the Supreme Court was better suited for this task.

15 Actual Malice

Between January and March 1964, Brennan toiled on the *Sullivan* opinion in his "chambers," which was really a small office in the Supreme Court building. It was a busy time for Brennan and his clerks.[1] *New York Times v. Sullivan* was one of nearly two dozen opinions Brennan was writing that term.[2] Brennan and his staff produced the *Sullivan* opinion under significant time pressure. Not only were there other cases competing for Brennan's time and attention, but Brennan was aware that the Alabama libel situation required a swift resolution, given the drain on the *Times'* resources, the progression of civil rights events calling out for media coverage, and the remainder of the Alabama cases coming up through the courts.

Brennan's talents for negotiation and compromise were on display during the opinion-writing process.[3] Brennan readily incorporated changes suggested by his colleagues and handled disagreements with grace and tact. It was more important to him that he achieve consensus rather than have the final product reflect his own preferences. He chose his words carefully, with the aim of minimizing disagreement and producing a unanimous opinion that would strengthen the impact of the Court's message.[4]

Over the course of two months, Brennan and his clerks wrote eight drafts of the *Sullivan* opinion, perhaps more than any other justice would have attempted.[5] Brennan abandoned his usual practice of having his law clerks write the opinion and wrote the first draft himself. In the end, Brennan held a majority that became the main rules of the *Sullivan* case: the actual malice rule, requiring that the libel plaintiff who was a public official show that the defendant acted with knowledge that a statement was false or reckless disregard of whether it was false or not; the requirement that the facts in a libel case involving a public official be proven with "clear and convincing" evidence; and independent review of the facts by an appeals court in a public official libel case. This set of rules, which had been mentioned by Wechsler but hadn't been discussed by the justices in their post-argument conference, had been developed in large part by Justice Brennan.

．　　．　　．　　．　　．

As Wechsler intended, his brief provided the template for the Court's opinion. Brennan drew heavily on Wechsler's structure, language, and ideas. Aside from the actual malice rule, almost all of the opinion came from Wechsler's brief.[6] Brennan's appropriation of Wechsler's rhetoric and ideas can be attributed to the eminence of Wechsler and his eloquent, academic brief, and to the time pressure Brennan faced in writing the opinion.

The first draft of the opinion was eleven pages long. Following Wechsler, Brennan laid out a complex, multistep argument explaining why libels of public officials were not categorically excluded from protections of the First Amendment.

In the first part of the three-part opinion, Brennan disposed of Sullivan's lawyers' arguments that the Fourteenth Amendment was directed against state action, rather than private action, and therefore, did not apply to a libel case. He wrote: "The test is not the form in which state power has been applied but, whatever the form, whether such power has in fact been exercised."[7] It's unclear whether the Court would have summarily disposed of the difficult state action issue presented by a civil libel suit had a more ordinary libel case come before it. Yet it seemed clear that this "private" libel suit was really an official, state undertaking.

In a footnote at the beginning of the opinion, Brennan tersely dismissed the ministers' claims of violations of the Fourteenth Amendment, stating that the decision rested on the First Amendment and that there was no need to go further.[8] In the same footnote, the opinion also rejected the *Times'* jurisdictional argument, claiming that it was "foreclosed from our review by the ruling of the Alabama courts that the *Times* entered a general appearance in the action and thus waived its jurisdictional objection."[9]

In Part II, the heart of the opinion, Brennan outlined his argument for extending constitutional protection to defamatory falsehoods about public officials. The national commitment to freedom of expression, he wrote, could not "be overpowered by mere labels such as "libel."

> Like insurrection, contempt, advocacy of unlawful acts, breach of the peace, obscenity, solicitation of legal business, and the various other formulae for the repression of expression that have been challenged in this Court, libel can claim no talismanic immunity from constitutional limitations. It must be measured by standards that satisfy the First Amendment.[10]

Citing passages by Holmes, Brandeis, and others, taken from Wechsler's brief, Brennan explained that "freedom of expression upon public questions" was at the core of the First Amendment's protections. This led to a discussion, again taken from Wechsler, on the Sedition Act of 1798. Brennan had been persuaded by Wechsler's analogy of the Alabama libel actions to punishment for sedition. Brennan's opinion declared the Sedition Act unconstitutional—it was found by history to be "inconsistent with the First Amendment."[11]

Throughout the Sedition Act discussion, Brennan seemed to be following Wechsler's position of an absolute view of the right to criticize government. However, the opinion stopped short of granting absolute immunity to criticize officials. Brennan then announced the main rule of *Sullivan,* allowing the libel plaintiff who was a public official to recover damages only if he could show that the defamatory falsehood was made with "actual malice," knowledge that a statement was false or "reckless disregard of whether it was false or not."[12]

Brennan stated that the actual malice rule was mandated by the First and Fourteenth Amendments in protecting critics of official conduct.

"This is a safeguard," he wrote, "which draws an appropriate line between an expression uttered with actual malice to harm the official by an accusation known to be unfounded in fact, or reckless of whether it is true or not, and an expression which is erroneous in fact but honestly believed to be true."[13]

The actual malice rule appears to have been drawn from one of Wechsler's three "accommodations." However, Wechsler had mentioned it only in passing, in a footnote in the brief. Wechsler, moreover, had proposed a version of the rule under which the aggrieved official must prove the critic's intent to defame, inferred from their knowledge that the accusation was unfounded. This was Wechsler's way of characterizing the good faith privilege or honest mistake privilege, the "minority rule" of privilege, as defined in cases such as *Coleman v. MacLennan*. Brennan described the "minority rule" as "a like rule" to the one envisioned by his actual malice standard. "Actual malice" was, in reality, different. Brennan was creating a new standard, but he went out of his way to make it seem as if the standard was already accepted in several states.[14]

Brennan, the consummate negotiator, chose "actual malice" as a way of providing First Amendment protection for speakers who criticized officials while at the same time allowing protection for reputation. This compromise was intended to please both the absolutist justices and the middle-of-the-road justices who preferred balancing approaches to the First Amendment. Actual malice, as a fault standard, is in many ways quite radical, given that the standard in most personal injury cases is negligence, which requires the plaintiff only to show that the defendant had been careless. (It will be recalled that libel was an anomaly in tort law in that it was strict liability, meaning that the defendant could be liable even if it published the defamatory statement with due care for the facts; merely publishing the statement was the basis of liability.) Actual malice was a more moderate stance, of course, compared to Wechsler's absolutist approach.

There was also a practical reason for the actual malice standard, tied to the facts of this case. Brennan knew that a fault standard of negligence wouldn't have protected the *Times*, as it failed to investigate the advertisement. Brennan may have felt, more generally, that a negligence standard may be too easy to prove in a libel case, especially when the trial involves a popular local plaintiff and an unpopular defendant. A negligence standard was never brought up in Wechsler's brief and was never once considered by the Supreme Court.

The opinion went on to conclude that Sullivan had not shown actual malice by the newly adopted standard of "clear and convincing evidence." The first draft concluded with one word, "reversed," without any statement about remanding the case to Alabama for further proceedings.[15]

The first draft offered another basis for reversing the judgment. The jury verdict did not meet the standards of the First Amendment because Sullivan had failed to prove with "clear and convincing evidence" that the statements in the ad were "of and concerning" Sullivan, that they referred to Sullivan. This suggestion had been proposed by several of the justices at the conference. However, this ground for the decision disappeared in the second draft, which was circulated to the justices on February 6.[16]

Warren and White signed on to this second draft. Yet Brennan's three other liberal allies—Black, Douglas, and Goldberg—made clear that they were holding fast to the absolutist line. Goldberg circulated a separate opinion in which he concurred in the Court's judgment but went on to say that a libel judgment based on criticism of a public official for his official conduct could not be justified even with a showing of actual malice. The following day, Black circulated an opinion concurring in the judgment on the same ground as Goldberg. Black opined that actual malice would not prevent Sullivan from recovering, since an Alabama jury could easily find that the *Times* acted with actual malice if it wanted to. Douglas joined Black's opinion.[17]

Brennan knew that normally the Supreme Court would allow lower courts to apply a new legal rule to the facts of a case. But he and the other justices had lost faith in Southern judges. Brennan wanted to prevent a new trial, knowing that if the case were sent back to Alabama, it would likely be a futile exercise, with the jury likely finding once again for Sullivan. In his third draft of his opinion circulated on February 17, Brennan reviewed the evidence in the case and held that it was insufficient to support a finding of actual malice as defined by the Court, and therefore Sullivan should not receive a new trial.[18]

Brennan was concerned with the possible reaction of Justice Harlan. Harlan was a deep believer in federalism, the division of power between the states and the national government. Harlan sent a letter to Brennan expressing his agreement with Parts I and II and also, surprisingly, agreeing that Sullivan should not have a new trial. No new trial would be warranted "on the basis that respondent would be afforded an opportunity to adduce further and sufficient evidence," he said. He believed that Sullivan had no additional evidence to offer. However, he stated in a note to Brennan that he wanted to offer his own "elaboration" of Part III. Harlan went on to suggest that Part III of the opinion should rely on the authority of 28 U.S.C. § 2106 of the judicial code, which authorized a federal appellate court to "direct the entry of such appropriate judgment, decree, or order as may be just under the circumstances." Because Brennan needed the support of Harlan and his allies, he incorporated Harlan's views into a new version of the opinion.[19]

Harlan's suggestion proved to be controversial, however, as 28 U.S.C. § 2106 had never been applied to a case from a state court and the question arose as to whether its application might overstep the court's appellate jurisdiction. Black sent a note to Brennan stating that "I do not see how John could possibly adhere to that position on more mature reflection. I can think of few things that would more violently clash with his ideas of 'federalism.' ... Construing the state as authorizing our Court to overturn state laws as to a right to a new trial would undoubtedly raise constitutional questions some of as I recall were discussed in the famous *cause celebre Cohens v. Virginia.*"[20] Brennan and Harlan conferred, after which Harlan retracted his proposal forbidding a new trial and inexplicably embraced the contrary view that since a new trial could not be absolutely prohibited, and since reversal was required because the Alabama courts had not applied the actual malice rule, there was no reason for the Court to concern itself with the evidence. Harlan now proposed that Part III be scrapped—that the opinion should state the actual malice rule, reverse for failure to apply the rule, and leave unanswered the question of how it should be applied to specific evidence.[21]

Brennan circulated his fifth draft of the opinion the next day, eliminating the references to 28 U.S.C. § 2106 and returning to an earlier draft, which reviewed the evidence and held that it was insufficient to support actual malice, yet omitting reference to the possibility of a new trial. It concluded, "The judgment of the Supreme Court of Alabama is reversed and the case is remanded for further proceedings not inconsistent with this opinion." Along with the draft, Brennan circulated a memorandum explaining his rejection of Harlan's approach:

> I am convinced ... that the analysis of the evidence to show its insufficiency under the constitutional rule we lay down is essential to the opinion. Since Sullivan did undertake to prove actual malice as a predicate for punitive damages, we of necessity must demonstrate the insufficiency of his evidence under the constitutional test of actual malice. Moreover, if Alabama would give Sullivan a new trial the parties should know that the evidence in this record will not support a judgment—that there is a large void to be filled. If we said nothing and we later overturned another judgment entered on this record, we might be rightly accused of having second thoughts because of the implication from our silence here that application of the valid rule to this evidence would be sustained.

Brennan reminded his colleagues of the other libel cases coming from the South. "There are a number of other libel suits pending both in Montgomery and in Birmingham and those concerned should know what to expect in the way of judicial superintendence from this Court over those proceedings."[22]

Harlan wrote to Brennan saying that he would dissent from the discussion of the evidence. He then circulated an opinion that agreed with Parts I and II of the Brennan opinion but went on to say, "I do not consider it appropriate for the Court to examine the sufficiency of the evidence at this stage, since other constitutional requirements compel a reversal of these judgments, however that issue is resolved."[23]

It was uncertain whether anyone would agree with Harlan. Stewart didn't. Nor did Warren. It was rumored that Clark and White were attracted to Harlan's view. Brennan was concerned that he would not speak for a majority and that the Court would not be able to signal to Alabama that it was determined to enforce the new constitutional law of libel it had created.[24]

Whenever Brennan wanted to find out what one of the other justices was thinking, he sent his clerks to gather information from the justice's clerks.

"Brennan's clerks were like honeybees in a field of clover," observes a biographer of Brennan. "They sent out feelers and brought back ideas. In many ways they were Brennan's personal trademark."[25] Brennan dispatched his clerks to talk with the clerks of Justice Clark, and they returned with disturbing news. Clark had originally been inclined to join Brennan's opinion, but he was now changing his position because he wanted to stay close to Harlan, his usual ally.[26]

Brennan walked down to Clark's office to discuss the matter. Before Brennan could say anything, Clark handed him a copy of a proposed opinion, which echoed Harlan's feelings. Brennan no longer had a majority for Part III of the opinion and wrote to Warren in despair:

> John [Harlan] has circulated a concurrence saying that it's inappropriate for us to dismiss the evidence since the judgment must in any event be reversed for unconstitutionality of the law of libel itself. Tom [Clark] seems to be leaning John's way in pressing me to omit Part III. I won't do that—I think it would be fatal to what we're trying to lay down. Even if we are only four, my thinking is that we should leave it in and add only that three of our brethren (Hugo, Bill, and Arthur) don't reach the question because they believe that evidence of actual malice is constitutionally inadmissible and not just subject to a test of sufficiency. What do you think of this program?[27]

Warren agreed with the idea, and a relieved Brennan set about to win the fifth vote for Part III from Black, Douglas, and Goldberg. Brennan proposed to Douglas that that the opinion should carry notes stating that all nine justices agreed with Parts I and II up to the statement that liability can exist if actual malice is shown, that all of the justices except Black, Douglas, and Goldberg agreed with that statement, and that all except Harlan and Clark agreed with the analysis of the evidence in Part III. Douglas and Goldberg agreed to this, but Black didn't, taking the position that Sullivan's evidence was sufficient to prove malice.[28]

Justice White then suggested a different basis for review of the evidence. He believed that the Alabama court's failure to instruct that malice was required for an award of general damages did not itself warrant a reversal, since the verdict might have consisted wholly of punitive damages, for which malice was required under Alabama law. Therefore, White argued, the rule of law applied in the Alabama courts was not necessarily erroneous in its failure to require a finding of malice, and the evidence must be

Figure 9. The Warren Court undertook a program of constitutional reform that transformed the lives of ordinary Americans as no previous Court had done. Photo: Warren Leffler, 1962. Library of Congress.

reviewed to determine whether the finding of malice was justified. This was incorporated into the sixth version of Brennan's opinion, circulated on March 4, to satisfy White and possibly attract Harlan. But Harlan stuck to his separate concurrence. The dispute had apparently ended, with the Douglas-Goldberg compromise the result.[29]

The next morning, Clark notified Brennan, unexpectedly, that he would withdraw his opinion and that he would join Brennan's opinion if there were a change in wording. Clark asked that the paragraph in Part III be changed to read: "Since respondent may seek a new trial, we deem that considerations of effective judicial administration require us to review the evidence in the present record to determine whether it could constitutionally support a judgment for respondent." The phrase "effective judicial administration" had achieved great significance during the term, "being employed in several different situations as sort of a 'judicial wonder drug,'" in the words of one of Brennan's clerks. Brennan did not understand the significance of the change but accepted the compromise, and it appeared in the final opinion.[30]

At the conference on Friday, March 6, the vote was taken, and Brennan had his majority. The opinion was approved for announcement the following Monday, during the Court's usual Monday morning ritual of reading opinions. This was just weeks after the Civil Rights Act of 1964 was passed by the House and sent to the Senate, where it would be approved three months later.

On Sunday evening, around eight o'clock, the phone rang at Brennan's home. It was Harlan. Harlan told Brennan that he decided to go along with the majority, out of respect for the work he had put into the opinion.[31] Harlan wrote a letter that was circulated to the Court the following day. "Dear Brethren, I have advised Brother Brennan, and I wish the other Brethren to know, that I am withdrawing my separate memorandum in this case, and am unreservedly joining the majority opinion. JMH."[32]

. . . . .

On Monday, March 9, Brennan announced the unanimous opinion in *New York Times v. Sullivan*. "We reverse the judgment," he declared. "We hold that the rule of law applied by the Alabama courts is constitutionally deficient for failure to provide the safeguards for freedom of speech and of the press that are required by the First and Fourteenth Amendments in a libel action brought by a public official against critics of his official conduct. We further hold that under the proper safeguards the evidence presented in this case is constitutionally insufficient to support the judgment for respondent."[33]

Brennan declared that libel could "claim no talismanic immunity from constitutional limitations."[34] Insofar as the judgment impaired "freedom of expression upon public questions," it represented a limitation on the "central meaning" of the First Amendment.[35] Here, Brennan issued one of the most notable passages of the opinion. Written by Brennan's clerk Stephen Barnett, it was one of the only phrases not taken from Wechsler's brief:

> Thus we consider this case against the background of a profound national commitment to the principle that debate on public issues should be uninhibited, robust, and wide-open, and that it may well include vehement, caustic, and sometimes unpleasantly sharp attacks on government and public officials ... The present advertisement, as an expression of grievance and

protest on one of the major public issues of our time, would seem clearly to qualify for the constitutional protection. The question is whether it forfeits that protection by the falsity of some of its factual statements and by its alleged defamation of respondent.[36]

The opinion then elaborated the grounds for disposing of the judgment against the *Times*. It rejected truth as a requirement for First Amendment protections: "erroneous statement is inevitable in free debate, and... it must be protected if the freedoms of expression are to have the 'breathing space' that they 'need to survive.'"[37] Brennan went on to say that "authoritative interpretations of the First Amendment guarantees have consistently refused to recognize an exception for any test of truth—whether administered by judges, juries, or administrative officials—and especially one that puts the burden of proving truth on the speaker."[38] Even a false statement could contribute to public discourse: it "make[s] a valuable contribution to public debate, since it brings about 'the clearer perception and livelier impression of truth, produced by its collision with error.'"[39]

Brennan rejected the notion that injury to reputation was sufficient grounds for repressing criticism of public officials: "Criticism of... official conduct does not lose its constitutional protection merely because it is effective criticism and hence diminishes... official reputations."[40] That "neither factual error nor defamatory content suffices to remove the constitutional shield from criticism of official conduct" was the lesson to be drawn from the "great controversy over the Sedition Act of 1798."[41] Brennan declared that the controversy over the Sedition Act "crystallized a national awareness of the central meaning of the First Amendment."[42] Citing Madison's report to the General Assembly of Virginia stating that the Constitution created a form of government under which "the people, not the government, possess the absolute sovereignty," he described how the act had been "condemned as unconstitutional in an attack joined in by Jefferson and Madison."[43]

The concept of the "chilling effect" was then applied to Alabama's rules of strict liability and the presumption of falsity. Citing his opinion in *NAACP v. Button*, Brennan wrote that "erroneous statement is inevitable in free debate, and... it must be protected if the freedoms of expression are to have the 'breathing space' that they 'need to survive.'"[44] "A rule compelling the critic of official conduct to guarantee the truth of all his factual assertions—and to do so on pain of libel judgments virtually unlimited in amount—leads to a comparable 'self-censorship.' Allowance of the defense of truth, with the burden of proving it on the defendant, does not mean that only false speech will be deterred.... Under such a rule, would-be critics of official conduct may be deterred from voicing their criticism, even though it is believed to be true and even though it is in fact true, because of doubt whether it can be proved in court or fear of the expense of having to do so. They tend to make only statements which 'steer far wider of the unlawful zone,'" he wrote, referencing his opinion in *Speiser v. Randall*. "The rule thus dampens the vigor and limits the variety of public debate. It is inconsistent with the First and Fourteenth Amendments."[45]

Then came the main rule of the case:

> We hold today that the Constitution delimits a State's power to award damages for libel in actions brought by public officials against critics of their official conduct. Since this is such an action, the rule requiring proof of actual malice is applicable. While Alabama law apparently requires proof of actual malice for an award of punitive damages, where general damages are concerned malice is "presumed."... Since the trial judge did not instruct the jury to differentiate between general and punitive damages, it may be that the verdict was wholly an award of one or the other. But it is impossible to know, in view of the general verdict returned. Because of this uncertainty, the judgment must be reversed and the case remanded.[46]

The next part of the opinion dealt with the evidentiary and new trial issues. "We deem that considerations of effective judicial administration require us to review the evidence in the present record to determine whether it could constitutionally support a judgment for respondent." "Applying these standards, we consider that the proof presented to show actual malice lacks the convincing clarity which the constitutional standard demands."[47]

The evidence was "constitutionally defective" in another respect—it was "incapable of supporting the jury's finding that the libelous statements were made 'of and concerning' respondent."[48] There was no reference to Sullivan in the ad, either by name or his official position. Several of the allegedly libelous statements about padlocking the dining hall and the arrest of King did not even concern the police and could not reasonably be seen as implicating Sullivan in the attacks. The proposition of the Ala-

Figure 10. Justice William Brennan, a champion of civil rights and
civil liberties, wrote the *New York Times v. Sullivan* opinion.
Library of Congress.

bama Supreme Court that criticism of government, "however impersonal
it may seem on its face," could be "personal criticism, and hence potential
libel," of government officials has "disquieting implications for criticism
of governmental conduct. For good reason, 'no court of last resort in this
country has ever held, or even suggested, that prosecutions for libel on
government have any place in the American system of jurisprudence,'"
Brennan wrote.[49]

There is no legal alchemy by which a State may thus create the cause of action that would otherwise be denied for a publication which, as respondent himself said of the advertisement, "reflects not only on me but on the other Commissioners and the community." Raising as it does the possibility that a good-faith critic of government will be penalized for his criticism, the proposition relied on by the Alabama courts strikes at the very center of the constitutionally protected area of free expression. We hold that such a proposition may not constitutionally be utilized to establish that an otherwise impersonal attack on governmental operations was a libel of an official responsible for those operations. Since it was relied on exclusively here, and there was no other evidence to connect the statements with respondent, the evidence was constitutionally insufficient to support a finding that the statements referred to respondent.[50]

The opinion disposed of the ministers' case tersely under the actual malice rule: "Even assuming that they could constitutionally be found to have authorized the use of their names on the advertisement, there was no evidence whatever that they were aware of any erroneous statements or were in any way reckless in that regard. The judgment against them is thus without constitutional support."[51]

In conclusion, Brennan wrote that "the judgment of the Supreme Court of Alabama is reversed and the case is remanded to that court for further proceedings not inconsistent with this opinion."[52]

. . . . . .

The separate concurring opinion by Justice Goldberg, joined by Douglas, stated enthusiastically the position of Wechsler and the *Times*.

"The First and Fourteenth Amendments to the Constitution afford to the citizen and to the press an absolute, unconditional privilege to criticize official conduct despite the harm which may flow from excesses and abuses," he wrote. "The theory of our Constitution is that every citizen may speak his mind and every newspaper express its view on matters of public concern and may not be barred from speaking or publishing because those in control of government think that what is said or written is unwise, unfair, false, or malicious."[53] Goldberg would retain an area of private life in which a public official would have the benefits of the ordinary rules of defamation. Justice Black would not.

In his separate concurring opinion, Black, also joined by Douglas, based his "vote to reverse on the belief that the First and Fourteenth Amendments not merely 'delimit' a State's power to award damages to 'public officials against critics of their official conduct' but completely prohibit a State from exercising such a power." With his native's view of the region—his knowledge of how Alabama juries worked, and how the segregationists could easily circumvent the "actual malice" rule if they wanted—he scoffed at the Court's new standard.[54]

"Malice," even as defined by the Court, is an elusive, abstract concept, hard to prove and hard to disprove. The requirement that malice be proved provides at best an evanescent protection for the right critically to discuss public affairs and certainly does not measure up to the sturdy safeguard embodied in the First Amendment. Unlike the Court, therefore, I vote to reverse exclusively on the ground that the *Times* and the individual defendants had an absolute, unconditional constitutional right to publish in the *Times* advertisement their criticisms of the Montgomery agencies and officials.[55] ...

The half-million-dollar verdict does give dramatic proof, however, that state libel laws threaten the very existence of an American press virile enough to publish unpopular views on public affairs and bold enough to criticize the conduct of public officials. The factual background of this case emphasizes the imminence and enormity of that threat. One of the acute and highly emotional issues in this country arises out of efforts of many people, even including some public officials, to continue state-commanded segregation of races in the public schools and other public places, despite our several holdings that such a state practice is forbidden by the Fourteenth Amendment. Montgomery is one of the localities in which widespread hostility to desegregation has been manifested. This hostility has sometimes extended itself to persons who favor desegregation, particularly to so-called "outside agitators," a term which can be made to fit papers like the Times, which is published in New York.

The scarcity of testimony to show that Commissioner Sullivan suffered any actual damages at all suggests that these feelings of hostility had at least as much to do with rendition of this half-million-dollar verdict as did an appraisal of damages. Viewed realistically, this record lends support to an inference that instead of being damaged Commissioner Sullivan's political, social, and financial prestige has likely been enhanced by the Times' publication. Moreover, a second half-million-dollar libel verdict against the Times based on the same advertisement has already been awarded to another Commissioner. There a jury again gave the full amount claimed. There is no reason to believe that there are not more such huge verdicts lurking just around the corner for the Times or any other newspaper or broadcaster which might dare to criticize public officials.

In fact, briefs before us show that in Alabama there are now pending eleven libel suits by local and state officials against the Times seeking $5,600,000, and five such suits against the Columbia Broadcasting System seeking $1,700,000. Moreover, this technique for harassing and punishing a free press—now that it has been shown to be possible—is by no means limited to cases with racial overtones; it can be used in other fields where public feelings may make local as well as out-of-state newspapers easy prey for libel verdict seekers.

In my opinion the Federal Constitution has dealt with this deadly danger to the press in the only way possible without leaving the free press open to destruction—by granting the press an absolute immunity for criticism of the way public officials do their public duty....

Stopgap measures like those the Court adopts are in my judgment not enough. This record certainly does not indicate that any different verdict would have been rendered here whatever the Court had charged the jury about "malice," "truth," "good motives," "justifiable ends," or any other legal formulas which in theory would protect the press. Nor does the record indicate that any of these legalistic words would have caused the courts below to set aside or to reduce the half-million-dollar verdict in any amount....

We would, I think, more faithfully interpret the First Amendment by holding that at the very least it leaves the people and the press free to criticize officials and discuss public affairs with impunity....

This Nation, I suspect, can live in peace without libel suits based on public discussions of public affairs and public officials. But I doubt that a country can live in freedom where its people can be made to suffer physically or financially for criticizing their government, its actions, or its officials....An unconditional right to say what one pleases about public affairs is what I consider to be the minimum guarantee of the First Amendment.[56]

Brennan had not gone as far as Black would have liked, but Black was nevertheless pleased with what Brennan had done. He conveyed this to Brennan in a handwritten note: "You know of course that despite my position and what I write, I think you are doing a wonderful job in the Times case and however it finally comes out it is bound to be a very long step toward preserving the right to communicate ideas."[57]

16 Free, Robust, and Wide Open

Roland Nachman received the news in a telegram from the clerk of the U.S. Supreme Court on March 9, 1964. "Judgment New York Times and Abernathy against Sullivan cases reversed today. Cases remanded. Advise associates," it read.[1] Nachman was stunned. He recalled, "I didn't conceive that [Wechsler's] would be a winning argument. It never entered my head that the case would come out the way it did."[2]

Nachman believed that the decision was the product of "extrinsic circumstances," as he put it. "There were a great many plaintiffs who came after us. That was one of the problems we had, to put it mildly," he later said. "Extrinsic circumstances over which the lawyers in the case had no control—including the amount of the verdict, the unfortunate political and social climate, and the proliferation of contemporaneous lawsuits brought by others—made this a very hard case for the plaintiff."[3] In later years, he was sanguine about his loss. He understood the importance of his work but often said that he "would rather be famous for a case he won rather than one he lost."[4] "My client," Nachman said, referring to the *Montgomery Advertiser*, "thought the greatest thing I ever did was lose the Sullivan case."[5]

Wechsler was teaching a class at Columbia when the decision came down. His secretary came into the classroom and handed him a note: "Judgment reversed, decision unanimous," it said. Wechsler read the note aloud, and the students cheered.[6]

Like Nachman, Wechsler was stunned by Brennan's use of the actual malice standard. "I wish [Brennan] hadn't used the word malice, but he did and it's there," he commented.[7] Nachman and Wechsler later saw each other in the Supreme Court building and agreed that Brennan had just "run away with the decision."[8] Even Wechsler was surprised that the Court went to such lengths to foreclose the possibility of another trial. "They didn't have to reach that second step," he said. "It showed a disposition to see this situation realistically for what it was and put a stop to it."[9]

King issued a public statement. "The Supreme Court has upheld the freedom of the press and speech so vital to those who are engaged in the struggle for full freedom. . . . This decision is an historic affirmation of the fact that forces of ill will can no longer silence the voices speaking for freedom."[10] The decision was issued on Abernathy's birthday. "It's the best birthday present I've ever received," he exulted. "Next year, I hope the gift will be freedom."[11] The SCLC celebrated the Court's ruling "that a suit in libel was not available as a formula for 'repression of expression.'" "Now, 'robust' and 'uninhibited' debate on public issues is guaranteed because one need no longer fear that a misstatement, strong language, or even error could lead to large dollar judgments, with the consequent jeopardy to one's savings, property, and possessions, as was the case with the four ministers," it announced. "When viewed in its historical perspective, this decision represent(s) a repudiation of those in the south who 'ingeniously' fashion 'evasive schemes' to perpetuate what Dr. King called 'a system of human values that came into being under a feudalistic plantation system which cannot survive.'"[12]

Though the press had avoided almost all involvement in the Alabama lawsuits, it wasted no time in lauding the decision and even taking credit for the outcome. Although *Sullivan*'s protections didn't apply only to the press, the *Sullivan* opinion was written with the press in mind, and news headlines declared *Sullivan* to be the greatest legal victory for the press since the Supreme Court's 1931 decision in *Near v. Minnesota*. The *Los Angeles Times* called *Sullivan* "A True Charter of Press Liberty" and predicted that "the inhibitions on many editors and publishers throughout the United States who have been plagued by the threat of catastrophic libel awards will fall away."[13] The *Atlanta Constitution* described an "An End to Intimidation."[14] The *New York Times* and the *Washington Post* printed the full text of the opinion. Several newspapers ran editorials.[15] The *Berkshire Eagle* deemed *Sullivan* to be a "modern-day Magna Carta."[16] Arthur B. Hanson, general counsel of American Newspaper Publishers of America, said that "no case in modern jurisprudence has had any greater effect on any field of law."[17] Newspapers praised the Court for writing an opinion that was not limited to the civil rights field. The *Boston Globe* lauded the Supreme Court for discouraging attempts to "limit criticism of official conduct... not only in the South."[18] None of the press accounts mentioned the ministers. The *Washington Post*'s editorial made no reference to the content of the ad and described the other defendants as "four Alabama citizens."[19]

Sulzberger issued a statement welcoming the decision: "The opinion of the court makes freedom of the press more secure than ever before," he announced. [20] A self-congratulatory editorial in the *Times* praised "the unanimous decision of the Supreme Court in a case involving this newspaper." "It is a victory of first importance in the long and never-ending struggle for the rights of a free press. But it is more than that. It is also a vindication of the right of a free people to have unimpeded access to the news and to fair comment on the news.... In its landmark decision yesterday, the Supreme Court of the United States has struck a solid blow not only for the freedom of the press but for the prerogatives of a free people."[21]

Sulzberger called Loeb after the decision was issued. He had trouble reaching him because Loeb's phone was busy. "I tried to telephone you yesterday evening to congratulate you and all those associated with our wonderful showing before the Supreme Court but was unable to reach you," he wrote to Loeb the following day. "The operator said your phone was in working order and legitimately busy (what girl were you talking to for so long?) We tried calling about five or six times. At any rate, I wanted then to congratulate you and I do congratulate you now, and I hope you will share these words with those who deserve them!"[22]

Sulzberger remained troubled by the seizure of the ministers' property and sought to "take steps to see that the four Negro ministers who were involved with us in the Alabama matter suffer no financial embarrassment."[23] Loeb deemed this inadvisable, pointing out that it was still possible for any of the plaintiffs to continue with the trials. If it became known that the *Times* was assisting the clergymen, "it would have a bad effect in Alabama in case a retrial is asked for by Sullivan or the other cases proceed to trial despite the Supreme Court's decision," Loeb said.[24] The Montgomery officials would eventually restore to the ministers the money they received from the sale of their property.[25] The ministers instructed Fred Gray to forward the funds to the SCLC, as their seized automobiles and legal fees had been paid for by that organization, through gifts from the public.[26]

After the Supreme Court decided the case, it was remanded to the Circuit Court of Montgomery County. Sullivan did have the right under the decision to seek a new trial and the same went for Mayor James. Loeb said that if Sullivan wanted to retry the case, the *Times* would remove the cases to federal court. This would now be possible because the ministers were no longer in the case.[27] Ultimately, Sullivan's lawyers did not seek a new trial.

The Supreme Court usually imposes on the losing side the cost of printing and modest fees—in this case, about thirteen thousand dollars. Nachman cleverly made a motion in the Court to divide the costs between Sullivan and the *Times*. He said that half of the record in the case pertained to the issue of whether the *Times* was subject to Alabama jurisdiction and that the Court held against the *Times* on this. The Court denied the motion without comment.[28]

Nachman finally conceded defeat to avoid the cost of further litigation. He sought an agreement with the *Times* in which the commissioners would abandon their cases if the *Times* voluntarily paid the costs in the *Sullivan* case and the firm's out-of-pocket expenses, around $4,700. Calvin Whitesell went to Birmingham to discuss this with Embry. Embry then called Loeb and recommended that the *Times* make this compromise. Loeb reminded him about the Ochs "no settlement" policy but said that he would discuss it with the *Times* executives. [29]

A few days later Loeb called Embry and reiterated that "because of a long standing policy of the owners of this corporation, which is a family owned affair, to not ever pay money in settlement of libel actions because of that being an encouragement to litigants to file suit for nuisance values, they could not permit the payment of money, by whatever name, to be made in a settlement in a libel action." However, he said, the executives might take a different stance when it came to forgiving the costs on the theory that it was not a payment of money "but a waiving or forgiveness of a debt."[30]

The *Times* agreed to this, and the *Sullivan* case ended. The transaction was consummated in September 1964.[31] Nachman wrote to Whitesell, "We have mourned enough about our fate in this case. I hope that we may be associated in a more profitable venture some day."[32] Nachman sent a check to Sullivan for $1,486.85. Sullivan, a man of limited means, had been paying for out-of-pocket expenses and was glad to recoup the sum. Nachman told him, "I need not restate our disappointment at the unfortunate end result of this case, but I am glad that we were able to get you out whole."[33]

Sullivan revolutionized the law of libel, as all recognized at the time. The decision was described as "stunning," "path breaking," and "a radical departure from understood law."[34] "Unquestionably," wrote legal scholar William Prosser, the ruling was "the greatest victory won by the defendants in the modern history of the law of torts."[35] An area of law that had been left to the states was now nationalized, with a constitutional floor established. No longer would localities have the power to censor the national press through libel suits, as Alabama had done. *Sullivan* made it easier for citizens to criticize government and public officials by diminishing officials' ability to recover damages for injury to their reputations. A public official suing for libel now had to prove the falsity of the statement and that it was made with actual malice. In one fell swoop, the Court radically shifted the centuries-old balance between the protection of free speech and the protection of reputation.

Sullivan represented a major alteration in the Court's thinking about the First Amendment. The decision seemed to offer a new paradigm for First Amendment jurisprudence, after years of government-friendly "ad hoc balancing" and unsatisfactory application of the "clear and present danger" rule. Under *Sullivan*, the First Amendment has a "central meaning"—the ban on seditious libel and the right of citizens to criticize their leaders. University of Chicago law professor Harry Kalven Jr., one of the era's leading First Amendment scholars, described *Sullivan* as "a happy revolution of free-speech doctrine."[36] Political theorist Alexander Meikeljohn called the decision an occasion for "dancing in the streets."[37] Declaring that freedom of speech is foundational to a political system based on sovereignty of the people, and that there is a "national commitment" to "uninhibited, robust, and wide-open" debate of public issues, Brennan's *Sullivan* opinion represented the most forceful and extensive articulation of the role of freedom of speech in democracy in the Supreme Court's history to that time.[38]

The Supreme Court saved the nation's newspaper of record from potential ruin. *Sullivan* not only reversed Sullivan's judgment but turned back the entire Southern "libel attack." It permitted the press to report fully and freely on the civil rights movement, coverage that could have been undermined if the next wave of libel suits had gone through the courts without *Sullivan's* protections.[39] As fears of segregationist "libel attacks" diminished in newsrooms, post-*Sullivan* media coverage of the civil rights movement was indeed "robust and wide-open." Media coverage of civil rights protests in Selma, Alabama, in 1965, and the segregationist backlash against those protests, helped to facilitate a national consensus on civil rights that led to the passage of the Voting Rights Act of 1965. Insofar as the success of the civil rights movement can be attributed, in significant part, to direct action protests and media coverage of those protests, *Sullivan* may have been one of the most consequential Supreme Court decisions for the advancement of the civil rights movement.[40]

· ·· · · · ·

The Court's adoption of the actual malice rule resulted, without doubt, from the extreme and idiosyncratic nature of the Alabama libel suits. Vindictive and retaliatory libel actions had certainly occurred in the past, but most libel suits did not involve a hostile community trying to quash criticism and literally to destroy a disfavored newspaper. The Supreme

Court likely would not have pursued its sweeping approach to libel if the first case it confronted in the field hadn't emerged from such dramatic facts. If the case had been more typical, the Court may well have imposed a negligence standard, the fault standard traditionally used in personal injury cases. But Brennan knew that a negligence standard wouldn't have protected the *Times*, which was admittedly careless in publishing the ad without checking the facts.

Sullivan's unusual procedural rules were also a result of the case's extreme circumstances. If the Court had simply reversed the case and sent it back to Alabama, as it would have under its typical procedures, the *Times* and the ministers would have been harassed, and the Alabama courts probably would have found for Sullivan again, requiring further appeals and expenses. To prevent that result, the Court boldly held that appellate judges must independently review the evidence to decide if it could support a finding of actual malice. To facilitate the conclusion that actual malice could not be shown in Sullivan's case, the Court adopted a rule that a finding of actual malice had to be supported by "clear and convincing" evidence, rather than the normal preponderance of evidence standard required to win a civil case. The Court concluded that the evidence was insufficient to support such a finding.

The *Sullivan* opinion was ambiguous in many respects. In particular, the opinion was unclear about what "actual malice" meant and how it would be proven, especially "reckless disregard of whether [a statement] was false or not." As clarified in subsequent cases, "reckless disregard" can only be shown by proving that the defendant "in fact entertained serious doubts as to the truth of his publication" or had a "high degree of awareness" of the statement's "probable falsity." This would mean that if reporters did not know of the truth or falsity of a statement—if they hadn't investigated a statement at all—they would not be in "reckless disregard" of its truth or falsity (an interpretation that was confirmed by the 1968 Supreme Court decision in *St. Amant v. Thompson*).[41] The actual malice rule encourages *not* investigating accuracy. The more journalists investigate, the more they may become aware of the possible falsity of a statement, making them more likely to be held liable for acting with actual malice.[42]

Technically, the Court did not have to adopt "actual malice" to dispose of Sullivan's case. There were less ambitious routes available, such as a limitation to recovery for proven economic loss. The $500,000 verdict was entered without a showing of any injury to Sullivan or harm to his livelihood. Probably the most obvious ground was to rule on the "of and concerning" point—that the advertisement said nothing about Sullivan. Yet many of the articles in the "libel attack" did mention the subjects by name, like Harrison Salisbury's articles on Bull Connor. A ruling on the "of and concerning" point would not have turned back the segregationist libel campaign.

Brennan also saw a First Amendment reason for adopting the actual malice standard, beyond protecting the *Times* and the ministers. Even under a negligence or carelessness standard, he implied, speakers would potentially censor themselves, since juries that were hostile toward the defendant could easily find negligent conduct if they wanted to. As such, the Court was willing to immunize false statements of fact carelessly made, to avoid "chilling" the expression of true statements. Freedom of speech needed "breathing room" to survive, Brennan wrote. *New York Times v. Sullivan* "protected falsity to protect truth."[43] This was the most controversial aspect of the opinion. It has been described as nothing less than a "bargain with the devil."[44]

.   .   .   .   .   .

New York Times v. Sullivan has survived in legal doctrine, history, and popular memory primarily as a case about freedom of speech. The civil rights context of the case has been diminished in most of the subsequent accounts of *Sullivan*. This reflects, in part, the way that the press memorialized *Sullivan*, as well as the *Times* and Wechsler's strategy of subduing the case's racial dimensions during the litigation. A reader of Brennan's opinion would learn more about the Sedition Act of 1798 than about the civil rights struggle from which the case emerged.

No one reading the headlines in 1964 could have ignored *Sullivan's* relation to the civil rights movement, however. *Sullivan* was the product of marches in the streets in Birmingham. It was the consequence of beaten and bloodied Freedom Riders and Bull Connor's attacks. It was the result of the slew of libel cases coming from the South and the threat they posed to the press. It was the vindication of a growing public consensus in favor of racial equality, which the Court's ruling reflected and reinforced. *Sullivan* was a freedom of speech case, but it was also a civil rights case and should be understood and memorialized as such. Harry Kalven Jr. described the decision as a reflection of "sociological reality," of "the pressures of the day created by the Negro protest movement."[45] The Supreme Court was "compelled by the political realities of the case to decide it in favor of the *Times*, yet equally compelled to seek high ground in justifying its result," he wrote.[46]

In many respects, the *Sullivan* decision followed more in line with the Court's rulings rejecting the South's efforts to interfere with the NAACP than its First Amendment decisions dealing with Communists. The Court's civil rights decisions based on the First Amendment encouraged it to begin the process of overturning precedents that had given the federal government a free hand to destroy radical groups during the Red Scare. Through its First Amendment cases involving the civil rights movement, the Court began to forge a general body of First Amendment law that was strongly protective of the right of dissenters to protest and to resist governmental intimidation.[47] Through cases like *Sullivan* and *NAACP v. Alabama*, the civil rights movement was a major force behind the expansion of First Amendment law.[48]

Sullivan itself was an easy case. L.B. Sullivan's reputation hadn't been harmed, the public interest in the ad was extremely compelling, and the libel suit was brought for obviously vindictive motives. Yet one might question the wisdom of *Sullivan's* actual malice rule when applied to more ordinary libel cases brought under less spectacular circumstances.[49] How should the First Amendment be weighed against reputation in a case in which a newspaper had grievously injured an official with careless falsehoods? Because of the unusual facts of *Sullivan*, the Court was not invited to take up that important question.

* * *

New York Times v. Sullivan proved to be just the beginning of the Supreme Court's intervention into libel law. In a series of cases decided between 1964 and 1974, known as *Sullivan's* "progeny," the Court extended *Sul-*

livan's protections and constitutionalized virtually all of the state law of defamation.

The first major extension was *Garrison v. Louisiana* (1964), which overturned the criminal libel conviction of a Louisiana district attorney and applied the actual malice rule to criminal libel.[50] Subsequent decisions defined *Sullivan*'s category of public official to include candidates for public office and public officials who appeared to have "control over the conduct of governmental affairs," no matter how lowly.[51]

Sullivan was rooted in traditional distaste for seditious libel. Yet the Court soon applied the *Sullivan* rule to situations having nothing to do with government or politics. In *Curtis Publishing Co. v. Butts*, and *Associated Press v. Walker*, cases from 1967 involving a football coach and a retired Army general, respectively (the latter was the Edwin Walker case brought over the Ole Miss rioting), *Sullivan*'s actual malice rule was applied to libel cases involving public figures as plaintiffs. Someone could be characterized as a "public figure" either by being someone who is pervasively famous (a celebrity, or politician, or other "household name," which the Court deemed a "general purpose public figure"), or by voluntarily injecting themselves into an important public controversy or even being drawn into such a controversy (a "limited purpose public figure").[52]

To justify this extension of *Sullivan*, the Court explained that public figures, including celebrities, often play a significant role in the determination of policies that are in the public interest, and therefore the public has an interest in knowing about their activities. In the modern era, "distinctions between governmental and private sectors are blurred," Warren wrote in his concurring opinion in *Associated Press*.[53] Furthermore, like public officials, public figures (at least those who voluntarily enter public affairs) can be said to have assumed the risk of criticism and harm to reputation, and thus have a lesser right to First Amendment protection. Public figures, moreover, have a public platform from which to respond to criticism, and the ability to engage in "self-help" or counter-speech in response to defamatory criticism.[54]

Gertz v. Robert Welch (1974) set the standard for libel cases involving "private figures," defined broadly as those who are not public figures. Under *Gertz*, private figures receive more protection for their reputations than public figures. States can impose liability in libel cases involving private figures under a negligence or carelessness standard. The plaintiff must show actual malice to receive punitive damages. The Court's rationale for greater protection for the reputations of private figures was that such individuals do not voluntarily expose themselves to the public and do not assume the risk of being defamed. Moreover, private figures are more vulnerable to injury because they do not (or did not, before the social media age) have a platform from which to respond to defamatory accusations.[55]

Under these "progeny" cases, private citizens who happen to "thrust themselves into the vortex" of a public controversy, to use the language of *Gertz*, have little ability to recover damages for defamatory falsehoods.[56] These "extension" cases arguably veered from the "central meaning" of the First Amendment established in *Sullivan*, the ban on seditious libel.[57] Brennan's clerk Steve Barnett once remarked that the actual malice rule "burst the bounds of its proper meaning" and became "a strange creature wandering the byways of the First Amendment with a life of its own."[58]

⋅   ⋅   ⋅

New York Times v. Sullivan permitted the press to take on, more boldly than in the past, its "fourth estate" role as guardian of the public's interest. In part because of *Sullivan's* protections, investigative reporting surged beginning in the 1970s and became an important check on government corruption and abuse.[59] Disclosures about the Vietnam War, and Watergate and related scandals, might have remained hidden if the press lacked the shield of *Sullivan*.[60] As a result of *Sullivan* and its progeny, there have been few efforts to weaponize libel law, and those that take place have not resulted in substantial damage awards.[61]

When the decision was issued, journalists celebrated *Sullivan* as an occasion for "dancing in the streets." Yet even within journalism, there were concerns that *Sullivan* might encourage careless reporting.[62] In journalism circles, there began to be discussion of a "social responsibility" theory of freedom of the press. Journalists would have to exercise restraint and follow professional ethics codes scrupulously, it was said, to resist the temptation to "abuse" their freedom.[63]

Critics allege that this state of affairs has come to pass. *Sullivan*, to some, has become a "license for shoddy journalism, transforming it into a profession where legal excuses are sought for falsehood."[64] *Sullivan's* "get out of jail free" card has fostered arrogance and journalistic irresponsibility, critics contend. Some have linked the worst excesses of journalism, including the rise of tabloids and talk radio, to the post-*Sullivan* emboldening of the press, although there is no evidence to suggest a direct connection. Twenty-first-century technologies seemingly enhance *Sullivan's* threat to the truth and to reputation. Even reputable media outlets, racing for clicks and confident of their *Sullivan* protections, tweet and post without confirming facts, writes Supreme Court justice Neil Gorsuch, who in 2021 argued that *Sullivan* and its extensions have created a "subsidy for published falsehood" that fosters the spread of misinformation online, prevents citizens from accessing facts they need to make informed political decisions, and undermines democracy.[65]

The assumption of *Sullivan* and the "progeny" cases that public figures can defend themselves through counter-speech has been proven to be untrue in an age when defamatory facts can be disseminated to the world with a click, claim Gorsuch and others.[66] Lies that go viral often can't be countered; in most cases, no amount of speech can undo the harm. Given that practically anyone can become a "public figure" under libel law by commenting on an issue on social media, *Sullivan* and its extensions leave a significant amount of injury unremedied and may discourage people from becoming involved in public affairs.[67]

Reputation remains an important personal interest that is essential to dignity and individual well-being. The protection of reputation also has social value; it is part of the protection of interpersonal respect and civility, values which are essential to meaningful public discourse and collective cooperation on social goals. To some critics, *New York Times v. Sullivan* has undermined the causes it tried to promote.[68]

* * * * *

What has been far less controversial than the "actual malice" rule is *Sullivan's* ringing tribute to the First Amendment. Although seditious libel ultimately did not endure as a paradigm in First Amendment law, *Times v. Sullivan* elevated free speech in the schema of American values, declaring it to be a preeminent value in a democratic society. *Sullivan* established the groundwork for an expansive body of free speech law that extended beyond libel. In *Time, Inc. v. Hill* (1967), the Court held that a family who brought an invasion of privacy claim based on a fictionalized account of their home invasion experience had to prove actual malice to recover.[69] *Hustler v. Falwell* (1988) held that constitutional libel standards applied in a case alleging that the publication of a parody constituted intentional infliction of emotional distress.[70] *Sullivan* enshrined a First Amendment commitment to protecting reporting on government, which can be seen in such historic opinions as *New York Times v. United States* (1971), the Pentagon Papers case, and *Richmond Newspapers v. Virginia* (1980), which declared a constitutional right of the press and the public to attend criminal trials.[71]

The "breathing space" concept has become central to First Amendment doctrine, and the phrase "uninhibited, robust, and wide-open debate" has acquired legal significance in its own right. It has been quoted in more than sixty Supreme Court opinions to justify the protection of speech in such fields as public employee speech, labor picketing, a candidate's right to appear on the ballot, door-to-door canvassing of voters, and the protest activities of a hate group.[72] That language, and idea of a "national commitment" to free expression, became important not only to legal doctrine but also to our "free speech tradition": the ideas and words that, along with court rulings, help give "actual meaning to freedom of expression."[73] *New York Times v. Sullivan* has come to stand for the proposition that the First Amendment "give(s) the benefit of the doubt to protecting rather than stifling speech."[74] This may be the most enduring legacy of the case. Few Supreme Court decisions have had greater impact on our First Amendment rights than *New York Times v. Sullivan*.

. . . . .

The libel suits over the "Heed Their Rising Voices" ad eventually and mercifully ended. The rest of the lawsuits were effectively nullified by the *Sullivan* decision. Yet the libel suits over the Harrison Salisbury "Fear and Hatred" articles were still ongoing after more than four years.

On July 14, 1964, former police lieutenant Joe Lindsey of Birmingham dropped his case against the *Times* based on *Sullivan*.[75] The other Birmingham plaintiffs did not. The remaining cases were consolidated by Judge Grooms in federal court. Grooms gave the other litigants the opportunity to amend their complaints to argue that the *Times* had shown actual malice. In September, Grooms threw out cases brought by the Birmingham mayor, Earl Morgan, and Commissioner James Waggoner. The Bull Connor case was allowed to stand because Connor was mentioned by name in Salisbury's article.[76]

The Connor case went to trial in the fall of 1964. The *Times* lawyers worked out a stipulation with the court that permitted Salisbury immunity while testifying, so that he wouldn't be arrested on the forty-two-count criminal libel indictment which was still standing in Bessemer. Beddow and Embry arranged for bail bondsmen to be available in case anything went wrong.[77]

Salisbury, Loeb, and Daly flew to the Tutwiler Hotel in Birmingham. They took three rooms with Salisbury's in the middle. They picked him up every morning, breakfasted together, and walked to court together. They dined together and went to bed at the same hour. This went on for three or four days. The lawyers didn't let him out of their sight. While Salisbury was testifying, word came to Judge Grooms that Bessemer sheriff's deputies were coming to arrest him.[78]

Grooms ordered federal marshals to surround the courtroom and advised the Bessemer district attorney that he would hold him in contempt. Reluctantly, the deputies turned back. Loeb and Daly told Salisbury nothing, fearing that it would upset him on the witness stand. Not until Salisbury was safely on the plane to New York did Loeb and Daly tell him why they had been so careful to guard him.[79]

James Simpson, an attorney for the former city officials, argued in his opening statement that the *Times* "maliciously" published the articles, which he said reflected on the good character and integrity of the former city leaders. Connor and Waggoner lost their city jobs when Birmingham dropped its city commission form of government. Connor contended that Salisbury's articles helped bring an end to the commission government and thus caused him to lose salary he would have made as police commissioner. "Salisbury came down here to stir up trouble and to get rid of Bull Connor," Connor's attorney said to the jury.[80] After eight and a half hours of deliberation, Connor won a $40,000 jury verdict against the *Times*.[81]

The *Times* appealed to the Fifth Circuit Court of Appeals. The case was finally disposed of on August 4, 1966, on the basis of the *Sullivan* rule. The court concluded that there was not "reckless disregard of the truth." The *Times* had "exhibited a high standard of reporting practices."[82]

Loeb wrote to Sulzberger on October 14, 1966. "I thought you would like to know that today we received a check of the clerk of the United States District Court for $3220.55, which represents payment by 'Bull' Connor of the bill of costs in connection with his libel suit," he wrote. "This is the final act in that series of cases which have been pending now for 6½ years."

> If you listen not too carefully you will hear me breathe the deepest sigh of relief in my life.
>
> It is wonderful to represent a client that will fight for a cause.
>
> Faithfully yours, Louis.[83]

Acknowledgments

I am grateful to the National Endowment for the Humanities for a Public Scholar Award to support the writing of this book, and to the Baldy Center for Law and Social Policy at the University at Buffalo for research support. Many thanks to James Goodale, former *New York Times* general counsel, for his insights on the impact of the libel suits on the *New York Times*; to Amy Nachman, for reminiscences and photos of Roland Nachman; to Miriam Trojanovic, for research assistance; and to John Schlegel, Fred Konefsky, Bob Slayton, and Caroline Funk for their encouragement and feedback.

Notes

1. New York Times Co. v. Sullivan, 376 U.S. 254, 267 (1964); Beauharnais v. Illinois, 343 U.S. 250, 266 (1952).

2. Harrison E. Salisbury, *Without Fear or Favor: The New York Times and Its Times* (New York: Times Books, 1980), 382; Louis Loeb, Memorandum to Harding F. Bancroft, Esq., December 2, 1960, New York Times Company Records, General Files, Manuscript and Archives Division, New York Public Library; John Herbers, "Libel Actions Ask Millions in South: 17 Suits by Public Officials Are Pending in Courts," *New York Times*, April 4, 1964, 12.

3. *Sullivan*, 376 U.S. at 270.

4. Henry Paul Monaghan, "A Legal Giant Is Dead," *Columbia Law Review* 100, no. 6 (2000): 1375. See also Lillian R. BeVier, "Intersection and Divergence: Some Reflections on the Warren Court, Civil Rights, and the First Amendment," *Washington and Lee Law Review* 59, no. 4 (2002): 1075; Floyd Abrams, "In Memoriam: William J. Brennan, Jr.," *Harvard Law Review* 111, no. 1 (1997): 18, 21; Frank B. Cross and James F. Spriggs II, "The Most Important (and Best) Supreme Court Opinions and Justices," *Emory Law Journal* 60, no. 2 (2010): 407, 432; Morton Horwitz, *The Warren Court and the Pursuit of Justice* (New York: Hill and Wang, 1998), 36; Jack M. Balkin and Sanford Levinson, "The Canons of Constitutional Law," *Harvard Law Review* 111, no. 963 (1998): 978; Geoffrey R.

Stone, "Justice Brennan and the Freedom of Speech: A First Amendment Odyssey," *University of Pennsylvania Law Review* 139 (1991): 1343.

5. "The Uninhibited Press, Fifty Years Later," *New York Times*, March 8, 2014.

6. *Sullivan*, 376 U.S. at 273.

7. Associated Press v. Walker, 388 U.S. 130 (1967); Curtis Publishing Co. v. Butts, 388 U.S. 130 (1967); Gertz v. Robert Welch, Inc., 418 U.S. 323 (1974).

8. See, e.g., David Logan, "Rescuing Our Democracy by Rethinking *New York Times Co. v. Sullivan*," *Ohio State Law Journal* 81, no. 5 (2020): 776; Berisha v. Lawson, 141 S. Ct. 2424, 2426 (2021) (Gorsuch, J., dissenting).

9. "Trump Renews Pledge to 'Take a Strong Look' at Libel Laws," *New York Times*, March 21, 2018.

10. Tah v. Global Witness Publishing, Inc., 991 F.3d 231, 251 (D.C. Cir. 2021) (Silberman, J., dissenting); McKee v. Cosby, 139 S. Ct. 675, 676 (2019) (Thomas, J., concurring).

11. Berisha v. Lawson, 141 S. Ct. at 2424–25, 2425–30 (Thomas, J., dissenting) (Gorsuch, J., dissenting).

12. Existing writings on *Sullivan*, including two book-length works, have addressed *Sullivan*'s context within the civil rights movement but have not explored, in depth, the case's impact on the civil rights movement, the defense strategies used by the Southern Christian Leadership Conference in the libel cases, or the legal strategies of the *New York Times* and the effects of the libel suits on press coverage of the civil rights movement.

The principal book-length writings on the history of *Sullivan* are *Make No Law: The Sullivan Case and the First Amendment* (New York: Vintage, 1991) by former *New York Times* Supreme Court reporter Anthony Lewis, and *New York Times v. Sullivan: Civil Rights, Libel Law, and the Free Press* by historians Kermit L. Hall and Melvin I. Urofsky (Lawrence: University of Kansas Press, 2011). Lewis's book focuses on the history of the First Amendment and the Supreme Court's deliberations in the case. The Hall and Urofsky book situates the *Sullivan* case within Alabama politics and the civil rights movement generally, but does not examine the SCLC's defense of the libel suits or make use of the archival records of the SCLC and the *New York Times*. Neither work investigates the lawsuits against the *Times* brought by officials in Birmingham, Alabama, lawsuits which were just as, if not more, threatening to the *Times* than the Montgomery cases, and that impacted the outcome of the *Sullivan* case.

Other notable book-length works addressing *Sullivan*'s relation to the civil rights movement include Aimee Edmondson's *In Sullivan's Shadow: The Use and Abuse of Libel Law during the Long Civil Rights Struggle* (Amherst: University of Massachusetts Press, 2019), describing segregationists' efforts to use libel law to impede civil rights reform both before and after *Sullivan*; Hank Klibanoff and Gene Roberts, *The Race Beat: The Press, the Civil Rights Struggle, and the Awakening of a Nation* (New York: Knopf, 2006), a history of press coverage of the civil rights movement, told from the perspective of reporters and editors; and the writings of Taylor Branch on Martin Luther King Jr. and the civil rights movement, *Parting the Waters: America in the King Years, 1954–63* (New York: Simon & Schuster, 1989), and *Pillar of Fire: America in the King Years, 1963–65* (New York: Simon & Schuster, 1999).

13. See, e.g., Richard A. Epstein, "Was *New York Times v. Sullivan Wrong?*" *University of Chicago Law Review* 53 (1986): 787; Frederick Schauer, "Do Cases Make Bad Law?" *University of Chicago Law Review* 73 (2006): 883, 902.

CHAPTER 1. ALL THE NEWS THAT'S FIT TO PRINT

1. The *Times* first used the title to describe itself in 1927, to entice libraries into archiving their paper. Colleen Mihal, "The New York Times," in *Encyclopedia of Journalism*, ed. Christopher H. Sterling (Thousand Oaks, CA: Sage, 2009), 1020.

2. Edwin Diamond, *Behind the Times: Inside the New* New York Times (Chicago: University of Chicago Press, 1995), 51.

3. "The Press: Without Fear or Favor," *Time*, May 9, 1950, 68.

4. Gay Talese, *The Kingdom and the Power: Behind the Scenes at the New York Times* (New York: World, 1969), 7.

5. "The Press: Without Fear or Favor," 74.

6. Andrew Porwancher, "Objectivity's Prophet: Adolph Ochs and the New York Times," *Journalism History* 36, no. 4 (2011): 186.

7. "Newspapers: A Family Enterprise," *Time*, June 28, 1963, 58.

8. "The Press: Without Fear or Favor," 74.

9. "The Press: Without Fear or Favor," 72.

10. Robert D. MacFadden, "150 Years and Counting," *New York Times*, November 14, 2001, H4.

11. Harrison E. Salisbury, *Without Fear or Favor: The New York Times and Its Times* (New York: Times Books, 1980), 28.

12. "Sulzberger Stressed News Coverage, Financial Strength, and Technical Progress," *New York Times*, December 12, 1968, 40.

13. Brooks Atkinson, "Arthur Hays Sulzberger," *New York Times*, December 15, 1968, E13.

14. "Sulzberger Stressed News Coverage," 40.

15. Atkinson, "Arthur Hays Sulzberger."

16. "Sulzberger Stressed News Coverage," 40.

17. "Sulzberger Stressed News Coverage."

18. Turner Catledge, "My Life and the Times," *New York Magazine*, January 11, 1971, 26.

19. "The Press: Without Fear or Favor," 68.

20. "The Press: Without Fear or Favor," 77.

21. David W. Dunlap, "Copy," *New York Times*, June 10, 2007.

22. "The Press: Without Fear or Favor," 68.

23. "The Press: Without Fear or Favor," 68.

24. "Changing Times," *Time*, June 28, 1948, 40.

25. Talese, *The Kingdom and the Power*, 33.

26. Salisbury, *Without Fear or Favor*, 5.

27. Dunlap, "Copy."

28. Salisbury, *Without Fear or Favor*, 6–7.

29. "Alfred A. Cook, 76, Law Expert, Dies," *New York Times*, January 3, 1950; Louis Loeb Oral History, New York Times Company Records, Oral History Files, Manuscripts and Archives Division, New York Public Library, 65.

30. Loeb Oral History, 224.

31. "Witty Pillar of the Bar," *New York Times*, July 13, 1967, 20; "Loeb Named Head of City Bar Group," *New York Times*, May 9, 1956, 34.

32. "Louis M. Loeb, 80; Was Times Counsel," *New York Times*, March 17, 1979, 24.

33. Paul Hoffman, *Lions in the Street: The Inside Story of the Great Wall Street Law Firms* (New York: Saturday Review Press, 1973), 98–99.

34. Salisbury, *Without Fear or Favor*, 125.

35. "Loeb Named Head of City Bar Group."

36. Loeb Oral History, 221, 224.

37. Jan Hoffman, "Oldest Law Firm Is Courtly, Loyal, and Defunct," *New York Times*, October 2, 1994, 33.

38. Clyde Haberman, "Publisher Who Transformed Times for a New Era," *New York Times*, September 30, 2012, 1.

39. Loeb Oral History, 222.

40. Loeb Oral History, 365.

41. Kimmerle v. New York Evening Journal, 186 N.E. 217, 218 (N.Y. 1933).

42. William Blake Odgers, *A Digest of the Law of Libel and Slander with the Evidence, Procedure, Practice, and Precedents of Pleadings, Both in Civil and Criminal Cases*, 3rd ed. (London: Stevens and Sons, 1896), 21.

43. *Restatement of the Law, Second, Torts 2d.* (St. Paul, MN: American Law Institute, 1965): § 559.

44. William Arthur and Ralph Crosman, *The Law of Newspapers* (New York: McGraw Hill, 1940), 72.

45. John Kelly, "Criminal Libel and Free Speech," *Kansas Law Review* 6, no. 3 (1958): 296.

46. Alfred Kelly, "Constitutional Liberty and the Law of Libel," *American Historical Review* 74, no. 2 (1968): 433.

47. Richard Donnelly, "The Right of Reply: An Alternative to an Action for Libel," *Virginia Law Review* 34, no. 8 (1948): 870.

48. *Sullivan*, 376 U.S. at 267.

49. Cooper v. Greeley & McElrath, 1 Denio 347, 365 (N.Y. Sup. 1845).

50. Van Vechten Veeder, "The History and Theory of the Law of Defamation, II," *Columbia Law Review* 4, no. 1 (1904): 33.

51. Quoted in Karen Haltunnen, *Confidence Men and Painted Women: A Study of Middle-Class Culture in America, 1830–1870* (New Haven, CT: Yale University Press, 1986), 47.

52. "The Right to a Good Name," *Outlook*, December 26, 1908, 891.

53. George Norris, "Forty Years with the New York Times: Libel and Other Miscellaneous Cases," 6, Box 196, Folder 17, Arthur Hays Sulzberger Papers, Manuscripts and Archives Division, New York Public Library.

54. To Ralph Beaver Strassburger, November 26, 1935, Box 196, Folder 17, Arthur Hays Sulzberger Papers.

55. "Ochs Policy on Libel," *Times Talk*, August 1951, published in *Nieman Reports*, October 1951, 29.

56. "Ochs Policy on Libel," 29.

57. Ochs to Alfred Cook, May 9, 1922, Box 86, Folder 6, Adolph S. Ochs Papers, Manuscripts and Archives Division, New York Public Library.

58. "George Norris, Lawyer, 81, Dies," *New York Times*, May 4, 1966, 47.

59. Norris, "Forty Years," 6.

60. "Ochs Policy on Libel," 30.

61. See Norris, "Forty Years."

62. Norris, "Forty Years," 1.

63. Norris, "Forty Years," 10.

CHAPTER 2. LIBEL AND THE PRESS

1. See Samuel Merrill, *Newspaper Libel: A Handbook for the Press* (Ticknor, 1888).

2. Edward W. Scripps, *I Protest: Selected Disquisitions of E.W. Scripps*, ed. Oliver Knight (Madison: University of Wisconsin Press, 1966), 88.

3. Samantha Barbas, "The Press and Libel before *New York Times v. Sullivan*," *Columbia Journal of Law & the Arts* 44, no. 4 (2021): 523.

4. Frederic Hudson, *Journalism in the United States* (New York: Harper, 1873), 74.

5. "These Jurors Set a Good Example," *The Fourth Estate: A Weekly Newspaper for Publishers, Advertisers, Advertising Agents and Allied Interests*, March 2, 1901, 11.

6. Smith v. Times Pub. Co., 178 Pa. 481, 486 (Pa. 1897).

7. *Proceedings of the Michigan Press Association at the 22nd Annual Meeting* (Bellevue, MI: Gazette Print, 1889), 75.

8. See Timothy W. Gleason, *The Watchdog Concept: The Press and the Courts in Nineteenth-Century America* (Iowa City: Iowa State Press, 1990).

9. Coleman v. MacLennan, 98 P. 281, 282, 291 (Kan. 1908).

10. Henry Schofield, *Essays on Constitutional Law and Equity, and Other Subjects* (Boston: Chipman Law, 1921), 570.

11. Van Vechten Veeder, "Freedom of Public Discussion," *Harvard Law Review* 23, no. 6 (1910): 419.

12. Burt v. Advertiser Newspaper Co., 154 Mass. 238, 243 (1891).

13. W.G. Nye, "The Libel Epidemic," *Printer's Ink*, February 17, 1909, 28.

14. David L. Lewis, *The Public Image of Henry Ford: An American Folk Hero and His Company* (Detroit: Wayne State University Press, 1987), 106.

15. "Roosevelt, Winning Libel Suit, Is Awarded 6 Cents," *San Francisco Call*, June 1, 1913, 1; "Henry Ford Files $1,000,000 Libel Suit; Resents Chicago Tribune's Charge of Anarchy in Connection with Enlistment of His Employees," *New York Times*, September 8, 1916.

16. See Stephen Banning, "The Professionalization of Journalism: A Nineteenth-Century Beginning," *Journalism History* 24, no. 4 (1999): 157–64; Michael Schudson, *Discovering the News: A Social History of American Newspapers* (New York: Basic Books, 1978), 7–9, 152–59.

17. H.L. Mencken, *Newspaper Days: 1899–1906* (New York: Alfred A. Knopf, 1940), 41.

18. By the 1930s, half of the major New York newspapers used lawyers as "censors." M. Marvin Berger, "Detecting Libel before It Appears," *Editor and Publisher*, May 29, 1937, 7.

19. Joseph Ruffner, "Libel," *The Washington Newspaper*, January 1922, 101.

20. Frank Thayer, "The Changing Libel Scene," *Wisconsin Law Review* 1943 (1943): 333.

21. Kathy Roberts Forde, *Masson v. New Yorker and the First Amendment* (Amherst: University of Massachusetts Press, 2008), 59.

22. Paul L. Murphy, *The Meaning of Freedom of Speech: First Amendment Freedoms from Wilson to FDR* (Westport, CT: Greenwood, 1972), 276.

23. David Riesman, "Democracy and Defamation: Fair Game and Fair Comment I," *Columbia Law Review* 42, no. 7 (1942): 1086.

24. Zechariah Chafee, *Government and Mass Communications: A Report from the Commission on Freedom of the Press* (Chicago: University of Chicago Press, 1947), 103.

25. Thomas Emerson, "Toward a General Theory of the First Amendment," *Yale Law Journal* 72 (1963): 909.

26. Sedition Act of 1918 (Pub.L. 65-150, 40 Stat. 553, enacted May 16, 1918).

27. Abrams v. United States, 250 U.S. 616, 630 (1919).

28. Whitney v. California, 274 U.S. 357, 375 (1927).

29. Gitlow v. New York, 268 U.S. 652, 666 (1925).

30. Stromberg v. California, 283 U.S. 359, 369 (1931).

31. Palko v. Connecticut 302 U.S. 319, 327 (1937).

32. Near v. Minnesota, 283 U.S. 697, 720 (1931).

33. Grosjean v. American Press Co., 297 U.S. 233, 250 (1936).

34. See Herndon v. Lowry, 301 U.S. 242 (1937); Cantwell v. Connecticut, 310 U.S. 296 (1940); Bridges v. California, 314 U.S. 252 (1941).

35. See Harry Kalven Jr., "The Metaphysics of the Law of Obscenity," *1960 Supreme Court Review* 1 (1960): 10.

36. Chaplinsky v. New Hampshire, 315 U.S. 568, 572 (1942).

37. Beauharnais v. Illinois, 343 U.S. 250, 266 (1952).

38. Brief for Respondent in Opposition at 45–47, *Sullivan*, 376 U.S. 254 (1964).

39. Harry Kalven Jr., "The Law of Defamation and the First Amendment," in *Conference on the Arts, Publishing, and the Law* (University of Chicago Law School Conference Series No. 10, 1952), 3.

CHAPTER 3. THE PAPER CURTAIN

1. Salisbury, *Without Fear or Favor*, 125.

2. Catledge, "My Life and The Times," 218–19.

3. Gay Talese, *Kingdom and the Power*, 147; "Catledge, Turner," in *The Scribner Encyclopedia of American Lives*, vol. 1, *1981–1985*, ed Kenneth T. Jackson, et al. (New York: Charles Scribner's Sons, 1998), 137–39.

4. See Michael J. Klarman, *From Jim Crow to Civil Rights: The Supreme Court and the Struggle for Racial Equality* (New York: Oxford University Press, 2004), 123.

5. Salisbury, *Without Fear or Favor*, 352.

6. "Race in the News," *New York Times*, August 11, 1946, 80.

7. David R. Davies, "An Industry in Transition: Major Trends in American Daily Newspapers, 1945–1965" (PhD diss., University of Alabama, 1997), chap. 6.

8. "John Popham, 89, Dies; Journalist Was Noted for Perceptive Coverage of South," *New York Times*, December 14, 1999, 13.

9. "All God's Chillun," *New York Times*, May 18, 1954, 28.

10. See Don Rodney Vaughan, "The New York Times and the Civil Rights Movement, 1954–1964" (PhD diss., University of Southern Mississippi, 2006).

11. John Popham, "Mississippi Jury Acquits 2," *New York Times*, September 24, 1955, 1.

12. Wayne Phillips, "Montgomery Is Stage for a Tense Drama," *New York Times*, March 4, 1956, E6.

13. Catledge, "My Life and The Times," 219.

14. "Report on the South: A Summary of the New York Times Survey: Extent to Which Integration Has Been Achieved," *New York Times*, March 18, 1956, 189.

15. Lucas A. Powe Jr., *The Warren Court and American Politics* (Cambridge, MA: Belknap Press, 2002), 61.

16. Powe, *The Warren Court and American Politics*, 68; on the Citizens' Councils, see Numan V. Bartley, *The Rise of Massive Resistance: Race and Politics in the South During the 1950's* (Baton Rouge: Louisiana State University Press, 1999), chap. 6.

17. Salisbury, *Without Fear or Favor*, 360.

18. Salisbury, *Without Fear or Favor*, 360.

19. Dennis Hevesi, "Claude Sitton, 89, Acclaimed Civil Rights Reporter, Dies," *New York Times*, March 11, 2015, A22.

20. Salisbury, *Without Fear or Favor*, 360.

21. Roberts and Klibanoff, *The Race Beat*, 191.

22. David E. Sumner, *The Magazine Century: American Magazines since 1900* (New York: Peter Lang, 2010), 117.

23. William H. Young, *The 1950s: American Popular Culture through History* (Westport, CT: Greenwood Press, 2004), 153.

24. Klarman, *From Jim Crow to Civil Rights*, 429.

25. Klarman, *From Jim Crow to Civil Rights*, 429.

26. Libel Defense|Resource Center, *Heed Their Rising Voices: A Tribute to Justice Brennan* (1993), 46.

27. Julian Bond, "The Media and the Movement: Looking Back from the Southern Front," in *Media, Culture, and the Modern African American Freedom Struggle*, ed. Brian Ward (Gainesville: University Press of Florida, 2001), 17.

28. Quoted in Angie Maxwell, *The Indicted South: Public Criticism, Southern Inferiority, and the Politics of Whiteness* (Chapel Hill: University of North Carolina, 2014), 3.

29. See Thomas C. Leonard, "Antislavery, Civil Rights, and Incendiary Material," in *Media and Revolution*, ed. Jeremy D. Popkin, (Lexington: University Press of Kentucky, 2014), 123.

30. David Wallace, *Massive Resistance and Media Suppression: The Segregationist Response to Dissent during the Civil Rights Movement* (El Paso: LFB Scholarly, 2013), 37.

31. David Wallace, "Piercing the Paper Curtain: The Southern Editorial Response to National Civil Rights Coverage," *American Journalism* 33, no. 4 (2016): 410.

32. Harold Lord Varney "Why Pick on Dixie?" *American Mercury*, July 1957, 1, 13.

33. William D. Workman, *The Case for the South* (New York: Devin-Adair, 1960), 63. This claim was not entirely groundless; some Northern newspapers didn't publish news of racial conflagrations in the North for fear of inflaming racial tensions. See Joseph Crespino, "Mississippi as Metaphor: Civil Rights, the South, and the Nation in Historical Imagination," in *Myth of Southern Excep-*

tionalism, ed. Matthew D. Lassiter and Joseph Crespino (New York: Oxford University Press, 2009), 109.

34. Tom Waring, "Paper Curtain over the South," *Charleston News and Courier*, October 10, 1955.

35. "The Paper Curtain," *Times and Democrat (Orangeburg)*, December 28, 1959, 4.

36. "Trouble in the Mixiecrats' Citadel," *Talladega Daily Home News*, February 18, 1957, 2.

37. Wallace, "Piercing the Paper Curtain," 421.

38. "The Abolitionist Hellmouths," *Montgomery Advertiser*, April 17, 1960, 14.

39. "Alarming Picture from NY Times," *Madisonville Messenger*, September 30, 1959, 6.

40. "Dishonest Journalism," *Talladega Daily Home News*, February 19, 1957, 2.

41. "Lifelong Damage Claimed by Caldwell in Libel Suit," *Miami News*, March 24, 1946, 1.

42. Jack E. Davis, "'Whitewash' in Florida: The Lynching of Jesse James Payne and Its Aftermath," *Florida Historical Quarterly* 68, no. 3 (1990): 293; Edmondson, *In Sullivan's Shadow*, 36–39.

43. "Public Opinion," *Tallahassee Democrat*, March 5, 1946, 4.

44. Tameka Bradley Hobbs, *Democracy Abroad, Lynching at Home: Racial Violence in Florida* (Gainesville: University Press of Florida, 2015), 186; "Caldwell Given $237,500 Verdict Against Collier's," *Tallahassee Democrat*, March 11, 1948, 1.

45. Snickered the *Tallahassee Democrat*, "Our neighbors earnestly hope that we will become more tolerant and less prejudiced. We return their good wishes with the kindly hope that they learn their own lesson." See "Settlement of the Caldwell-Collier's Suit," *Tallahassee Democrat*, August 26, 1949, 6.

46. "Folsom, Aides File $6 Mill Libel Suit," *Troy Messenger*, October 30, 1950, 1.

47. "Author of Sin Story Identified as Minister," *Alabama Journal*, July 19, 1957, 1.

48. "City Witnesses Deny Magazine's Veracity," *Alabama Journal*, November 28, 1957, 2.

49. "Ending City Officials' Suit," *Montgomery Advertiser*, January 26, 1958, 1.

50. Harold Cross, "Current Libel Trends," *Nieman Reports*, January 1951, 2.

CHAPTER 4. HEED THEIR RISING VOICES

1. Claude Sitton, "Negro Sitdowns Stir Fear of Wider Unrest in South," *New York Times*, February 15, 1960, 1.

2. "Greensboro Lunch Counter Sit-In," Library of Congress, https://www.loc.gov/exhibits/odyssey/educate/lunch.html

3. Daniel H. Pollitt, "Dime Store Demonstrations: Events and Legal Problems of First Sixty Days," *Duke Law Journal* 1960, no. 3 (1960): 318.

4. Robert Heinrich, "Montgomery: The Civil Rights Movement and Its Legacies" (PhD diss., Brandeis University, 2008), 1, 21.

5. James Baldwin, "The Dangerous Road before Martin Luther King," *Harper's Magazine*, February 1961, 35.

6. Wesley Phillips Newton, *Montgomery in the Good War: Portrait of a Southern City, 1939–1946* (Tuscaloosa: University of Alabama Press, 2000), 4.

7. "Montgomery: Testing Ground," *New York Times*, December 16, 1956, 5.

8. "Montgomery: The Civil Rights Movement and Its Legacies," 29.

9. King, *Stride Toward Freedom: The Montgomery Story* (New York: Harper & Row, 1986), 185.

10. J. Mills Thornton, III, *Dividing Lines: Municipal Politics and the Struggle for Civil Rights in Montgomery, Birmingham, and Selma* (Tuscaloosa: University of Alabama Press, 2002), 112.

11. Philip Lee, "The Case of Dixon v. Alabama: From Civil Rights to Students' Rights and Back Again," *Teachers College Record* 116 (2014): 2.

12. "City Leaders Issue Words of Warning," *Montgomery Advertiser*, February 26, 1960, 1; Bernard Lee affidavit, February 1961, 2, Abernathy v. Patterson, Box 787, Folder 7, American Civil Liberties Union Papers.

13. D. Hines and Bob Ingram, "Expel Negro Sitdowners, College Told: Alabama State President Given Mandate in Governor's Office," *Montgomery Advertiser*, February 26, 1960, 1, 2.

14. Bernard Lee affidavit, 2–3.

15. Bernard Lee affidavit, 3–4; "Press Stirs Sullivan Ire on Coverage," *Montgomery Advertiser*, March 1, 1960, 1.

16. "Negroes 'Visit' State Capitol," *Alabama Journal*, March 1, 1960, 1.

17. "Alabama Expels 9 Negro Students: Governor Calls Action Needed to Prevent Bloodshed—Nashville Arrests 50," *New York Times*, March 3, 1960, 15.

18. Bernard Lee affidavit, 6.

19. "Sullivan Statement on Capitol Meeting," *Montgomery Advertiser*, March 6, 1960, 1.

20. Nat Hentoff, "Our Far-Flung Correspondents: A Conversation in Alabama," *New Yorker*, July 16, 1960, 48.

21. Claude Sitton, "Negroes Dispersed in Alabama March," *New York Times*, March 7, 1960, 1.

22. Hentoff, "Our Far-Flung Correspondents," 48.

23. "Police Thwart Negro Services at Capitol," *Montgomery Advertiser*, March 7, 1960, 1; Claude Sitton, "Negroes Dispersed in Alabama March," *New York Times*, March 7, 1960, 1, 14.

24. "Capital Police Head Asks Negro College Closing," *Selma Times-Journal*, March 10, 1960, 1.

25. "King Sends Appeal to Ike," *Alabama Journal*, March 10, 1960, 1.

26. "King Sends Appeal to Ike," 1; "Alabama Protest Sends 37 to Jail: Police Halt a Demonstration on Montgomery Campus—Flogging Investigated," *New York Times*, March 9, 1960, 19.

27. "Everywhere: Tension," *U.S. News and World Report*, March 21, 1960, 74.

28. "Capital Profile," *Montgomery Advertiser*, October 4, 1959, 5; "Sullivan Stayed in Headlines Despite Quiet Nature," *Montgomery Advertiser*, June 13, 1977, 11.

29. "Sullivan Stayed in Headlines despite Quiet Nature," 11.

30. Brief for Petitioner at 10, *Sullivan*, 376 U.S. 254 (1964).

31. Thornton, *Dividing Lines*, 109.

32. Advertisement, *Alabama Journal*, February 27, 1959, 14.

33. Advertisement, *Alabama Journal*, February 20, 1959, 23.

34. Thornton, *Dividing Lines*, 110.

35. William MacDonald interview, Kermit Hall Papers.

36. "Battle against Tradition: Martin Luther King Jr.," *New York Times*, March 21, 1956, 28.

37. Branch, *Parting the Waters*, 203.

38. Brief for Petitioner at 9–10, *Sullivan*, 376 U.S. 254 (1964); "King Arrested for Loitering in Montgomery," King Institute, Stanford University, https://king institute.stanford.edu/encyclopedia/king-arrested-loitering-montgomery

39. Aldon Morris, *The Origins of the Civil Rights Movement: Black Communities Organizing for Change* (New York: Free Press, 1984), 87–99.

40. Claude Sitton, "Dr. King, Symbol of the Segregation Struggle," *New York Times* Magazine, January 22, 1961, SM10.

41. Adam Fairclough, "The Preachers and the People," *Journal of Southern History* 52, no. 3 (1986): 433. On the history of the SCLC, see Adam Fairclough, *To Redeem the Soul of America: The Southern Christian Leadership Conference and Martin Luther King, Jr.* (Athens: University of Georgia Press, 2001); Eugene Walker, *A History of the Southern Christian Leadership Conference, 1955-1965* (Durham, NC: Duke University Press, 1978).

42. Fairclough, "The Preachers and the People," 435.

43. Branch, *Parting the Waters*, 282.

44. Leonard Rubinowitz, "Martin Luther King's Perjury Trial," *Indiana Journal of Law and Social Equality* 5, no. 2 (April 2017): 240.

45. Branch, *Parting the Waters*, 277.

46. Emilie Raymond, *Stars for Freedom: Hollywood, Black Celebrities, and the Civil Rights Movement* (Seattle: University of Washington Press, 2015), 77–82.

47. King to Jackie Robinson, June 19, 1960, in *The Papers of Martin Luther King, Jr.*, vol. 5, *Threshold of a New Decade, January 1959–December 1960* (Berkeley: University of California Press, 2005), 476.

48. "Quaker Believes Jails Will Advance Cause of Negroes," *Decatur Daily*, April 11, 1960, 3.

49. Branch, *Parting the Waters*, 168–73; on Rustin, see John D'Emilio, *Lost Prophet: The Life and Times of Bayard Rustin* (New York: Free Press, 2010).

50. "Fund to Defend King Established," *Atlanta Daily World*, March 6, 1960.

51. "Raise $20,000 for Southwide Fund," *New York Amsterdam News*, March 19, 1960, 4.

52. "M.L. King Fund Grows," *New York Amsterdam News*, March 5, 1960, 30.

53. See Morris, *Origins of the Civil Rights Movement*, 227, on newspaper ads as a major source of contributions to the SCLC from liberal Northern whites.

54. Advertisement, "Heed Their Rising Voices," *New York Times*, March 29, 1960, 25.

55. Advertisement, "Heed Their Rising Voices."

56. "Amendment XV," *New York Times*, March 19, 1960, 20. The Civil Rights Act provided for federal inspection of local voter registration rolls and penalties for voter obstruction.

57. Lewis, *Make No Law*, 5.

58. Brief for Petitioner at 16–17, *Sullivan*, 376 U.S. 254 (1964).

59. Brief for Petitioner at 15, *Sullivan*.

60. Monroe Green, "Censorship of Advertising in Newspapers," *Advertising Agency and Advertising & Selling*, July 1952, 66.

61. "New York Times Advertising Acceptability Standards," April 1, 1960, Alabama Department of History and Archives.

62. "New York Times Jubilee Supplement," *New York Times*, September 18, 1901; Meyer Berger, *The Story of the New York Times* (New York: Simon and Schuster, 1951), 271; Andrew Porchwancher, "Objectivity's Prophet: Adolph S. Ochs and *The New York Times*, 1896–1935," *Journalism History* 36, no. 4 (2011): 190.

63. "New York Times Advertising Acceptability Standards."

64. Brief for Petitioner at 16–17, *Sullivan*.

65. Notes contained in Box 1, M. Roland Nachman Jr. Records from Times v. Sullivan and Related Cases, Alabama Department of Archives and History.

66. Handwritten notes contained in Box 1, Roland Nachman Records; Advertisement, "Heed Their Rising Voices."

67. Jack Newfield, *Somebody's Gotta Tell It: The Upbeat Memoir of a Working-Class Journalist* (New York: St. Martin's Press, 2002), 53.

CHAPTER 5. MONTGOMERY V. THE NEW YORK TIMES

1. *Sullivan*, 376 U.S. at 305n3.

2. "How Richard Nixon's Downfall Started in Our Newsroom," *Montgomery Advertiser*, April 22, 1979, 5.

3. "How Richard Nixon's Downfall Started in Our Newsroom," 5.

4. Katherine Q. Seelye, "Ray Jenkins, Newspaperman Who Covered Civil Rights Era, Dies at 89," *New York Times*, March 23, 2020; Charlotte Grimes, "Civil Rights and the Press," *Journalism Studies* 6, no. 1 (2007): 130.

5. "Liberals Appeal for Funds to Defend M.L. King," *Alabama Journal*, April 5, 1960, 9.

6. Roberts and Klibanoff, *The Race Beat*, 229.

7. "Tell It Not in Gath," *Time*, April 23, 1956, 62.

8. Branch, *Parting the Waters*, 152; Roberts and Klibanoff, *The Race Beat*, 122.

9. On Hall, see Daniel Webster Hollis III, *An Alabama Newspaper Tradition: Grover Hall and the Hall Family* (Tuscaloosa: University of Alabama Press, 1983).

10. King, *Stride Toward Freedom*, 176.

11. Branch, *Parting the Waters*, 152, 183.

12. "Tell It Not in Gath," *Time*, April 23, 1956, 62.

13. "Published in Askelon," *Montgomery Advertiser*, May 11, 1956, 4.

14. This was a reference from the Bible to David's order not to let the Philistines know of King Saul's death, lest the enemy gloat.

15. "Tell It Not in Gath," *Time*, April 23, 1956, 62.

16. "House Commends Advertiser Drive," *Alabama Journal*, April 3, 1956, 1.

17. "Militant Editor Honored," *Clarke County Democrat*, April 25, 1957, 4.

18. Roberts and Klibanoff, *The Race Beat*, 211.

19. "Hypocrisy of North Incenses Southerner," *U.S. News & World Report*, February 24, 1956, 47–48.

20. "The Sidewalks of New York," *Montgomery Advertiser*, February 2, 1958, 8.

21. "Will They Purge Themselves?" *Montgomery Advertiser*, April 7, 1960, 4.

22. "Will They Purge Themselves?"

23. Susan Lindley Smith, "Casual Conversation or Constitutional Conspiracy: Controverting the Origins of *New York Times v. Sullivan*," *Free Speech Yearbook* 42, no. 1 (2012): 10.

24. Justice Hugo Black would assert that the record of the case "lends support to an inference that instead of being damaged, Sullivan's political, social, and financial prestige has been enhanced by the Times' publication." *Sullivan*, 376 U.S. at 294.

25. Smith, "Casual Conversation," 10.

26. Smith, "Casual Conversation," 10.

27. On Jews in Montgomery in the 1950s, see Clive Webb, "Closing Ranks: Montgomery, Jews and Civil Rights, 1954–1960," *Journal of American Studies* 32, no. 3 (1998): 463–81.

28. "Nachman Won before He Lost," *Montgomery Advertiser*, December

9, 2015, A8; Bruce Weber, "M. Roland Nachman, Lawyer in Times v. Sullivan Libel Case, Dies at 91," *New York Times*, December 5, 2015; "An Oral History of M. Roland Nachman," https://www.youtube.com/watch?v=ZlPEXFGIx-M.

29. Author's interview with Amy Nachman, August 2020.

30. Author's interview with Amy Nachman, August 2020.

31. "An Oral History of M. Roland Nachman," https://www.youtube.com/watch?v=ZlPEXFGIx-M.

32. "Jury Awards Davis $67,500 Verdict from Jet Magazine," *Alabama Journal*, May 9, 1959, 9.

33. Kermit Hall, "'Lies, Lies, Lies': The Origins of *New York Times Co. v. Sullivan*," *Communication Law and Policy* 9, no. 4 (2004): 415.

34. *Sullivan*, 376 U.S. at 267.

35. Nachman interview, September 1990, Box II, Anthony Lewis Papers, Library of Congress.

36. Loeb to Parks, April 15, 1960, New York Times Company Records, General Files.

37. Ala. Code, tit. 7, § 913 (1940) (Recomp. 1958).

38. L.B. Sullivan to Fred Shuttlesworth, March 8, 1960, contained in Box 1, Roland Nachman Records.

39. "Administration Charges 'Lies,'" *Huntsville Times*, April 8, 1960, 3.

40. "Gallion Plans to Take Action on Times Ad," *Alabama Journal*, April 3, 1960, 19.

41. "Patterson Advised to Sue N.Y. Times," *Birmingham News*, April 21, 1960, 4.

42. "Retraction by Times Asked on Dr. King Ad," *New York Times*, April 9, 1960, 12.

43. "Unworthy Newspaper Policy," *Alabama Journal*, April 18, 1960, 4.

44. Garst to Mr. Neuhut, April 15, 1960, New York Times Company Records, General Files.

45. McKee to Garst, April 14, 1960, New York Times Company Records, General Files.

46. Brief for Petitioner at 18–19, *Sullivan*, 376 U.S. 254 (1964).

47. Brief for Petitioner at 3, *Sullivan*.

48. Brief for Petitioner at 3, *Sullivan*.

49. Undated, Box 1, Roland Nachman Records.

50. Ala. Code tit. 7 § 199(1) (1940) (Recomp. 1958).

51. "The Alabama Actions against the Times," Bulletin of the American Society of Newspaper Editors, contained in Turner Catledge Papers, Box 2.

52. According to legal historian Christopher Schmidt, this "race-conscious use of race-neutral law" represented a new strategy used by segregationists. As Schmidt observes, segregationists by 1960 were increasingly waging their battles against the civil rights movement through laws that said nothing about race—

laws regulating disorderly conduct, trespass, disturbing the peace, and even tax laws: "Increasingly, Southern leaders came to see direct legal methods of segregation as ineffective and costly. These forms of explicit discrimination cast the South in an unfavorable light; in the eyes of most Americans outside the South, racial discrimination as a formal state policy was no longer tolerable. For those dedicated to blocking or limiting the impact of the Civil Rights Movement, a new approach was needed." See Christopher W. Schmidt, *"New York Times v. Sullivan* and the Legal Attack on the Civil Rights Movement," *Alabama Law Review* 66, no. 2 (2014): 295.

53. William Workman, "Montgomery Press Strikes Back at Northern Press Propaganda," *Greenville* (South Carolina) *News*, April 24, 1960, 42.

54. Lucille Woodham, "Jus Ramblin," *Florala News*, April 21, 1960, 6.

55. Loeb Oral History, 322.

56. Loeb Oral History, 322.

57. "Former Supreme Court Justice Dies," *Montgomery Advertiser*, January 14, 1992, 4.

58. Eric Embry interview, June 4, 1990, Anthony Lewis Papers.

CHAPTER 6. BIRMINGHAM V. THE NEW YORK TIMES

1. Gay Talese, *The Kingdom and the Power*, 113–14.

2. "Harrison Evans Salisbury," in *The Scribner Encyclopedia of American Lives*, vol. 3, *1991–1993*, ed. Kenneth T. Jackson et al. (New York: Charles Scribner's Sons, 2001): 472; "Harrison E. Salisbury, 84, Author and Reporter, Dies," *New York Times*, July 7, 1993, D19.

3. "Harrison Evans Salisbury," 472.

4. Harrison Salisbury, *Disturber of the Peace: Memoirs of a Foreign Correspondent* (London: Unwin Hyman, 1989), 204.

5. Salisbury, "Fear and Hatred Grip Birmingham," *New York Times*, April 12, 1960, 28.

6. Salisbury, *A Time of Change*, 50.

7. Salisbury, *A Time of Change*, 42, 49.

8. Salisbury, *A Time of Change*, 49–50.

9. Salisbury, *A Time of Change*, 51.

10. "Birmingham: Integration's Hottest Crucible," *Time*, December 15, 1958.

11. J. Mills Thornton, *Dividing Lines, Municipal Politics and the Struggle for Civil Rights in Montgomery, Birmingham, and Selma* (University of Alabama Press, 2002), 231–32.

12. Salisbury, *A Time of Change*, 51.

13. Salisbury, "Fear and Hatred Grip Birmingham," 28.

14. Salisbury, *A Time of Change*, 53.

15. Salisbury, "Fear and Hatred Grip Birmingham," 28.

16. "Fear and Hatred Grip Birmingham," 28.

17. "Fear and Hatred Grip Birmingham," 28.

18. "Race Issues Shakes Alabama Structure," *New York Times*, April 13, 1960, 1, 33.

19. Salisbury, *Without Fear or Favor*, 381.

20. Diane McWhorter, *Carry Me Home: Birmingham, Alabama: The Climactic Battle of the Civil Rights Revolution* (New York: Simon and Schuster, 2001), 158.

21. Scribner Christopher MacGregor, *Renewing Birmingham, Federal Funding and the Promise of Change* (Athens: University of Georgia Press, 2002), 94–95.

22. McWhorter, *Carry Me Home*, 158.

23. "A City Gripped by Fear, Hatred," *Birmingham News*, April 13, 1960, 10.

24. Jonathan Foster, *Stigma Cities: The Reputation and History of Birmingham, San Francisco, and Las Vegas* (Norman: University of Oklahoma Press, 2018), 40.

25. "A Grave Disservice," *Birmingham News*, April 15, 1960, 14.

26. "Times' Attack on Alabama Stirs Statewide Indignation," *Birmingham News*, April 25, 1960, 12.

27. Letters contained in Box 16, Turner Catledge Papers.

28. "Suit Planned by Commission against Times," *Birmingham News*, April 16, 1960, 1.

29. "Paper Will Check Salisbury Story," *Selma Times*, April 27, 1960, 1.

30. "The Times Target of New Libel Suits," *Birmingham News*, May 31, 1960, 25.

31. "Commission Seeks Times Retraction in Bessemer Area," *Birmingham News*, April 26, 1960, 22.

32. "City Detective Sues Times for $100,000," *Birmingham News*, July 19, 1960, 1.

33. "The Libel Suits," *Andalusia Star-News*, April 28, 1960, 4.

34. Alex Jones and Susan Tifft, *The Trust: The Private and Powerful Family behind the New York Times* (Boston: Little, Brown, 1999), 320.

35. Thomas Daly to Harding F. Bancroft, December 2, 1960, New York Times Company Records, General Files.

36. On the possibility of the *Times* being bankrupted because of the libel suits, see James Goodale, former general counsel of the *Times*, "Is the Public Getting Even with the Press in Libel Cases?" *New York Law Journal*, August 11, 1982.

37. Loeb Oral History, 318.

38. Claude Sitton interview, https://newseumed.org/tools/video-page/silencing-press

39. Sitton interview.

40. Loeb to Dryfoos, January 26, 1961, New York Times Company Records, General Files.

41. This was especially true after Harrison Salisbury was indicted on charges of criminal libel; see chapter 7.

CHAPTER 7. DOING BUSINESS IN ALABAMA

1. Epigraph: "Some Is Unfit," *Alabama Journal*, September 5, 1960, 4.
"Alabama Governor Sues for $1,000,000," *New York Times*, May 31, 1960, 20.

2. "Folsom, Aides File $6 Mill Libel Suit," *Troy Messenger*, October 30, 1950, 1.

3. Harvey H. Jackson, *Inside Alabama: A Personal History of My State* (Tuscaloosa: University of Alabama Press, 2004), 244–45.

4. "The South: Crisis in Civil Rights," *Time*, June 2, 1961.

5. "Governor Patterson to Sue NY Times for Publishing Ad," *Centreville Press*, May 5, 1960, 9.

6. "Patterson Sues New York Times," *Chattanooga Times*, May 31, 1960, 17.

7. Brief for Respondent in Opposition at 9–10, *Sullivan*, 376 U.S. 254 (1964).

8. "Times Retracts Statement in Ads," *New York Times*, May 16, 1960, 22.

9. Letter to the editor, *New York Times*, May 18, 1960, contained in New York Times Company Records, General Files.

10. Nat Hentoff, "The Soft Decay of the New York Times," *Village Voice*, June 1, 1960.

11. Loeb to Hentoff, June 13, 1960, New York Times Company Records, General Files.

12. "The Times Retracts," *Greenville News*, May 20, 1960, 4.

13. "The *Times* Acknowledges Error," *Montgomery Advertiser*, May 17, 1960, 4.

14. "Fall Out from an Error," *Montgomery Advertiser*, May 22, 1960, 10.

15. Branch, *Parting the Waters*, 312.

16. Fred D. Gray, *Bus Ride to Justice*, rev. ed. (Montgomery: NewSouth Books, 2012), 162.

17. "Gray, Fred David Sr," Stanford University: The Martin Luther King, Jr. Research and Education Institute, https://kinginstitute.stanford.edu/encyclopedia/gray-fred-david-sr.

18. Jonathan L. Entin, "Symposium: In Honor of Fred Gray: Making Civil Rights Law from Rosa Parks to the Twenty-First Century," *Case Western Reserve Law Review* 67, no. 4 (2017): 1026.

19. Leonard S. Rubinowitz, "The Courage of Civil Rights Lawyers: Fred Gray and His Colleagues," *Case Western Reserve Law Review* 67, no. 4 (2017): 1227–75.

20. Richard Severo, "Ralph David Abernathy, Civil Rights Pioneer, Is Dead at 64," *New York Times*, April 18, 1990, B7.

21. "Solomon Seay Sr.," *Encyclopedia of Alabama*, http://encyclopediaofala bama.org/article/h-3825

22. King, *Stride Toward Freedom*, 73.

23. "Rev. Joseph E. Lowery, Civil Rights Leader and King Aide, Dies at 98," *New York Times*, March 28, 2020.

24. "Insistent Integrationist," *New York Times*, May 11, 1963, 8.

25. On Shuttlesworth, see Andrew M. Manis, *A Fire You Can't Put Out: The Civil Rights Life of Birmingham's Reverend Fred Shuttlesworth* (Tuscaloosa: University of Alabama Press, 1999).

26. Paul Hemphill, *Leaving Birmingham: Notes of a Native Son* (Tuscaloosa: University of Alabama Press, 2000), 142–43.

27. "Rev. Fred L. Shuttlesworth, an Elder Statesman for Civil Rights, Dies at 89," *New York Times*, October 6, 2011, A33.

28. Branch, *Parting the Waters*, 289.

29. Gray, *Bus Ride to Justice*, 166.

30. Gray, *Bus Ride to Justice*, 166.

31. Martin Luther King, Jr. to Fred Gray, December 14, 1960, Box 79, Folder 6, Martin Luther King, Jr. Papers, Howard Gotlieb Archival Research Center, Boston University.

32. Fred Gray to Martin Luther King, Jr., January 12, 1961, Box 79, Folder 6, Martin Luther King, Jr. Paper, Howard Gotlieb Archival Research Center, Boston University.

33. International Shoe Co. v. Washington, 326 U.S. 310 (1945).

34. Scripto, Inc. v. Carson, 362 U.S. 207 (1960).

35. See Brief for Tribune Company as Amicus Curiae Supporting Petitioner, *Sullivan*, 376 U.S. 254 (1964).

36. "Developments in the Law: Defamation," 69 *Harvard Law Review* (1956): 875.

37. Motion to Quash Service of Process, Box 1, Roland Nachman Records.

38. Quoted in *Essential Liberty: First Amendment Battles for a Free Press* (Columbia University Graduate School of Journalism, 1992), 46–47.

39. "Suit against Times Argued in Alabama," *New York Times*, July 27, 1960, 18; Transcript of Record, 242.

40. Anthony Lewis, *Make No Law*, 26; The Reminisces of Herbert Wechsler, 307.

41. "Times Loses Point in Alabama Suits," *New York Times*, August 6, 1960, 8.

42. Ray Jenkins, "New York Times Can Be Sued by Alabama," *Alabama Journal*, August 6, 1960, 1.

43. The relevant code, Alabama Code Section 199(1), stated that "any nonresident person, firm, or any corporation... shall, by the doing of such business or the performing of such work, or services, be deemed to have appointed the secretary of state... agent of such nonresident, upon whom process may be served in any action accrued or accruing from the doing of such business, or the per-

forming of such work, or service, or as an incident thereto by any such nonresident or his agent, servant, or employee." Ala. Code tit. 7 § 199(1) (1940) (Recomp. 1958).

44. Because the circumstances were different, Jones in Montgomery and Grooms of Birmingham based their decisions on different reasons. The question of doing business in Alabama was not involved in Judge Grooms's ruling in Birmingham. Grooms's ruling was based on the contention that Salisbury's stories resulted from "work or service" he performed.

45. "Howzzat?," *Birmingham News*, May 28, 1960, 6.

46. James Clayton, "Case of Birmingham v. New York Times," *Washington Post*, September 10, 1960.

47. Clayton, "Case of Birmingham v. New York Times."

48. John Kelly, "Criminal Libel and Free Speech," 6 *Kansas Law Review* (1957): 301.

49. Kelly, "Criminal Libel and Free Speech," 301–18.

50. Garrison v. Louisiana, 379 U.S. 64, 69 (1964).

51. Zechariah Chafee, *Government and Mass Communications* (Chicago: University of Chicago Press, 1947), 115.

52. Kelly, "Criminal Libel and Free Speech," 320.

53. Alabama Code, Tit. 14, § 350 (1940).

54. Salisbury, *Without Fear or Favor*, 383.

55. Howard Sullinger to Harrison Salisbury, August 24, 1960, Harrison Salisbury Papers, 1927–1999, Rare Book & Manuscript Library, Columbia University Libraries, New York.

56. Orvil E. Dryfoos to Sulzberger, August 29, 1960, New York Times Company Records, General Files.

57. Salisbury, *A Time of Change*, 56.

58. Salisbury, *Without Fear or Favor*, 383.

59. Salisbury, *Without Fear or Favor*, 383.

60. "State Finds Formidable Club to Swing at Out of State Press," *Montgomery Advertiser*, September 25, 1960, 7.

61. James Clayton, "Case of Birmingham vs. New York Times," *Washington Post*, September 10, 1960, E1.

62. Lawyers for the *Atlanta Constitution* were said to have advised editors not to send reporters to Birmingham. See Schmidt, *"New York Times v. Sullivan* and the Legal Attack," 329.

CHAPTER 8. "THIS NEW WEAPON OF INTIMIDATION"

1. John Bodnar, *Remaking America: Public Memory, Commemoration, and Patriotism in the Twentieth Century* (Princeton, NJ: Princeton University Press, 1993), 220.

2. "Montgomery Salutes Civil War Centennial," *Birmingham News*, November 1, 1960, 7.

3. "Walter Burgwyn Jones," *Clarke County Democrat*, August 8, 1963, 4.

4. William MacDonald interview, Kermit Hall Papers, M.E. Grenander Department of Special Collections and Archives, University of Albany.

5. "Judge Walter B. Jones Is Dead at Age 74," *Alabama Journal*, August 1, 1963, 1.

6. Marvin E. Frankel, "The Alabama Lawyer: Has the Official Organ Atrophied," *Columbia Law Review* 64, no. 7 (1964): 1247; Walter B. Jones, "We Must Save the Constitution," *Alabama Lawyer* (1958), 36.

7. "The Jones Law," *New Republic*, August 6, 1956, 4; Powe, *The Warren Court and American Politics*, 100.

8. "Justice and Judge Jones," *New Republic*, June 4, 1956, 134.

9. "Off the Bench," *Montgomery Advertiser*, March 4, 1957, 4.

10. "Off the Bench," *Montgomery Advertiser*, September 1, 1958, 4.

11. "Off the Bench," *Montgomery Advertiser*, May 16, 1957, 12.

12. Salisbury, *Without Fear or Favor*, 385; William MacDonald interview, Kermit Hall Papers.

13. "Another Symbol of Progress in Montgomery," *Montgomery Advertiser*, July 25, 1958, 31.

14. Walter B. Jones, "Dignity in Our Court Rooms," *Alabama Lawyer* 193 (1960), 193.

15. "Judge Walter B. Jones Is Dead at Age 74," *Alabama Journal*, August 1, 1963, 1.

16. "Jurors Selected for Times Suit," *Montgomery Advertiser*, November 1, 1960.

17. "Times Asks New Trial in Alabama," *Asheville Citizen-Times*, March 4, 1961, 2.

18. Loeb Oral History, 325; *Essential Liberty*, 52.

19. Branch, *Parting the Waters*, 370.

20. Transcript of Record, *New York Times v. Sullivan* (TR), 597.

21. Salisbury, *Without Fear or Favor*, 385.

22. Nachman's notes are contained in Box 1, Roland Nachman Records.

23. TR, 605.

24. *Sullivan*, 376 U.S. at 291.

25. *Sullivan*, 376 U.S. at 291.

26. TR, 627–69.

27. TR, 703.

28. TR, 706.

29. TR, 706.

30. TR, 721–22.

31. TR, 725.

32. TR, 725.

33. TR, 742.

34. TR, 765.

35. TR, 754.

36. Brief for Respondent in Opposition at 55, *Sullivan*, 376 U.S. 254 (1964).

37. Brief for Respondent in Opposition at 55.

38. Gray, *Bus Ride to Justice*, 167; "Opposing Sides Give Final Arguments in Times Libel Suit," *Alabama Journal*, November 3, 1960, 1.

39. "$500,000 Damages Awarded Sullivan by Times Suit Jury," *Montgomery Advertiser*, November 4, 1960, 1.

40. "Times, 4 Clerics Lose Libel Case," *New York Times*, November 4, 1960, 67.

41. "Blackjacking the Press," *Nation*, November 26, 1960, 407.

42. "Opposing Sides Give Final Arguments in Times Libel Suit," *Alabama Journal*, November 3, 1960, 1.

43. "$500,000 Damages Awarded Sullivan by Times Suit Jury," *Montgomery Advertiser*, November 4, 1960, 1.

44. TR, 819.

45. TR, 824.

46. "$500,000 Damages Awarded Sullivan by Times Suit Jury," *Montgomery Advertiser*, November 4, 1960, 1.

47. "4 Ala. Leaders, Times, Lose $500,000 Libel Suit," *Jet*, November 17, 1960.

48. "Alabama Et Al. vs. the New York Times," *Times Talk*, March 1961.

49. "$500,000 Damages Awarded Sullivan by Times Suit Jury," *Montgomery Advertiser*, November 4, 1960, 1.

50. Brief for Tribune Company as Amicus Curiae Supporting Petitioner at 12, *Sullivan*, 376 U.S. 254 (1964).

51. "Must Stick to the Truth," *Alabama Journal*, November 4, 1960, 4.

52. "Times, 4 Clerics Lose Libel Case," *New York Times*, November 4, 1960, 67.

53. Memorandum to Harding F. Bancroft, December 2, 1960, New York Times Company Records, General Files.

54. Loeb to Dryfoos, January 26, 1961, New York Times Company Records, General Files.

55. Klibanoff and Roberts, *The Race Beat*, 240.

56. On the history of the ASNE, see Paul Alfred Pratted, *Gods within the Machine: A History of the American Society of Newspaper Editors, 1923–1993* (Westport, CT: Greenwood, 1995).

57. Klibanoff and Roberts, *The Race Beat*, 241.

58. Klibanoff and Roberts, *The Race Beat*, 241.

59. Memo for Dryfoos, Bradford, Catledge from Bancroft, November 30, 1960, New York Times Company Records, General Files.

60. Catledge to Lee Hills, December 30, 1960, Box 2, Turner Catledge Papers.

61. Catledge to Felix McKnight, December 30, 1960, Box 2, Turner Catledge Papers.

62. "Libel Brief Filed by 3 Newspapers," *New York Times*, April 13, 1961, 26.

63. Alan Reitman to Spencer Coxe, April 4, 1961, American Civil Liberties Union Papers.

64. "Times and Clerics Lose in Libel Suit; Montgomery Mayor Granted $500,000 Damages on Ad—Appeal Is Planned," *New York Times*, February 2, 1961, 17.

65. "Libel in Alabama Denied by Times," *New York Times*, January 31, 1961, 14.

66. "Charles Conley," NYU Alumni Magazine, https://blogs.law.nyu.edu/magazine/2011/charles-conley-1921–2010/

67. Motion to Declare Void the Jury, contained in Box 1, Roland Nachman Records.

68. "Negroes Integrate Circuit Courtroom," *Alabama Journal*, January 31, 1961, 1.

69. "Alabama Mayor Testifies in Suit," *New York Times*, February 1, 1961, 33; "Negroes Mix Circuit Court At Libel Trial," *Montgomery Advertiser*, February 1, 1961, 1.

70. Fred Shuttlesworth, "A Southerner Speaks," *New Pittsburgh Courier*, February 18, 1961, 8.

71. "Judge Seats Races Apart in Libel Suit," *Birmingham News*, February 1, 1961, 26.

72. Walter B. Jones, "Judge Jones on Courtroom Segregation," *Alabama Lawyer* 22, no. 2 (1961): 190–92.

73. "Mayor Gains Libel Verdict of $500,000," *Montgomery Advertiser*, February 2, 1961, 1.

CHAPTER 9. A CIVIL RIGHTS CRISIS

1. "Leaders Come to the Defense of the New York Times," *Atlanta Daily World*, May 14, 1960, 8.

2. "Leaders Come to the Defense of the New York Times"; resolution adopted by the Board of Directors of the SCEF, Atlanta, April 29, 1961, Box 115, Folder 2, Martin Luther King, Jr. Papers.

3. Adam Fairclough, "The Preachers and the People: The Origins and Early Years of the Southern Christian Leadership Conference," *Journal of Southern History* 53, no. 3 (August 1986): 440.

4. Wyatt Tee Walker oral history interview, by David P. Cline in Richmond, Virginia, July 9, 2014, Library of Congress, https://www.loc.gov/item/2016655400/.

5. Fairclough, *Southern Christian Leadership Conference*, 96.

6. Clayborne Carson and Dr. Clarence B. Jones, "Session VII: Concluding Keynote: A Conversation with Dr. Clarence B. Jones," *Northwestern Journal of Law & Social Policy* 10, no. 3 (2016): 698.

7. Clarence B. Jones, *What Would Martin Say?* (New York: HarperCollins, 2008), 21. https://www.college.columbia.edu/cct_archive/jan_feb08/cover.html

8. Jones to King, November 27, 1962, Reel 16, Southern Christian Leadership Conference Papers.

9. Clayborne Carson and Dr. Clarence B. Jones, "Session VII: Concluding Keynote: A Conversation with Dr. Clarence B. Jones," *Northwestern Journal of Law & Social Policy* 10, no. 3 (2016): 698.

10. "Southern Christian Leadership Conference Treasurers' Report, Fiscal Year September 1, 1960–August 31, 1961," *SCLC Newsletter* 1, no. 4 (February 1962): 3–4.

11. Gray, *Bus Ride to Justice*, 162.

12. "Clerics Lose Plea for 2d Libel Trial," *New York Times*, January 19, 1961, 22.

13. Gray, *Bus Ride to Justice*, 169.

14. "Abernathy Car Sold for $400 to Pay on Judgment," *Alabama Tribune*, March 3, 1961.

15. "Car Impounded as Libel Payment," *New York Times*, February 4, 1961, 42.

16. "Pastor's Land Sold in Libel Judgment," *New York Times*, March 22, 1961, 34.

17. See SCLC Records, Reel 20; "Rev. Abernathy Gets Aid from West Coast Baptists," *Atlanta Daily World*, March 29, 1961, 2.

18. "Abernathy of Montgomery," *SCLC Newsletter* 1, no. 2 (August 1961): 3.

19. Martin Luther King, Jr., introduction to *The Papers of Martin Luther King, Jr.*, vol. 7, *To Save the Soul of America*, ed. Clayborne Carson and Tenisha Hart Armstrong (Oakland: University of California Press, 2014), 7.

20. Andrew M. Manis, *A Fire You Can't Put Out: The Civil Rights Life of Birmingham's Reverend Fred Shuttlesworth* (Tuscaloosa: University of Alabama Press, 1999), 238.

21. McWhorter, *Carry Me Home*, 181; "Braveheart: Fred Shuttlesworth," *The Best of Emerge Magazine*, 1998, 505.

22. Branch, *Parting the Waters*, 393.

23. Joseph Echols Lowery oral history interview, by Joseph Mosnier in Atlanta, Georgia, June 6, 2011, Library of Congress https://www.loc.gov/item/2015669122/.

24. Branch, *Parting the Waters*, 393.

25. "Report of the Director: Semi-Annual Report, November 1–April 30, 1960," 3, 7.

26. "Four Ministers Sue Alabama Officials," *New York Times*, February 23, 1961, 28.

27. See complaint, *Abernathy v. Patterson*, ACLU Papers, November 2, 1961.

28. MLK to Eugene Cotton and Richard Watt, November 2, 1961, Box 115, Folder 2, Martin Luther King, Jr. Papers.

29. Jack Bass, *Taming the Storm: The Life and Times of Judge Frank M. Johnson, Jr., and the South's Fight over Civil Rights* (Athens: University of Georgia Press, 2003), 161

30. "4 Ministers Lose Libel Case Round," *New York Times*, November 2, 1961, 34.

31. "High Court Rejects Plea in Libel Case," *New York Times*, February 20, 1962, 13.

32. Susan E. Tifft and Alex S. Jones, *The Trust: The Private and Powerful Family behind the New York Times* (New York: Back Bay Books, 2000), 255.

33. Sulzberger to Loeb, March 22, 1961, New York Times Company Records, General Files.

34. Loeb to Sulzberger, March 23, 1961, New York Times Company Records, General Files.

35. Joseph Echols Lowery, oral history interview, 2011, Library of Congress.

36. Minutes, Joint Committee of SCLC's Administrative Committee and New York Administrative Staff, n.d., Box 109, Folder 3, Martin Luther King, Jr. Papers.

37. Branch, *Parting the Waters*, 580.

38. See Leonard S. Rubinowitz, Michelle Shaw, and Michal Crowder, "A 'Notorious Litigant' and 'Frequenter of Jails': Martin Luther King, Jr., His Lawyers, and the Legal System," *Northwestern Journal of Law & Social Policy* 10, no. 3 (2016): 494.

39. "Lawyers Will Aid in Alabama Suits," *New York Times*, May 9, 1961, 23.

40. Press release, Lawyers Advisory Committee on the Alabama Libel Suits, April 28, 1961, William Hammatt Davis Papers, Wisconsin Historical Society.

41. Statement by Dr. Martin Luther King at Lawyers' Advisory Committee Meeting, May 8, 1961, William Hammatt Davis Papers.

42. Kheel Remarks, May 8, 1961, William Hammatt Davis Papers; "18 Attorneys to Aid Defense in Libel Suits," *Chicago Tribune*, May 9, 1961.

43. William Rogers interview, Kermit Hall Papers.

44. "SCLC to Carry Libel Suit to Supreme Court," *Alabama Tribune*, May 19, 1961, 1.

45. "Grossly Unjust, Says Times; Asks New Trial," *Montgomery Advertiser*, December 12, 1960, 1.

46. "Times Claims Jurors Pressured into Verdict," *Alabama Journal*, March 3, 1961, 15.

47. "Times Claims Jurors Pressured into Verdict."

48. "Times Attorneys Call Jury Biased," *New York Times*, March 4, 1961, 9.

49. "Judge Denies Bid for Retrial," *Alabama Journal*, March 3, 1961, 15

50. "Sellers Suing the N.Y. Times," *Alabama Journal*, March 18, 1961, 1.

51. "Three Times Suits Are Taken to Federal Court," *Birmingham News*, April 14, 1961, 34.

52. Bass, *Taming the Storm*, 161.

53. Parks v. New York Times Co., 195 F. Supp. 919 (1961).

54. Parks v. New York Times Co., 308 F. 2d 474 (1962).

55. "Times Revenues at a Record High," *New York Times*, April 5, 1961, 51.

56. Lord Day & Lord to Haskins & Sells, February 1961, New York Times Company Records, General Files.

57. "N.Y. Times Earnings Off in Banner Year," *Boston Globe*, April 6, 1961, 14.

58. "Times Rattled," *Alabama Journal*, April 27, 1961, 4.

59. "Times Rattled."

CHAPTER 10. THE IRON CURTAIN

1. George Lewis, *Massive Resistance: The White Response to the Civil Rights Movement* (London: Bloomsbury Academic, 2006), 139.

2. Raymond Arsenault, *Freedom Riders: 1961 and the Struggle for Racial Justice* (New York: Oxford University Press, 2007), 218.

3. Bernard Schwartz, *Inside the Warren Court, 1953–69* (New York: Doubleday, 1983), 203.

4. Manis, *A Fire You Can't Put Out*, 276.

5. "Montgomery Tension High after Threats of Bombing," *New York Times*, May 23, 1961, 1.

6. Klarman, *From Jim Crow to Civil Rights*, 428.

7. Arsenault, *Freedom Riders*, 219.

8. Sitton interview, https://newseumed.org/tools/video-page/silencing-press.

9. Sitton interview; "Montgomery Tension High after Threats of Bombing."

10. Salisbury, *Without Fear or Favor*, 384.

11. Bancroft to Dryfoos, December 6, 1960, New York Times Company Records, General Files.

12. Salisbury, *Without Fear or Favor*, 386.

13. Bancroft to Dryfoos, December 6, 1960, New York Times Company Records, General Files.

14. Roberts and Klibanoff, *The Race Beat*, 251.

15. "Tele-Follow Up Comment," *Variety*, May 24, 1961, 29.

16. W. Edward Harris, *Miracle in Birmingham: A Civil Rights Memoir, 1954–1965* (Indianapolis: Stonework Press, 2004), 75.

17. "CBS Reports Turns Camera on Birmingham," *New York Times*, May 19, 1961, 63.

18. "On 'Who Speaks for Birmingham,'" *Birmingham News*, May 19, 1961, 8.

19. Roberts and Klibanoff, *The Race Beat*, 251.

20. "3 in Birmingham Sue CBS for $1,500,000," *New York Times*, December 9, 1961, 54.

21. Edmondson, *In Sullivan's Shadow*, 124.

22. "Federal Court Finds for Times, Ending an Alabama Case," *New York Times*, June 15, 1961, 22.

23. "Victory for the Times," *St. Louis Post-Dispatch*, June 16, 1961; "Reporting Alabama," *Washington Post*, June 17, 1961.

24. Catledge to Hills, June 29, 1961, Box 2, Turner Catledge Papers.

25. Catledge to McGill, March 20, 1962, Box 2, Turner Catledge Papers.

26. Catledge to McGill, March 20, 1962, Box 2, Turner Catledge Papers.

27. Louis Loeb Oral History.

28. Sitton interview, https://newseumed.org/tools/video-page/silencing -press

29. Harding F. Bancroft to Orvil E. Dryfoos, June 21, 1961, Box 4, Orvil Dryfoos Papers. The *Times* continued to rely on wire services for its news from Birmingham and Montgomery. See Salisbury to Arthur Frisch, May 10, 1962, Harrison E. Salisbury Papers.

30. Harding F. Bancroft to Orvil E. Dryfoos, October 11, 1961, Box 4, Orvil Dryfoos Papers.

31. Loeb to Sweetzer, April 23, 1962, New York Times Company Records, General Files.

32. Daniel to Catledge, April 17, 1962, Box 2, Turner Catledge Papers.

33. Daniel to Catledge, April 17, 1962, Box 2, Turner Catledge Papers.

34. Michal R. Belknap, *The Supreme Court under Earl Warren, 1953–1969* (Columbia: University of South Carolina Press, 2005), 152.

35. "Justice Thomas Seay Lawson," *Alabama Lawyer* 64, no. 6 (2003): 292.

36. Brief, New York Times v. Sullivan, 273 Ala. 656, 672 (1962), contained in Roland Nachman Records.

37. Brief, New York Times v. Sullivan, 112, contained in Roland Nachman Records.

38. New York Times v. Sullivan, 273 Ala. 656, 672 (1962).

39. *Sullivan*, 273 Ala. at 670.

40. *Sullivan*, 273 Ala. at 674–75.

41. *Sullivan*, 273 Ala. at 686.

42. *Sullivan*, 273 Ala. at 686.

43. *Sullivan*, 273 Ala. at 676.

44. *Sullivan*, 273 Ala. at 687.

45. *Sullivan*, 273 Ala. at 681.

46. "Times Libel Ruling Upheld in Alabama," *New York Times*, August 31, 1962, 22.

47. Sulzberger to Catledge, October 1, 1962, Box 2, Turner Catledge Papers.

48. Catledge to Sulzberger, October 1, 1962, Box 2, Turner Catledge Papers.

CHAPTER 11. MAKE NO LAW

1. "Minority Opinion," *Time*, June 22, 1962, 55.

2. Robert G. McCloskey, "Reflections on the Warren Court," *Virginia Law Review* 51, no. 7 (1965): 1236.

3. McCloskey, "Reflections on the Warren Court," 1230. On the Warren Court, see Powe, *The Warren Court and American Politics*; Belknap, *The Supreme Court under Earl Warren*.

4. McCloskey, "Reflections on the Warren Court," 1230.

5. Samantha Barbas, *Newsworthy: The Supreme Court Battle over Privacy and Press Freedom* (Stanford: Stanford University Press, 2017), 155.

6. Burt Neuborne, "The Gravitational Pull of Race on the Warren Court," *Supreme Court Review* 2010, no. 1 (June 2011): 65.

7. Lucy v. Adams, 350 U.S. 1 (1955).

8. 352 U.S. 903 (1956).

9. *New Orleans City Park Improvement v. Detiege*, 358 U.S. 54 (1958).

10. 364 U.S. 339, 340 (1960).

11. Michael Klarman, "An Interpretive History of Modern Equal Protection," *Michigan Law Review* 90, no. 2 (1991): 272–73.

12. NAACP v. Alabama, 357 U.S. 449, 455 (1958).

13. 364 U.S. 479, 489 (1960).

14. NAACP v. Button, 371 U.S. 415, 417 (1963).

15. Dennis v. United States, 341 U.S. 494, 508–9 (1951).

16. See Yates v. United States, 354 U.S. 298, 299 (1957); Scales v. United States, 367 U.S. 203 (1961) *reh'g denied* 366 U.S. 978 (1961).

17. 354 U.S. 476, 493 (1957).

18. 357 U.S. 513, 529 (1958).

19. 361 U.S. 147, 153–54 (1959).

20. Geoffrey R. Stone, "Justice Brennan and the Freedom of Speech: A First Amendment Odyssey," *University of Pennsylvania Law Review* 139, no. 5 (1991): 1333.

21. Laurent B. Frantz, "The First Amendment in the Balance," *Yale Law Journal* 71, no. 8 (1962): 1435.

22. Alexander Meiklejohn, *Free Speech and Its Relation to Self-Government* (New York: Harper Brothers, 1948), 100.

23. Alexander Meiklejohn, "The First Amendment Is an Absolute," *Supreme Court Review* 1961 (1961): 255.

24. Meiklejohn, "Absolute," 259.

25. Steve Suitts, *Hugo Black of Alabama: How His Roots and Early Career Shaped the Great Champion of the Constitution* (Montgomery: NewSouth Books, 2017), 18.

26. Horwitz, *The Warren Court*, 5.

27. Sylvia Snowiss, "The Legacy of Justice Black," *Supreme Court Review* (1973), 196.

28. "Justice Black Dies at 85; Served on Court 34 Years," *New York Times*, September 25, 1971, 1.

29. Tracy S. Uebelhor, *Presidential Profiles: The Truman Years* (New York: Facts on File, 2006), 42.

30. Hugo Black, "The Bill of Rights," *New York University Law Review* 35 (1960): 874–75; Charles Black, "Mr. Justice Black, the Supreme Court, and the Bill of Rights," *Harper's*, February 1961, 63.

31. Hugo Black and Edmond Cahn, "Mr. Justice Black and First Amendment Absolutes: A Public Interview," *New York University Law Review* 37 (1962): 553, 557; Anthony Lewis, "Black Doubts Suits for Libel Are Legal," *New York Times*, June 11, 1962, 1.

32. "Minority Opinion," *Time*, June 22, 1962, 55.

33. Beauharnais v. Illinois, 343 U.S. 250, 270 (1952) (Black, J., dissenting).

34. "Mr. Justice Black and First Amendment Absolutes: A Public Interview," 553, 557.

35. Noted *Time* magazine, "in extending protection last week to liars, libelers and slanderers. Justice Black found himself almost alone. In the controversy that predictably followed publication of his remarks, few voices were raised in his defense." "Minority Opinion," 55.

36. John Herbers, "Libel Actions Ask Millions in South: 17 Suits by Public Officials are Pending in Courts," *New York Times*, April 4, 1964, 12.

37. Herbers, "Libel Actions Ask Millions in South."

38. Klibanoff and Roberts, *The Race Beat*, 358.

39. Edmondson, *In Sullivan's Shadow*, 148–53.

40. Edmondson, *In Sullivan's Shadow*, 174–79.

41. Kermit L. Hall and Melvin I. Urofsky, *New York Times v. Sullivan: Civil Rights, Libel Law, and the Free Press* (Lawrence: University Press of Kansas, 2011), 85.

42. "Libel or Revenge," *Columbia Journalism Review*," Fall 1963, 2.

43. "U.S. Court Shifts Times Libel Rule," *New York Times*, November 17, 1962, 10.

44. Branch, *Parting the Waters*, 581.

45. King, *The Papers of Martin Luther King, Volume VII*, 37; Branch, *Parting the Waters*, 583, 590.

46. Leonard E. Ryan, "Suits in Alabama Stir New Protest; Concern over Libel Actions Voice by More Lawyers Letter Sent to Lawyers Cites Officials' Suits 'Powerful New Weapon,'" *New York Times*, October 14, 1962, 74.

47. "The Montgomery, Alabama Libel Suits: A Summary" in Box 787, Folder 7, American Civil Liberties Union Papers; "Suits in Alabama Stir New Protest."

48. "Lawyers Act Improperly," *Alabama Journal*, October 19, 1962, 4.

49. Nachman to Simpson, October 23, 1962, Box 4, Roland Nachman Records.

CHAPTER 12. HERBERT WECHSLER

1. Loeb Oral History, 329–31.

2. "Herbert Wechsler, Legal Giant, Is Dead at 90," *New York Times*, April 28, 2000, C21.

3. David A. Anderson, "Wechsler's Triumph" *Alabama Law Review* 66 (2014): 231.

4. Philip A. Lacovara, "Herbert Wechsler," *Columbia Law Review* 78, no. 5 (1978): 966.

5. Henry Paul Monaghan, "A Legal Giant Is Dead," *Columbia Law Review* 100 (2000): 1376.

6. The Reminiscences of Herbert Wechsler, Columbia Center for Oral History, Columbia University.

7. Louis Henkin, "Herbert Wechsler, 4 December 1909–26 April 2000," *Proceedings of the American Philosophical Society* 146, no. 3 (2002): 315.

8. The Reminiscences of Herbert Wechsler.

9. Anders Walker, "American Oresteia: Herbert Wechsler, the Model Penal Code, and the Uses of Revenge," *Wisconsin Law Review* (2009): 1022.

10. Anders Walker, "Neutral Principles: Rethinking the Legal History of Civil Rights, 1934-1964," *Loyola University Chicago Law Journal* 40, no. 3 (2009): 387.

11. David L. Shapiro, "Herbert Wechsler—A Remembrance," *Columbia Law Review* 100, no. 6 (2000): 1377.

12. "Herbert Wechsler, Legal Giant, Is Dead at 90."

13. Herbert Wechsler, "Toward Neutral Principles of Constitutional Law," *Harvard Law Review* 73, no. 1 (1959): 1–35.

14. David Kennedy and William Fisher, eds., *The Canon of American Legal Thought* (Princeton, NJ: Princeton University Press, 2006), 313.

15. Wechsler, "Toward Neutral Principles of Constitutional Law," 34.

16. Lewis interview with Wechsler, 1990, Anthony Lewis Papers.

17. The Reminiscences of Herbert Wechsler, 298.

18. The Reminiscences of Herbert Wechsler, 301.

19. The Reminiscences of Herbert Wechsler, 304.

20. The Reminiscences of Herbert Wechsler, 304.

21. "The Press: Without Fear or Favor," *Time Magazine*, May 8, 1950, 68.

22. Robert Friedman, "Freedom of the Press: How Far Can They Go," *American Heritage* 33, no. 6 (October/November 1982).

23. Wechsler interview, 1984, Anthony Lewis Papers.

24. The Reminiscences of Herbert Wechsler, 305.

25. The Reminiscences of Herbert Wechsler, 304.

26. "Marvin Frankel, Federal Judge and Pioneer of Sentencing Guidelines, Dies at 81," *New York Times*, March 5, 2002, C15.

27. The Reminiscences of Herbert Wechsler, 306.

28. The Reminiscences of Herbert Wechsler, 308.

29. Wechsler interview, Anthony Lewis Papers.

30. Wechsler interview, Anthony Lewis Papers.

31. Zechariah Chafee, "A History of the Law of Sedition," in *Free Speech in the United States* (Cambridge, MA: Harvard University Press, 1941): 497–98.

32. David A. Anderson, "Seditious Libel," in *Encyclopedia of the American Constitution*, 2nd ed., ed. Leonard W. Levy and Kenneth L. Karst (New York: Macmillan Reference USA, 2000) 5: 2352; Harold L. Nelson, "Seditious Libel in Colonial America," *American Journal of Legal History* 3, no. 2 (1959): 160–72; Alfred H. Kelly, "Constitutional Liberty and the Law of Libel: A Historian's View," *American Historical Review* 74, no. 2 (December 1968): 429–34.

33. Anderson, "Seditious Libel."

34. Gordon T. Bell, "The Sedition Act of 1798: A Brief History of Arrests, Indictments, Mistreatment & Abuse," Freedom Forum Institute, 2011.

35. *Sullivan*, 376 U.S. at 275.

36. *Sullivan*, 376 U.S. at 276. See David Jenkins, "The Sedition Act of 1798 and the Incorporation of Seditious Libel into First Amendment Jurisprudence," *American Journal of Legal History* 45, no. 2 (2001): 154–213.

37. Abrams v. United States, 250 U.S. 616, 630 (1919).

38. Beauharnais v. Illinois, 343 U.S. 250, 289 (1952) (Jackson, J., dissenting).

39. Beauharnais v. Illinois, 343 U.S. at 272 (Black, J., dissenting).

40. Brief for Petitioner on Writ of Certiorari at 2, *Sullivan*, 376 U.S. 254 (1964).

41. Petition for certiorari at 12.

42. Petition for certiorari at 13.

43. Petition for certiorari at 13.

44. Petition for certiorari at 15.

45. Petition for certiorari at 17, 20.

46. Petition for certiorari at 19, 20.

47. Jones to King, November 27, 1962, Reel 20, SCLC Records.

48. Petition for certiorari at 9, Abernathy v. Sullivan, 371 U.S. 946 (1963).

49. Petition for certiorari at 18, Abernathy v. Sullivan.

50. Brief for Respondent in Opposition at 6, 18, *Sullivan*, 376 U.S. 254 (1964).

51. Brief for Respondent in Opposition, 6, 19; Valentine v. Chrestensen, 316 U.S. 52 (1942).

52. Brief for Respondent in Opposition, 33.

53. "114 Day Newspaper Strike Ends," *New York Times*, April 1, 1963, 1.

54. "Orvil E. Dryfoos Dies at 50," *New York Times*, May 26, 1963, 1.

CHAPTER 13. BEFORE THE COURT

1. Powe, *The Warren Court and American Politics*, 223; Aldon D. Morris, *Origins of the Civil Rights Movement: Black Communities Organizing for Change* (New York: Free Press, 1984), 258–59.

2. Powe, *The Warren Court and American Politics*, 224–25.

3. Andrew Manis, "Fred Lee Shuttlesworth," in Encyclopedia of Alabama, http://encyclopediaofalabama.org/article/h-1093.

4. Branch, *Parting the Waters*, 771–72.

5. Richard Kluger, *Simple Justice: The History of Brown v. Board of Education and Black America's Struggle for Equality,* rev. ed. (New York: Vintage Books, 2004), 550; Anthony Lewis, "The Justices' Supreme Job," *New York Times,* June 11, 1961, 4.

6. Powe, *The Warren Court and American Politics*, 303.

7. "Justice Black Dies at 85; Served on Court 34 Years," *New York Times*, September 25, 1971, 1; Alden Whitman, "William O. Douglas Is Dead at 81; Served 36 Years on Supreme Court," *New York Times*, January 20, 1980, 1.

8. "Tom C. Clark, Former Justice, Dies; On the Supreme Court for 18 Years," *New York Times*, June 14, 1977, 72.

9. Lesley Oelsner, "Harlan Dies at 72; On Court 16 Years," *New York Times*, December 30, 1971, 1.

10. Daniel M. Berman, "Mr. Justice Brennan: A Preliminary Appraisal," *Catholic University Law Review* 7 (1958): 11, 14–15.

11. Nat Hentoff, "The Constitutionalist," *New Yorker*, March 12, 1990, 60.

12. John C. P. Goldberg, "Judging Reputation: Realism and Common Law in Justice White's Defamation Jurisprudence," *University of Colorado Law Review* 74, no. 4 (2003): 1471.

13. Eric Pace, "Arthur J. Goldberg Dies at 81; Ex-Justice and Envoy to U.N.," *New York Times*, January 20, 1990, A1.

14. The clerks' memoranda are contained in the William O. Douglas Papers, Library of Congress, and John Marshall Harlan Papers, Mudd Manuscript Library, Princeton University.

15. Loeb Oral History, 332.

16. Lewis, *Make No Law*, 113.

17. William H. Davis to Kheel, January 14, 1963, William Hammatt Davis Papers, Wisconsin Historical Society.

18. Wechsler interview, Anthony Lewis Papers.

19. Marvin E. Frankel, "Herbert Wechsler: A Junior's Appreciation," *Columbia Law Review* 78, no. 5 (1978): 962.

20. Mary Ann Watson, *The Expanding Vista: American Television in the Kennedy Years* (Durham, NC: Duke University Press, 1994), 105.

21. Lewis, *Make No Law*, 115.

22. Likewise, Wechsler may have believed that an argument based on race would not have satisfied the criteria of "neutral principles" he advocated.

23. Brief for Petitioners at 39, *Sullivan*, 376 U.S. 254 (1964).

24. Brief for Petitioners, 40.

25. Brief for Petitioners, 41.

26. Brief for Petitioners, 43.

27. Brief for Petitioners, 44.

28. Brief for Petitioners, 44.

29. Brief for Petitioners, 47.

30. Brief for Petitioners, 49.

31. Brief for Petitioners, 55.

32. David A. Anderson, "Wechsler's Triumph" *Alabama Law Review* 66, (2014): 241–42; Brief for Petitioners, 52–53.

33. Brief for Petitioners, 62, 64–65.

34. Brief for Petitioners, 66, 68.

35. Brief for Petitioners, Abernathy v. Sullivan, 52, 29.

36. Brief for Respondent, 8–9, *Sullivan*, 376 U.S. 254 (1964).

37. Brief for Respondent, 33, *Sullivan*.

38. Motion of Washington Post Company for Leave to File a Brief as Amicus Curiae, 3.

39. See Brief of American Civil Liberties Union and New York Civil Liberties Union as Amicus Curiae.

40. Bruce Weber, "M.R. Nachman, Lawyer in Libel Case, Dies at 91," *New York Times*, December 7, 2015, A20.

41. Nachman to Douglas Stripp, November 13, 1963, Box 4, Roland Nachman Records.

CHAPTER 14. ARGUMENTS

1. Anthony Lewis, "Judicial Powers Extended in Supreme Court's Term," *New York Times*, June 29, 1964, 1.

2. Walter F. Murphy, "Deeds under a Doctrine: Civil Liberties in the 1963 Term," *American Political Science Review* 59, no. 1 (March 1965): 64–79.

3. Anthony Lewis, "The Justices' Supreme Job," *New York Times*, June 11, 1961, SM31.

4. William Rogers interview, Kermit Hall Papers.

5. Wachtel to Abernathy, September 13, 1963, Reel 16, SCLC Records.

6. Branch, *Pillar of Fire*, 204.

7. Loeb Oral History, 334–35.

8. The oral argument can be accessed on Oyez.org.

9. Nachman's notes for the oral argument are contained in Box 2, Roland Nachman Papers.

10. Branch, *Pillar of Fire*, 204.

11. Branch, *Pillar of Fire*, 204.

12. Branch, *Pillar of Fire*, 44.

13. Branch, *Pillar of Fire*, 207.

14. Oral argument, *Abernathy v. Sullivan*, Oyez.org.

15. "High Court Hears Libel Arguments," *New York Times*, January 8, 1964, 19.

16. William Rogers interview, Kermit Hall Papers.

17. Joseph B. Russell, Letter to the Editor, *Columbia College Today*, March/April 2008.

18. Del Dickson, ed., *The Supreme Court in Conference: The Private Discussions behind Nearly 300 Supreme Court Decisions* (New York: Oxford University Press, 2001), 380.

19. Seth Stern and Stephen Wermiel, *Justice Brennan: Liberal Champion* (Boston: Houghton Mifflin Harcourt, 2010), 203.

20. Nina Totenberg et al., "A Tribute to Justice William J. Brennan, Jr.," *Harvard Law Review* 104, no. 1 (1990): 34.

21. Owen Fiss, "A Life Lived Twice," *Yale Law Journal* 100, no. 5 (1991): 1128

22. On Brennan's philosophies, see Daniel M. Berman, "Mr. Justice Brennan after Five Years," *Catholic Law Review* 11, no. 1 (1962): 2; Robert O'Neil, "Clerking for Justice Brennan," *Journal of Supreme Court History* 3 (1991): 11–13; Hentoff, "The Constitutionalist"; "Justice Brennan's Vision," *New York Times*, July 25, 1997.

23. Geoffrey R. Stone, "Justice Brennan and the Freedom of Speech: A First Amendment Odyssey," *University of Pennsylvania Law Review* 139 (1991): 1344.

24. Speiser v. Randall, 357 U.S. 513, 526 (1958).

25. A "chilling effect" has been defined by one scholar as an effect that occurs "when individuals seeking to engage in activity protected by the First Amendment are deterred from so doing by governmental regulation not specifically directed at that protected activity." Frederick Schauer, "Fear, Risk and the First Amendment: Unraveling the 'Chilling Effect,'" *Boston University Law Review* 58 (1978): 693.

26. Smith v. California, 361 U.S. 147 (1959).

27. NAACP v. Button, 371 U.S. 415, 433 (1963).

CHAPTER 15. ACTUAL MALICE

1. Stephen Barnett interview, Anthony Lewis Papers.

2. Anthony Lewis, "The Justices' Supreme Job," *New York Times*, June 11, 1961, 1.

3. On the behind-the-scenes deliberation in the *Sullivan* case, see the unpublished memorandum written by Brennan's clerks, "October Term 1963," contained in Anthony Lewis Papers; Lee Levine and Stephen Wermiel, *The*

Progeny: Justice William J. Brennan's Fight to Preserve the Legacy of New York Times v. Sullivan (Chicago: American Bar Association, 2014); Lee Levine and Stephen Wermiel, "Behind the U.S. Reports: Justice Brennan's Unpublished Opinions and Memoranda in New York Times v. Sullivan and Its Progeny," *Communication Law and Policy* 19, no. 2 (2014): 227; W. Wat Hopkins, "Justice Brennan, Justice Harlan and New York Times Co. v. Sullivan: A Case Study in Supreme Court Decision Making," *Communication Law and Policy* 1, no. 4 (1996): 469.

4. Totenberg, "Tribute to Justice William J. Brennan, Jr.," 33.

5. The drafts and correspondence on the *Sullivan* case are contained in the William J. Brennan, William O. Douglas, Hugo Lafayette Black, Arthur Goldberg, and Byron White papers, all housed at the Library of Congress. See also John Marshall Harlan Papers, Mudd Manuscript Library, Princeton University, and Tom C. Clark Papers, Tarleton Law Library, University of Texas.

6. David A. Anderson, "Wechsler's Triumph," *Alabama Law Review* 66 (2014): 251.

7. *Sullivan*, 376 U.S. at 265.

8. *Sullivan*, 264n4.

9. *Sullivan*, 264n4.

10. *Sullivan*, 269. Following Wechsler, Brennan dismissed the argument that commercial advertisements were unprotected by the First Amendment. The "Heed Their Rising Voices" ad communicated information and opinions upon a public issue, thereby invoking the guarantees of freedom of speech. *Sullivan*, 267.

11. *Sullivan*, 276.

12. *Sullivan*, 280.

13. Hopkins, "Justice Brennan, Justice Harlan," 480.

14. Anderson, "Wechsler's Triumph," 242.

15. Unpublished memorandum, October Term 1963, 2.

16. Unpublished memorandum, October Term 1963, 2.

17. Unpublished memorandum, October Term 1963, 3.

18. Unpublished memorandum, October Term 1963, 2–3.

19. Unpublished memorandum, October Term 1963, 4.

20. Black to Brennan, undated, Hugo Lafayette Black Papers; unpublished memorandum, October Term 1963, 5.

21. Unpublished memorandum, October Term 1963, 6; Harlan to Brennan, March 3, 1964.

22. Memorandum to the Conference, March 3, 1964, William J. Brennan Papers.

23. Unpublished memorandum, October Term 1963, 8.

24. Unpublished memorandum, October Term 1963, 8.

25. Kim Isaac Eisler, *The Last Liberal: William J. Brennan, Jr. and the Decisions That Transformed America* (Washington, DC: Beard Books, 2005), 189.

26. Eisler, *The Last Liberal*, 189.

27. Hopkins, "Justice Brennan, Justice Harlan," 489.

28. Unpublished memorandum, October Term 1963, 8.

29. Unpublished memorandum, October Term 1963, 11.

30. Unpublished memorandum, October Term 1963, 11.

31. Lewis, *Make No Law*, 223.

32. Harlan, Memorandum to the Conference, March 9, 1964, William J. Brennan Papers.

33. *Sullivan*, 376 U.S. at 264–65.

34. *Sullivan*, 269.

35. *Sullivan*, 269, 273.

36. *Sullivan*, 270–71.

37. *Sullivan*, 271–72.

38. *Sullivan*, 271.

39. *Sullivan*, 279n19.

40. *Sullivan*, 273.

41. *Sullivan*, 273.

42. *Sullivan*, 273.

43. *Sullivan*, 274.

44. *Sullivan*, 272.

45. *Sullivan*, 279.

46. *Sullivan*, 283–84.

47. *Sullivan*, 284–86.

48. *Sullivan*, 288.

49. *Sullivan*, 291.

50. *Sullivan*, 292.

51. *Sullivan*, 292.

52. *Sullivan*, 292.

53. *Sullivan*, 298.

54. *Sullivan*, 293.

55. *Sullivan*, 293.

56. *Sullivan*, 294–96.

57. Black to Brennan, undated, Hugo Lafayette Black Papers.

CHAPTER 16. FREE, ROBUST, AND WIDE OPEN

1. John Davis, Clerk of the U.S. Supreme Court, to Nachman, March 9, 1964, Roland Nachman Records.

2. Lewis, *Make No Law*, 161.

3. Lewis, *Make No Law*, 161.

4. Bruce Weber, "M.R. Nachman, Lawyer in Libel Case, Dies at 91," *New York Times*, December 7, 2015.

5. Richard Friedman, "Freedom of the Press: How Far Can They Go," *American Heritage* (October–November 1982).

6. Wechsler interview, Anthony Lewis Papers.

7. Wechsler interview, Anthony Lewis Papers.

8. The Reminiscenses of Herbert Wechsler.

9. Friedman, "Freedom of the Press, How Far Can It Go."

10. "SCLC Board Members, New York Times Win Reversal in $500,000 Libel Suit Brought by Alabama Police Official," SCLC Newsletter, March 1964, 2.

11. "Overrule Libel Suit Against Clerics, N.Y. Times," *Jet*, March 26, 1964, 45.

12. Harry Wachtel, "Attorney in Times Libel Verdict Points Up Significance and Dangers of Decree," SCLC Newsletter, June 1964, 8.

13. "A True Charter of Press Liberty," *Los Angeles Times*, March 12, 1964.

14. "An End to Intimidation," *Atlanta Constitution*, March 11, 1964.

15. On news coverage of *Sullivan*, see Jeffrey B. Hedrick, "A Content Analysis of Editorial Regionalism in the 1960s: Midsize Newspaper Coverage of New York Times v. Sullivan (1960–1964)" (PhD diss., Bowling Green State University, 2006).

16. "Keeping Opinions Free," *Berkshire Eagle*, March 10, 1964.

17. Friedman, "Freedom of the Press, How Far Can It Go."

18. "The Right to Criticize," *Boston Globe*, March 11, 1964, quoted in Schmidt, "New York Times v. Sullivan and the Legal Attack on the Civil Rights Movement," 324.

19. Editorial, "Criticizing Public Servants," *Washington Post*, March 10, 1964, A16.

20. "Decision Welcomed by Times Publisher," *New York Times*, March 10, 1964.

21. Editorial, "Free Press and a Free People," *New York Times*, March 10, 1964, 36.

22. Sulzberger to Loeb, March 10, 1964, New York Times Company Records, General Files.

23. A.H. Sulzberger to A.O. Sulzberger, March 10, 1964, New York Times Company Records, General Files.

24. Bancroft to Sulzberger, March 10, 1964, New York Times Company Records, General Files.

25. Fred Gray, *Bus Ride to Justice*, 170.

26. Abernathy to Gray, October 15, 1964, Reel 20, SCLC Records.

27. H. Bancroft to file, March 10, 1964, New York Times Company Records, General Files.

28. "Sullivan to Pay Costs of Libel Suit Case," *New York Times*, April 7, 1964, 23.

29. Embry to Whitesell, April 29, 1964, Roland Nachman Records.

30. Embry to Whitesell, April 29, 1964, Roland Nachman Records.

31. Nachman to Whitesell, September 11, 1964, Roland Nachman Records.

32. Nachman to Whitesell, September 11, 1964, Roland Nachman Records.

33. Nachman to Sullivan, September 11, 1964, Roland Nachman Records.

34. Kermit Hall, "New York Times v. Sullivan, The Case and Its Times," *Drake Law Review* 1, no. 21 (1990): 23.

35. William L. Prosser, *Handbook of the Law of Torts*, 4th ed. (Eagan, MN: West, 1971), § 118, at 819.

36. Harry Kalven Jr., "The *New York Times* Case: A Note on 'The Central Meaning of the First Amendment,'" *Supreme Court Review* 191 (1964): 205.

37. The vision of the First Amendment in *Sullivan* was not unlike that espoused by Meikeljohn, who believed that the First Amendment absolutely protected "political speech," speech related to self-governance. See "The *New York Times* Case," 221n125; William Brennan, "The Supreme Court and the Meiklejohn Interpretation of the First Amendment," *Harvard Law Review* 79 (1965): 17.

38. *Sullivan*, 376 U.S. at 270.

39. Roberts and Klibanoff, *The Race Beat*, 364.

40. Walker, "Rethinking Neutral Principles," 433; David J. Garrow, *Protest at Selma: Martin Luther King, Jr., and the Voting Rights Act of 1965* (New Haven, CT: Yale University Press, 2015).

41. St. Amant v. Thompson, 390 U.S. 727, 733 (1968).

42. William P. Marshall and Susan Gilles, "The Supreme Court, The First Amendment, and Bad Journalism," *Supreme Court Review* 1994 (1994): 184-86; Berisha v. Lawson, 594 U.S. 2424, 2428.

43. Powe, *The Fourth Estate*, 104.

44. Kalven, "The *New York Times* Case," 192.

45. Kalven, "The *New York Times* Case," 192.

46. Kalven, "The *New York Times* Case," 193-94.

47. Nadine Strossen, "Freedom of Speech in the Warren Court," in *The Warren Court: A Retrospective*, ed. Bernard Schwartz (New York: Oxford University Press, 1996), 77-78.

48. "[T]he Negro," Harry Kalven observed, was "winning back... the freedoms the Communists seemed to have lost for us." Kalven, *The Negro and the First Amendment* (Columbus: Ohio State University Press, 1965), 6.

49. See, e.g., Richard A. Epstein, "Was New York Times v. Sullivan Wrong?," *University of Chicago Law Review* 53 (1986): 787; Frederick Schauer, "Do Cases Make Bad Law?" *University of Chicago Law Review* 73 (2006): 883, 902.

50. Garrison v. Louisiana, 379 U.S. 64 (1964).

51. Monitor Patriot Co. v. Roy, 401 U.S. 265, 277 (1971).

52. Curtis Pub. Co. v. Butts, 388 U.S. 130 (1967); Associated Press v. Walker, 388 U.S. 130 (1967).

53. Associated Press v. Walker, 388 U.S. at 163 (Warren, J., concurring).

54. Associated Press v. Walker, 388 U.S. at 163.

55. Gertz v. Robert Welch, Inc., 418 U.S. 323 (1974).

56. Gertz v. Robert Welch, Inc., 418 U.S. at 352.

57. Anthony Lewis, *Freedom for the Thought That We Hate: A Biography of the First Amendment* (New York: Basic Books, 2010), 57. See also Anthony Lewis, "New York Times v. Sullivan Reconsidered: Time to Return to The Central Meaning of the First Amendment," *Columbia Law Review* 83 (1983): 603.

58. "Heed Their Rising Voices, A Tribute to Justice Brennan," 36–37.

59. Other factors behind the rise of investigative reporting include popular disillusionment with authority in the 1960s, an unpopular war in Vietnam, and the growing power and prestige of the media industries. Mark Feldstein, "A Muckraking Model: Investigative Reporting Cycles in American History," *Harvard International Journal of Press/Politics* 11, no. 2 (2006): 110–11.

60. Archibald Cox, *The Role of the Supreme Court in American Government* (New York: Oxford University Press, 1976), 40.

61. See David Logan, "Rescuing Our Democracy by Rethinking *New York Times Co. v. Sullivan*," *Ohio State Law Journal* 81, no. 5 (2020): 759–814. Yet in the long run, *Sullivan* did not protect the press completely from the burdens of libel because it did little to reduce the costs of defending libel suits. "Actual malice" proved to be expensive to litigate, since it depends on a factual determination of the defendant's actions prior to publication. See Lucas A. Powe, *The Fourth Estate and the Constitution: Freedom of the Press in America* (Berkeley: University of California Press, 1991), 121; David A. Anderson, "Libel and Press Self-Censorship," *Texas Law Review* 53 (1975): 422–81.

62. *Times* editors Lester Markel and John Oakes wrote to Wechsler expressing their fears that the decision "may be opening the way to complete irresponsibility in journalism." Markel and Oakes to Wechsler, September 18, 1964, New York Times Company Records, General Files.

63. Richard D. Yoakam and Ronald T. Farrar, "The *Times* Libel Case and Communication Law," *Journalism Quarterly* 42, no. 4 (December 1965): 661–64.

64. Anthony Lewis, "The Sullivan Decision," *Tennessee Journal of Law and Policy* 1, no. 1 (2004): 146.

65. Berisha v. Lawson, 141 S. Ct. 2424, 2424–25, 2425–30 (2021) (Thomas, J., dissenting) (Gorsuch, J., dissenting).

66. Gorsuch is not the only Supreme Court justice to express dissatisfaction with *Sullivan*. Justice Byron White later expressed regret for the "actual malice" rule, convinced that the Court struck an "improvident balance" between the "public's interest in being fully informed about public officials and public affairs" and the competing interest in reputation. Dun & Bradstreet, Inc. v. Greenmoss Builders, Inc., 472 U.S. 749, 767 (White, J., concurring). See also Elena Kagan, "A Libel Story: Sullivan Then and Now," *Law & Social Inquiry* 18 (1993): 197.

67. Berisha v. Lawson, 141 S. Ct. at 2424–25, 2425–30.

68. See, for example, Kagan, "A Libel Story," 197; Logan, "Rethinking *New York Times v. Sullivan*," 761; F. Trowbridge vom Baur, "License to Defame Gov-

ernment Officials: New York Times v. Sullivan Should Be Overruled," *Federal Bar News & Journal* 30, no. 12 (1983): 501–6; Ronald A. Cass, "Weighing Constitutional Anchors: *New York Times Co. v. Sullivan* and the Misdirection of First Amendment Doctrine," *First Amendment Law Review* 12 (2014): 399; Natasha Cooper, "Reevaluating New York Times v. Sullivan in the Wake of Modern Day Journalism," *ABA Journal*, February 27, 2019; Benjamin Barron, "A Proposal to Rescue *New York Times v. Sullivan*," *American University Law Review* 57, no. 1 (October 2007): 73–127; Bollinger, *Images of a Free Press*, 36 (noting the "effects on public discussion of uninhibited defamatory statements" and the "risks to democracy of a completely free press").

69. Time, Inc. v. Hill, 385 U.S. 374 (1967).

70. Hustler Magazine, Inc. v. Falwell, 485 U.S. 46 (1988).

71. New York Times Co. v. United States, 403 U.S. 942 (1971); Richmond Newspapers, Inc. v. Virginia, 448 U.S. 555 (1980).

72. Anderson, "The Promises of New York Times v. Sullivan," 8–9.

73. Strossen, "Freedom of Speech in the Warren Court," 72.

74. Fed. Election Com'n v. Wisconsin Right To Life, Inc., 551 U.S. 449, 451 (2007) (citing New York Times Co. v Sullivan, 376 U.S. 254, 269–70 (1964)).

75. "Suit against Times Ended in Alabama," *New York Times*, July 14, 1964, 17.

76. "Times Is Cleared in Two Libel Suits," *New York Times*, September 18, 1964, 22.

77. Salisbury, *Without Fear or Favor*, 389; *A Time of Change*, 59.

78. Salisbury, *Without Fear or Favor*, 389.

79. Salisbury, *Without Fear or Favor*, 389.

80. "Times Libel Case Is Given to Jury," *New York Times*, September 23, 1964, 41.

81. "Libel Jury Finds against the Times," *New York Times*, September 25, 1964, 26.

82. "Court Voids Bull Connor Libel Award," *Atlanta Constitution*, August 5, 1966. Despite this, Salisbury couldn't go back to Alabama until the late 1960s. The *Times* was unable to get the indictment dismissed against Salisbury before then, because the *Times* was advised by the attorneys in Alabama that the district attorney in Bessemer was still bitter and wouldn't get rid of it. But the DA was finally replaced, and the Alabama lawyers were in a position to get the indictment quashed. After more than half a decade, Salisbury was free to set foot in the state. Loeb Oral History, 346.

83. Loeb to Sulzberger, October 14, 1966, New York Times Company Records, General Files.

Archival Collections

American Civil Liberties Union Papers, accessed through New York Public
   Library
Hugo Lafayette Black Papers, Library of Congress
William J. Brennan Papers, Library of Congress
Turner Catledge Papers, Mississippi State University Libraries
Tom C. Clark Papers, Tarleton Law Library, University of Texas
William Hammatt Davis Papers, Wisconsin Historical Society
William O. Douglas Papers, Library of Congress
Orvil Dryfoos Papers, Manuscripts and Archives Division, New York Public
   Library
Arthur Goldberg Papers, Library of Congress
Kermit Hall Papers, M.E. Grenander Department of Special Collections and
   Archives, University of Albany
John Marshall Harlan Papers, Mudd Manuscript Library, Princeton University
Martin Luther King Jr. Papers, Howard Gotlieb Archival Research Center,
   Boston University
Anthony Lewis Papers, Library of Congress
M. Roland Nachman Jr. Records from Times v. Sullivan and Related Cases,
   Alabama Department of Archives and History
New York Times Company Records, General Files, Manuscripts and Archives
   Division, New York Public Library

Adolph S. Ochs Papers, Manuscripts and Archives Division, New York Public
Library
Harrison Salisbury Papers, Rare Book & Manuscript Library, Columbia University Libraries
Southern Christian Leadership Conference (SCLC) Records
Arthur Hays Sulzberger Papers, Manuscripts and Archives Division, New York
Public Library
Herbert Wechsler Papers, Rare Book & Manuscript Library, Columbia University
Byron White Papers, Library of Congress

Index

Note: Italic page numbers indicate photographs.

Founded in 1893,
UNIVERSITY OF CALIFORNIA PRESS
publishes bold, progressive books and journals
on topics in the arts, humanities, social sciences,
and natural sciences—with a focus on social
justice issues—that inspire thought and action
among readers worldwide.

The UC PRESS FOUNDATION
raises funds to uphold the press's vital role
as an independent, nonprofit publisher, and
receives philanthropic support from a wide
range of individuals and institutions—and from
committed readers like you. To learn more, visit
ucpress.edu/supportus.